DESTINATION USA

EAST

Produced by the
Publications Division of the Automobile Association
Fanum House,
Basingstoke, Hampshire RG21 2EA

Produced by the Publications Division of the
Automobile Association
Researched and written by **Roland Weisz**
Editor **Richard Powell**
Art Editors **Keith Russell** and **M A Preedy**
Picture Research **Sally Howard**
Editorial Contributors **Barry Francis, Gail
Harada, Roger Prebble** and **Pat Rowlinson**
Editorial Adviser **Professor Esmond Wright**,
Director of the Institute of United States Studies,
University of London
Maps produced by the Cartographic Department of
the Automobile Association. Based on cartography
supplied by the American Automobile Association.
All maps © 1981 The American Automobile
Association

The contents of this book are believed correct at the
time of printing. Nevertheless, the Publishers cannot
accept any responsibility for errors and omissions, or
for changes in details given.
© The Automobile Association 1982 56339
All rights reserved. No part of this publication may
be reproduced, stored in a retrieval system, or
transmitted in any form or by any means – electronic,
mechanical, photocopying, recording, or otherwise –
unless the written permission of the Publisher has
been given beforehand.

ISBN 0 86145 106 6

The Publishers would like to acknowledge the
extremely valuable help given to them in the
preparation of this book by the American Automobile
Association (AAA), 8111 Gatehouse Road, Falls
Church, Virginia 22047.
The AAA has prepared all the town plans and route
maps. They have also devised the routes followed by
the motor tours and the route information has been
checked by AAA road reporters, who make an annual
survey of all US roads. The names, addresses and
telephone numbers of museums, places of interest
and public buildings are in general based on the
information supplied by the AAA and every effort
has been made to ensure that it is accurate. The
publishers are also grateful to the following for
providing facilities and help during the preparation of
material for this book: Pan American World Airways
Inc; the Hertz Corporation; Budget Rent-A-Car;
Florida Division of Tourism; The United States
Travel and Tourism Administration.
Professor Esmond Wright, Director of the Institute
of United States Studies, the University of London,
has provided valuable help in the reading of the
manuscript.

Filmset in Monophoto Plantin by
Servis Filmsetting Ltd, Manchester
Litho reproduction by
Mullis·Morgan Ltd, London

Printed and bound by Graficromo, S. A., Cordoba

Published by the Automobile Association,
Fanum House, Basingstoke, Hampshire RG21 2EA

The Publishers would like to thank the following
organisations, photographers and picture libraries for
the use of photographs in this book:
J Allan Cash Ltd; Colorific!; Florida Division of
Tourism; Maryland Office of Tourist Development;
Miami Beach Visitor Convention; New York State
Department of Commerce; Picturepoint; Spectrum;
State of New York Division of Tourism; Richard
Surman; United States Travel and Tourism
Administration; Virginia State Travel Service; ZEFA.

Contents

Interstate Routes in Eastern USA	4	Washington DC	46
Introduction	5	Washington Directory	52
Useful Information	6		

The Empire State: New York	54
The Sunshine State: Florida	8
Motor Tours: Around Long Island	62
Motor Tour: Coastal Florida	17
Along the Hudson River	65
Miami	24	New York	68
Miami Directory	30	New York Directory	75

The Mid-Atlantic States: Delaware, Maryland, Pennsylvania, Virginia, West Virginia	32
New England: Connecticut, Massachusetts, Rhode Island	78
Motor Tours: Annapolis and Chesapeake Bay	41
Motor Tour: Cape Cod and Rhode Island	85
The Pennsylvania Dutch Country	43
Boston	91
Boston Directory	94

Cover photographs:

U *The Space Shuttle, Kennedy Space Center, Florida*
S *A typical street scene in downtown New York*
A *Mayflower II, at Plymouth, Massachusetts*

Title page photographs:

U *The Empire State Building, New York*
S *The Back Bay area, Boston*
A *The Shenandoah National Park, Virginia*

Introduction

As a practical, on the spot guide, this book will delight the first-time traveller to the United States. It is packed with fact and practical information – where to stay, where to eat, and what to see. For those who have crossed the Atlantic before, these pages can serve as a happy reminder of past trips, or assist and suggest further exploration of this exciting continent. Others, who prefer to travel from the comfort of their own armchairs, will find the photographs and text make a valuable addition to the fireside library. This book helps you to enjoy the best the USA has to offer:

Destination USA East deals specifically with those Atlantic states around the great cities of Miami, Washington, New York and Boston, which are the most popular ports of entry for transatlantic visitors. A sister volume concentrates on the cities and states of the Pacific and Gulf coasts. Each of the four areas described here is divided into three sections. Firstly, the states and cities are introduced; secondly, detailed motor tours are given, accompanied by clearly marked maps; the final section is devoted to the major city of the area. Details of hotels, restaurants, and places of interest are listed.

The Sunshine State – *Florida's Miami Beach*

The Mid-Atlantic States – *Valley Forge in Pennsylvania*

The Empire State – *The Catskill Mountains of New York*

Southern New England – *Gloucester, on the Massachusetts coast*

Useful Information

Although the British and Americans may speak the same language, remember that America is a foreign country, with attitudes and customs often radically different to those we are used to in Europe. To help the tourist adjust a little more smoothly to the American lifestyle we have listed here some of the things you need to know for a visit to the United States.

ENTRY REGULATIONS

To enter the United States you require two essential documents; a visa, and a full British passport, which must be valid for at least six months after your intended return home. NB – the one-year British Visitors' Passport is not valid for the USA. Most travel agents carry application forms for visas, and may undertake to obtain the visa on your behalf. Otherwise, apply to the American Embassy, Visa Branch, 5 Upper Grosvenor Street, London W1A 2JB, tel 01 499 3443 (recorded information), and enclose a stamped addressed envelope, your passport, and evidence of your intention to leave the USA after your holiday (such as your return ticket or a letter from your employer stating that you will be returning to work). Normally you should allow at least four weeks for your application to be completed, but in an emergency you can apply personally to the Visa Branch (open 8am to 3pm, Monday to Friday, except for public holidays, 25 May and 3 July), but you may have to queue for anything up to three hours. Visas may also be obtained from the American Consulates in Edinburgh and Belfast. The addresses are: American Consulate General, 3 Regent Terrace, Edinburgh EH7 5BW; American Consulate General, Queen House, 14 Queen Street, Belfast BT1 6EQ.

CUSTOMS REGULATIONS

When you reach the USA, you will have to pass through immigration. This is usually a formality, but immigration officials will want to know where you intend to stay. You are allowed to bring the following duty-free items into the USA: one US quart of spirits or wine (persons ages 21 or over, although local state laws may vary); 200 cigarettes, or 50 cigars, or 3lbs of tobacco, or proportionate amounts of each; $100 worth of gifts, provided you are staying more than 72 hours and have not visited in the previous six months. You may bring $5,000 in personal funds into the USA.

CURRENCY

The basic unit of American currency is the dollar bill ($1.00 = 100 cents). Paper notes come in $1, $2, $5, $10, $20, $50, $100, $500 and $1,000 denominations, all of which are printed in the same colour and are the same size. Coins are minted in denominations of 1c (penny), 5c (nickel), 10c (dime), 25c (quarter), 50c and $1. You can exchange your own currency into US dollars at most major American banks. It is always best to change your currency at airports or in the larger cities, where you will receive a better exchange rate. Normal banking hours are 9am to 3pm, Monday to Friday. Credit cards such as American Express, Access (American Master Card), Barclaycard/VISA and Diners Club are accepted almost everywhere, and travellers cheques, either in sterling or dollars, are usually accepted by banks, hotels, restaurants or shops.

TRAVEL

AIR: More than 600 cities are covered by the internal flight network, and it is the best way to travel large distances. Foreign travellers can claim special discount fares on many airlines. A Visit USA Fare (VUSA) worth a 40% discount is one example, and there are several go-as-you-please packages. Ask your travel agent for details.

RAIL: Inter-city trains are generally cheaper than going by air over shorter distances. AMTRAK is the major passenger railway network, and their agents in Britain are Thomas Cook (England and Wales) and Thistle Air (Scotland). Your travel agent will be able to make arrangements for you.

BUSES: Luxurious coaches provide the most economical method of long distance travel. Greyhound and Trailways are the largest bus companies, and together with their smaller counterparts cover 120,000 miles of America's excellent highways. Passes entitling you to unlimited, nationwide travel can be bought in advance in the UK through your travel agent.

MOTORING: Major roads in America are well-surfaced, wide, and well signposted. Americans tend to think in terms of how long a journey may take, although distances are calculated in miles. Local roads are not so well surfaced and are often narrow. Controlled access highways are variously known as interstates, expressways or toll roads. Roads designated US, followed by a number, are similar to British main trunk roads. Interstate roads are equivalent to motorways. State Routes are main roads within a state, and Local Routes are minor roads. Toll roads and turnpikes charge a toll of 2–3 cents per mile and as access is limited on these super-highways, you should plan your exit points and rest stops well in advance. Often you will find that the cashier at petrol stations (gas stations) sits behind a bullet-proof kiosk, and may insist that you pay before filling up. When buying petrol, remember that American pints, quarts and gallons are smaller than the Imperial equivalents by about one-fifth, therefore a US gallon is about four-fifths of a British one. Hire cars usually use only lead-free petrol, a more expensive grade. There will be a notice in the car stating whether it uses this grade or not.

CAR HIRE: Hire cars are available at airports, car hire agencies, and rental offices in hotels. Local AAA clubs will recommend reputable agencies. There is usually a wide choice of vehicles, which you are able to inspect before you hire. Campers – motorised caravans – are readily available and come with all mod cons, but it is best to reserve one to avoid disappointment. The American Automobile Association can supply a list of approved camping sites to members of the British AA. Their address is the American Automobile Association (AAA), 8111 Gatehouse Road, Falls Church, Virginia 22047. Some car hire companies will rent to drivers of 18 years of age, others require you to be over 21, and in some areas drivers must be over 25. The major credit cards are universally acceptable, and travellers' cheques are taken. You will be asked to produce your passport and driving licence as proof of identification. Prices vary from one region to another, and include oil, maintenance and liability insurances. State and local taxes are additional, and petrol is usually extra. Most American cars have automatic transmission, and are often air-conditioned, a necessity in some regions where the summers can be very hot.

DRIVING REGULATIONS

Rules and hints are listed here which will help you to drive safely in America. Driving in the USA is not difficult, but it is helpful, and polite, to forearm yourself with knowledge of those general practices Americans take for granted. Each state has its own traffic regulations, however, so this list is only general. Local AAA offices will give advice about local regulations

1 Drive on the right of the road.
2 Keep to the speed limits; 20–25 miles per hour in cities and congested areas, 55 miles per hour on open roads.
3 Report any accident to the nearest police department immediately.
4 Strictly observe all traffic lights and stop, slow and caution signs. Normally, however, cars can filter right on red, provided they have first halted and checked that the road is clear. This does not apply in New York.
5 Do not pass on bends, at junctions or near the top of hills.
6 Do not pass school buses which have stopped to allow children to get on or off. This applies both when you are following the bus and when you are approaching it.
7 Observe reduced speed limits in all school zones.

8 Do not park on the highway in rural areas. If you must stop, pull right off the road.
9 Observe parking zone laws in cities, or your car may be towed away. Always park facing the flow of traffic and never double-park. Kerbside colour codes are: red for no parking; yellow for unloading commercial vehicles; white for unloading passengers; blue for parking for handicapped people; green for short-term (this often means literally 12 minutes). These may vary from state to state.
10 Always signal when you turn, stop or change lanes. Remember, however, that on many multi-lane highways Americans may overtake you on both sides, and may themselves change lane without signalling.

Watch your positioning on near-side lanes of highways. These sometimes become exit lanes only, and you may not see the sign saying 'Right Lane Must Exit' until too late. Many stretches of roadway on fast highways are heavily studded. This is an effective deterrent to speeding, as the noise of the drumming of the tyres is most alarming. On urban highways, keep an eye on the speed limits. You can move within moments from a 40 mph zone to a 45 mph zone, and back down to a 30 mph zone.
11 Cars carrying fewer than four people may be barred from certain privileged lanes of highways, especially at rush hours. These express lanes by-pass hold-ups at junctions, and are designed to encourage car-sharing.
12 Keep a lookout for cyclists – they are allowed to ride towards oncoming traffic.
13 Always lock your car when it is unattended.
14 Never pick up hitch-hikers.
15 Never call a sidewalk a pavement. To an American, the pavement is the roadway, and using the English term could lead to confusion if you have to have dealings with the police.

USEFUL WORDS

Although English is spoken throughout the USA, there are some variations in vocabulary which it is essential to know. The following is a brief list of English-American equivalents.

American	English
apartment	flat
balcony	gallery
bathroom/comfort station/rest room	lavatory
check	bill
booth	kiosk
broil	grill
call collect (phone)	reverse charges
candy	sweets
cookies	biscuits
crepes	pancakes
drugstore	chemist
elevator	lift
fabric	material
faucet	tap
flashlight	torch
first floor	ground floor
french fries	chips
gas (gasoline)	petrol
grill	broil
grits (breakfast)	semolina
hashbrowns	fried potatoes
hood (car)	bonnet
jello	jelly
jelly	jam
line	queue
long distance	trunk call
mail	post
mezzanine	dress circle
on the rocks (drinks)	with ice
orchestra	stalls
panty hose	tights
pastrami	peppered beef
pavement	roadway
potato chips	crisps
purse	handbag
sidewalk	pavement
stick shift	gear lever
straight up (drinks)	neat
streetcars	trams
subway	underground
trunk (car)	boot
vest	waistcoat
washcloth	face flannel
wholewheat bread	brown bread
windshield	windscreen

MEDICAL TREATMENT

The charges for medical treatment are high in the USA, so it is essential that you insure yourself before you leave. If you need a doctor or dentist, your hotel will contact one for you. Alternatively your embassy or consulate will supply a list of approved doctors.

HOTELS AND RESTAURANTS

It is worth taking a little time in selecting your hotel, and advisable to make reservations. Breakfast is seldom included in the price of a room. Remember many hotels in the cities offer cheap weekend rates to keep the rooms filled. Restaurants are not over expensive by British standards, and American food at its best is excellent. Portions are often larger than you are probably used to, and salad is frequently served without question as a first course. It is common to wait for a 'hostess' to show you to your table, and send someone to take your order. Tipping is expected – 12½% or 15% is normal. Sometimes restaurants serve meals or bar drinks more cheaply during a 'happy hour', between 4 and 7pm.

PUBLIC HOLIDAYS

There are a number of public holidays celebrated in America which may be unfamiliar to the tourist. The principle ones are:

Washington's Birthday	Third Monday in February
Memorial Day	Last Monday in May
Independence Day	4 July
Labor Day	First Monday in September
Columbus Day	Second Monday in October
Veterans' Day	11 November
Thanksgiving Day	Fourth Thursday in November

Lincoln's Birthday, Armistice Day and Yom Kippur are designated public holidays in certain states or areas.

TOURIST INFORMATION

There are State Tourist Departments in every state, whose staff will help you with advice and information on every aspect of your holiday. They will also supply literature and maps to help you get the best out of your visit. Addresses of these departments may be obtained from the United States Travel Services, US Department of Commerce, 22 Sackville Street, London W1.

TELEPHONES

Public telephones are plentiful in the USA, and are found in restaurants, garages, hotel foyers, tobacconists, railway stations, airports and in telephone boxes on the pavements. Local calls cost from 10 to 20 cents, and for long-distance calls you need a good supply of 25c pieces. Many large hotels and organisations have free phone numbers, for which you do not need to pay. The code for these is 800. Some hotels also have 'courtesy phones' at airports, which are also free of charge. The STD system is universal but if you do need to contact the operator, dial 0. Instructions on how to use the telephone are clearly printed beside the instrument.

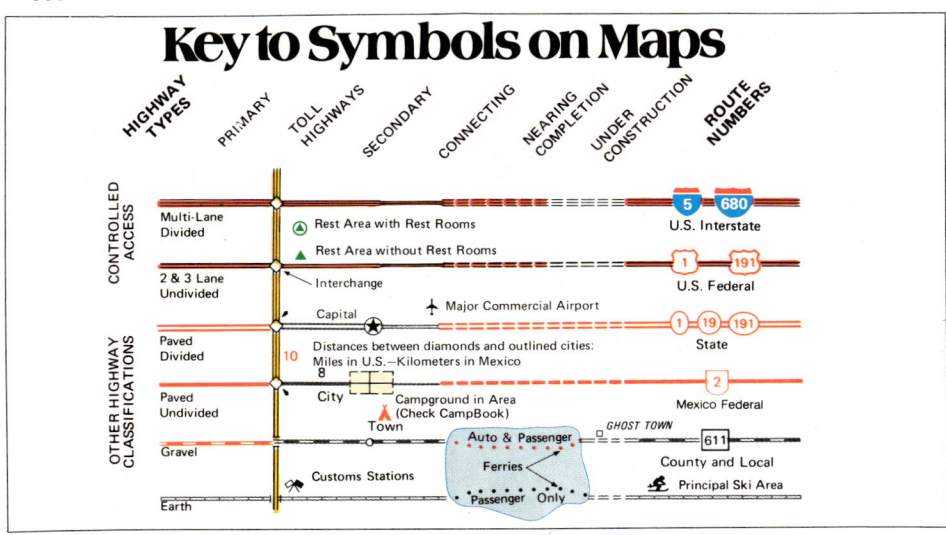

The Sunshine State
–Florida

This is America's vacationland, a sub-tropical playground which specialises in holidays: exotic, adventurous, lazy, luxurious, and always fun.

Florida can cater for those in search of the high life – luxury hotels, white beaches and unlimited sun – in the high-rise coastal resorts of the type epitomised by Miami, the queen of them all.

If in search of the Bohemian way of life, then the Florida Keys, a string of islands which stretch from Miami 135 miles out into the Gulf of Mexico, provide superb natural scenery and a taste of sun soaked Latin-America. Key West, the last in the chain, was much favoured by novelist and adventurer Ernest Hemingway.

For the family, Florida offers an unbelievable variety of entertainment, from Disney World, a magnificent extravaganza of fantasy and fun, to Marineland, where the creatures of the sea take part in a non-stop variety act, and the Kennedy Space Center, where the story of man's quest for the stars is told.

At the other end of the scale, in the deep south, lie the Everglades, a unique natural wonderland of swamps and mangroves which hide a remarkable flora and fauna, including the endangered Everglades crocodile. In contrast the cool woodlands of pine and oak in the north of the state harbour a multitude of game for the hunter – in Osceola and Apalachicola National Forests bears still roam.

Fishing, in both the sea and the many inland waters, provides excellent sport, and the same waters play host to a myriad enthusiastic sailors, amateur and professional. In Fort Lauderdale the boat is as common a method of transport as the car.

Good food is important to all Americans, and there are over 23,000 restaurants in Florida to prove that this state is no laggard in this matter. Naturally, fresh, succulent seafood caught around this most productive of coasts heads the menus in the

majority of restaurants – oysters, shrimps, crabs, crawfish, clams, scallops and fish of all kinds prepared in an astounding variety of dishes to tempt the palate.

Sea, sun, good food and a warm welcome – Florida takes great care of its visitors – add up to a great holiday, and as the Florida Division of Tourism tells us 'When you need it bad, we've got it good.'

The shining white sands and clear waters of Miami Beach are a perfect antidote to cold, dreary northern winters. Holidaymakers from many countries come here to sail, swim, fish or simply soak up the tropical sunshine

Land of sunshine, sweet orange blossom, white beaches and dazzling blue seas, Florida is that low-lying, rich, green finger of southern-most America which separates the Atlantic Ocean from the Gulf of Mexico. More than 8,000 miles of coast, with numerous bays, inlets and islands, create the perfect setting for those in search of a sub-tropical holiday. It is a state which can justifiably claim to rival the best that California can offer on the Pacific west coast, with the advantage of being barely half the distance from New York and the other great east-coast cities.

Nine million people live in Florida. Another 23 million visit each year, and tourism is the main business of the 'Sunshine State'; it has been since Henry Plant built a railway through central Florida to Tampa in 1881, and Henry Flagler built his Florida East Coast line in 1883. These two millionaires initiated a remarkable burst of resort and hotel building which reached its peak in the 1920s, at the same time embarking on feverish promotion advertising the state's warm winters to the fur-wrapped rich in the north, which today has culminated in Florida being America's foremost holiday state.

Florida is a triumph for those early developers who wrested an almost instant civilisation out of the swamps and jungles of this most southern extremity of the United States. Driving along its broad, mature highways which, even when they cut through the densest hinterland, are never far from evidence of the sophisticated society which now inhabits these lands, the visitor might find it hard to accept that most of it sprang up in less than a hundred years. Of course, it needs more than climate and money to create such a tourist trap, and Florida has an abundance of natural attractions.

If the peninsula is described as the chunky high heel on the foot of the American continent, then high up in the north-west, tucked into the instep of the shoe, is Miracle Strip, 150 miles of brilliant white, sandy quartz beaches stretching from Pensacola at the extreme western point of the state to Apalachicola. Inland, around Tallahassee, the state capital, the terrain changes to rolling hills, great oaks hung with Spanish moss, and crystal-clear lakes fed by artesian wells. Cool green forests of pine grow up around the Georgia border, while in the south are the majority of Florida's 30,000 lakes, the king of them all being one of the southernmost, the 700-square-mile Lake Okeechobee. At the peninsula's tip, land and sea mingle in the Everglades, a labyrinth of waterways wound round huge cypress and mangrove swamps, and filtered through acres of shallow sheets of water filled with sawgrass – altogether a unique wildlife sanctuary where 400 species of birds alone have been recorded.

However, it is Florida's magnificent coastline which is the star attraction. The

JACKSONVILLE

Hotels

DAYS INN: 5649 Cagle Rd, tel 733 3890. 266 rooms. Inexpensive.

JACKSONVILLE HILTON: 565 S Main St, tel 398 3561. 226 rooms. Expensive.

RODEWAY INN: 1057 Broward Rd, tel 757 0990. 187 rooms. Inexpensive.

Restaurants

STRICKLAND'S TOWN HOUSE RESTAURANT: 3510 Phillips Hwy, Maryport, tel 396 1682. Fishing village atmosphere. Moderate.

VALLE'S STEAKHOUSE: 5555 University Blvd, tel 731 5411. Large menu, steak and seafood. Moderate.

Places of Interest

CUMMER GALLERY OF ART: 829 Riverside Av. Features art from the 5th century to present. Sculpture, tapestries and furniture.

FORT CAROLINE NATIONAL MEMORIAL: 12713 Fort Caroline Rd. Reconstructed French colony of 1564 which began permanent European settlement in N America. 140 acres.

JACKSONVILLE ART MUSEUM: 4160 Boulevard Center Dr. African, oriental and pre-Columbian art and modern exhibitions.

FOR MORE INFORMATION: Jacksonville-Jacksonville Beach Visitor & Convention Bureau, 240 W Monroe St, tel 353 9736.

FLORIDA

Daybreak and city lights in Jacksonville, a busy port and thriving commercial centre on the St Johns River

peninsula is hung with an island necklace, which terminates in a 135-mile ribbon of islands known as the Florida Keys, which appear on the map as a pendulum pivoted on the southern tip of the state, frozen at the zenith of its swing, stretched out towards the shores of Cuba, just 90 miles away.

At the southern tip of the mainland is Miami, attached to the most famous holiday island of them all – Miami Beach, a 10-mile-long, 100-yard-wide expanse of sand which has attracted a staggering 90,000 permanent population into its seven-and-a-half square miles of city.

Further up the Atlantic coast, the hundreds of islands were formed by the action of the Intra-coastal waterway, which separates them from the mainland and washes hundreds of miles of white beaches clean on either side of its channel as it cleaves its way down to Key West on the tip of the Florida Keys. The waterway divides near Stuart, some hundred miles north of Miami, one branch cutting inland to cross the state – on its way feeding Lake Okeechobee. Past the lake it becomes the Caloosahatchee River. In that guise it meanders on to meet the warm waters of the Gulf of Mexico at Fort Myers, where it turns north again, creating a similar string of islands along much of the west coast.

Florida is divided into six main regions, each with its own characteristic holiday appeal. The North-west, a camper's paradise, has some 25 state parks, where camping and picnicking are encouraged. There are also 100 camp grounds, 17 canoe trails, and lakes and streams offering fine freshwater fishing. The coastal waters team with blue marlin, dolphin and king mackerel.

Inland, and almost as far as it is possible to go from Florida's most internationally celebrated holiday city, Miami, is the state capital, Tallahassee. A wild frontier-style town when it was founded nearly 160 years ago, it has assumed gentler, softer contours now that it is the home of two of Florida's universities. It boasts fine state capital buildings, and proudly guards the 150-year-old restored remains of the Columns, once the financial, political and social centre of the capital. Since it was moved from its original site to 100 North Duval Street it has housed the headquarters of the Chamber of Commerce. Apart from its famous parks and shady tree-lined streets, Tallahassee has also nearby the world's deepest artesian spring – most of Florida's 17 spectacular springs are found in this area.

The North-east Region, on the other hand, is rich in the remains of the primitive beginnings of the state. The early inhabitants of the land were the Indians who ruled the territory well into the 19th century, and several decades after the state was admitted to the Union in 1821.

In the area dominated by Jacksonville, Florida's most populous city, some 30 miles from the Georgia border, skyscrapers stand shoulder to shoulder with French and Spanish fortresses that sprang up over 400 years ago after Juan Ponce de Leon, Puerto Rico's Spanish Governor, landed between the St Augustine estuary and the St John's River. He had hoped to find the legendary Fountain of Youth, but ended up claiming the land in the name of Spain in April 1513. He called it La Florida. As a result of his action, Florida nearly five centuries later can lay claim to St Augustine as the oldest city in the United States – a distinction that every other American state envies.

St Augustine served as a fort and became the site of the first permanent European settlement in the United States. Though de Leon claimed the land it was Pedro Menendez de Aviles, sent by King Philip of Spain in 1564 to consolidate the territory, who drove the encroaching French Huguenots from Fort Caroline, established as their stronghold a year earlier a few miles across

TALLAHASSEE

Hotels

HOLIDAY INN: 2 locations; 1302 Apalachee Pkwy, tel 877 3141. 168 rooms. Downtown, 316 W Tennessee St, tel 222 8000. 160 rooms. Moderate.

TALLAHASSEE MOTOR HOTEL: 1630 N Monroe St, tel 224 6183. 92 rooms. Moderate.

Restaurants

JOE'S STEAK AND SPAGHETTI HOUSE: 1713 Mahan Dr, tel 877 1253. Excellent Italian dishes. Moderate.

MORRISON'S CAFETERIA: 2415 N Monroe Av, tel 385 2111. Wide variety, good food. Inexpensive.

Places of Interest

FLORIDA STATE CAPITOL: S Monroe St. 22-storey tower.

MACLAY STATE GARDENS: 5 miles NE on US 319. 308 acres of delightful gardens. Maclay House serves as a centre for information on camellias.

TALLAHASSEE JUNIOR MUSEUM: 6½ miles SW at Lake Bradford. Excellent educational museum for children. Mainly natural sciences.

WAKULLA SPRINGS: Junc SR 61 and SR 267, 13 miles S. State's deepest spring. See marine life through glass-bottomed boats. Jungle cruise.

FOR MORE INFORMATION: Tallahassee Chamber of Commerce, PO Box 1639, tel 224 8116.

PENSACOLA

Hotels

RAMADA INN: 6550 Pensacola Blvd, tel 477 0711. 104 rooms. Moderate-Expensive.

RODEWAY INN: 710 N Palafox, tel 438 4922. 157 rooms. Inexpensive.

Restaurants

DRIFTWOOD RESTAURANT: 27 W Garden St, tel 433 4559. Deliciously prepared seafood. Moderate.

THE OYSTER BAR: 709 N Navy Blvd, tel 455 3925. Inexpensive-Moderate.

Places of Interest

PENSACOLA HISTORICAL MUSEUM: 405 S Adams St at Zaragosa St. Displays local artefacts, supplies walking tours.

US NAVAL AVIATION MUSEUM: Naval Air Station. Over 75 historic aircraft and Skylab Command Module.

FOR MORE INFORMATION: Pensacola Tourist Information Centre, 803 N Palafox, tel 433 3065.

A gleaming 22-storey tower, now the seat of Florida's legislature in Tallahassee, soars above the dome of the original state capitol building of 1845

FLORIDA

the St Johns River at what is now Jacksonville.

Still preserving strong traces of its Spanish origins, St Augustine reflects the country's as well as the state's passion for the past. Its narrow streets, flanked by walled patios, lead to restored houses and craft shops. Though the city was under the influence of successive masters, the English were much in evidence in the 17th century as they moved southwards down the coast. By 1763 St Augustine, after serving as a seat of government for 30 missions, became an English possession. Twenty years later the whole of Florida was traded back to Spain, and after nearly 40 years of Spanish rule it was ceded to the Union, by which time St Augustine had already become well populated by migrating Americans from the north. During the Revolutionary War, it turned into a haven for fleeing loyalists from nearby states. In the Indian Seminole War, in the 1830s, it once more assumed the role of a military fort.

Thanks to almost uninterrupted sunshine, and a beach that at the turn of the century drew the first contingent of wealthy holiday makers from the sun-starved north, St Augustine soon bore the marks of 20th-century commercialism.

Fifty miles down the coast, in the Central East Region, Daytona Beach is where the pioneers of the motor car first tested the high-speed capabilities of their machines during the first decades of this century, attracted by 23 miles of the most firmly-packed sand in the world. These activities turned Daytona Beach into a kind of race track, and speed kings like the late Sir Malcolm Campbell repeatedly set up world records there. Even today, beach motorists

ST AUGUSTINE

Hotels

BY THE SEA COURT: 57 Comares Av, tel 829 8646. 16 rooms. Expensive.

MARION MOTOR LODGE: 120 Avenida de Menendez, tel 829 2261. 31 rooms. Inexpensive.

PONCE DE LEON LODGE: Ponce de Leon Blvd, tel 824 2821. 200 rooms. Expensive.

Restaurants

THE CHIMES RESTAURANT: 12 Avenida de Menendez, tel 829 8141. Steak and seafood dishes, and delicious waffles for breakfast. Moderate.

EDDY'S CARAVAN RESTAURANT: 2500 Ponce de Leon Blvd, tel 824 3123. Alaskan king crab a speciality. Moderate-Expensive.

Places of Interest

ALLIGATOR FARM: 1¾ miles SE on SR A1A, Anastasia Island. Zoo and museum.

CASTILLO DE SAN MARCOS NATIONAL MONUMENT: Castillo Dr and Avenida de Menendez. Oldest masonry fort in US, begun in 1672. Impressive.

CROSS AND SWORD: 2 miles S on SR A1A at St Augustine Amphitheatre. Nightly (ex Sun) dramatisation of city's early history.

LIGHTNER MUSEUM: King and Cordova Sts. Essentially Victoriana.

OLDEST HOUSE: 14 St Francis St. 1710 house and museums of history and architecture.

POTTER'S WAX MUSEUM: 1 King St. Spectacular wax replicas of the famous.

SAN AUGUSTIN ANTIGUO: St George St. 18th-century Spanish colonial village. 8 buildings in all, mostly reconstructions.

ZORAYADA CASTLE: 83 King St. 1:10 scale replica of a Spanish castle.

FOR MORE INFORMATION: St Augustine Area Chamber of Commerce, 10 Castillo Dr, tel 829 5681.

DAYTONA BEACH

Hotels

BEACHCOMBER: 2000 N Atlantic Av, tel 252 8513. 184 rooms. Expensive.

CASTAWAY BEACH MOTEL: 2075 S Atlantic Av, tel 255 6461. 300 rooms. Moderate.

DAYTONA SANDS BEACH MOTEL: 2523 S Atlantic Av, tel 767 2551. 50 rooms. Moderate-Expensive.

Restaurants

CHEZ BRUCHEZ: 304 Seabreeze Blvd, tel 252 6656. Sea fresh seafood. Moderate.

MORRISON'S: 200 N Ridgewood Av, tel 258 6396. Good simple fare. Inexpensive.

SAN REMO RESTAURANT: 1290 S Ridgewood Av, tel 252 1357. Italian-American cuisine. Moderate.

VALLE'S STEAK HOUSE: 2600 Valusia Av, tel 255 0532. Moderate.

Places of Interest

DAYTONA INTERNATIONAL SPEEDWAY: 1801 Speedway Blvd. Races scheduled throughout year.

MUSEUM OF ARTS AND SCIENCES: 1040 Museum Blvd. One of Florida's major art museums.

FOR MORE INFORMATION: Daytona Beach Area Chamber of Commerce, PO Box 874, tel 255 0981.

Racing is no longer permitted on the sands at Daytona, but events like this can be seen at Daytona International Speedway

Several period riverboats are in use as passenger ferries at Walt Disney World

almost out-number sunbathers. Although car racing is banned on the sands, the town is still a centre for the sport. On Daytona Beach and adjoining Ormond Beach, visitors can still bring their cars to the water's edge.

Only about 20 miles inland from Daytona is DeLand, once ambitiously planned as the 'Athens of Florida', but now a relaxed and dignified university town which has the distinction of housing a seat of learning named after a hat! For it is here that John B Stetson produced his famous American wide-brimmed hat much favoured by Texan oil millionaires on (and off) the screen. The company helped to establish the university and has given it support. In the town, moss-hung oaks line the streets, and nearby is a 1,600-acre park noted for its bird life and accessible only by boat. Around the city are other recreation areas where artesian springs are the major tourist draw.

After World War II, as the tourist traffic along Florida's eastern seaboard multiplied, a new spectator sport was unfolding in the late 1950s at an obscure air-force base called Cape Canaveral, another 50 miles down the coast. Re-named for several years Cape Kennedy in deference to the memory of the assassinated President, it reverted to its original Spanish name when the greatest show on and off the earth was given the full multi-media treatment at the Kennedy Space Center, situated on the cape – a triangular spit jutting far out into the Atlantic Ocean. This 140,000-acre site has been the hub of America's manned flight launches since Alan B Shepard went into sub-orbit on 5 May 1961, and has since been visited by millions of tourists.

A rival attraction 30 miles inland, in the Central Region, has already drawn more than 100 million people to a rather different setting. A few miles south-west of Orlando, Central Florida's top town, Walt Disney World stands on 43 square miles of reclaimed swampland at Lake Buena Vista, a more ambitious counterpart of the nearly 30-year-old original Disneyland in California. Over the past 10 years Disney World has not merely grown into a vast entertainment complex, it has also become the embodiment of Walt Disney's dream to confront crowds at leisure with a new concept in international understanding. Exhibitions presenting the differing cultures of mankind are part of a complex plan to build an Experimental Prototype Community of Tomorrow, at a cost of £300 million. Two of the major exhibition areas are due to open in the autumn of 1982.

The main business, meanwhile, of entertaining some 14 million visitors every year goes on with professional zeal and enthusiasm. Whatever appeals most, whether it is the Magic Kingdom with its Cinderella Castle, Frontierland, Fantasyland, Adventureland or Tomorrowland, or the more practical (though no less fantastic) facilities of the hotels (the Polynesian Village on Seven Seas Lagoon comes complete with a rushmat-style bamboo-curtained hotel), Disney World makes make-believe respectable for young and old alike.

ORLANDO

Hotels

ALTAMONTE SPRINGS INN: 151 N Douglas Av, tel 862 5521. 216 rooms. Expensive.

DAVIS PARK MOTEL: 221 E Colonial Dr, tel 425 9065. 75 rooms. Moderate.

GOLD KEY INN: 7100 S Orange Blossom Trail, tel 855 0050. 204 rooms. Expensive.

JAMAICA INN: 3300 W Colonial Av, tel 293 7221. 100 rooms. Moderate.

QUALITY INN: 7600 International Dr, tel 351 1600. 322 rooms. Moderate.

Restaurants

MAISON & JARDIN: 430 S Wymore Rd, Altamonte Springs, nr Orlando, tel 862 4410. Prize-winning dishes. Expensive.

PURPLE PORPOISE SEAFOOD RESTAURANT: 220 N Orlando Av, tel 644 1861. Famous fresh seafood. Moderate.

Places of Interest – See tour page 22.

FOR MORE INFORMATION: Greater Orlando Chamber of Commerce, PO Box 1234, tel 425 1234.

The 19th-century Moorish-style buildings of the University of Tampa were originally opened as the Tampa Bay Hotel

Due south at Kissimmee, once a small trading post and now enshrined in Florida's annals as the home of Tupperware International (there is a museum of food containers to prove it!) a new theme park called Little England is due to join the list of visitor attractions in the area which include Reptile World Serpentarium, Alligatorland Safari, and Gatorland Zoo.

But what really sets the Central Region of Florida apart from the rest is its concentration of citrus groves. They provide a quarter of the world's citrus fruit output, and contribute much of the crop of oranges, grapefruit and tangerines which make up 30 per cent of Florida's entire agricultural yield. A motorist on the way, say, to Sea World, the world's largest marine park 15 minutes south of Orlando, or to Cyprus Gardens at the town of Winter Haven, or to any one of the 13 lakes within the boundaries of Lakeland, can find the most succulent fruits within arm's reach on most stretches of highways. (see the tour on pages 17–23 for details of these and other places worth visiting.)

Rivalling the East coast for its abundance of beaches and of its cities, the South-west Region of Florida, from the Crystal Bay, 400 miles south to Everglades City, is an endless stretch of beaches lapped by the Gulf of Mexico. As in so many other parts of Florida, the giant entertainment centres dominate the holiday scene. At Tampa, Florida's third largest city, Busch Gardens, with its rare and exotic jungle animals, is second only to Walt Disney World in popularity. With its Latin Quarter, Tampa expresses the more cosmopolitan influence of the Tampa Bay area. On the other hand, St Petersburg, at the mouth of Tampa Bay, was for several decades a spa for the elderly. Although it is no longer devoted to such a role, preferring to see itself as a modern, active community, St Petersburg still supports a large retired population.

A little way up on the coast Tarpon Springs has a thriving Greek community enjoying the benefits of a lucrative sponge diving industry. Despite the growing popularity of synthetic sponges, the sponge divers can still be seen washing and cutting the abundant marine vegetation they harvest from the bottom of the Gulf of Mexico, and there is an exhibition of sponges at the Spongeorama Center and Theater in town. Bakeries and restaurants specialise in Greek dishes, and Greek music drifts from the white façades of houses lining the cobblestone streets.

Further down the coast, the names of the resorts have a distinct Mediterranean flavour. Madeira Beach, Venice, Naples, Marco Island and even the Isle of Capri, are just some of the warm European place-names to be found on this golden Gulf of Mexico riviera. Sarasota, the largest city on this stretch of coast, lays claim to being more beautiful than the Bay of Naples. Yet the city has a much more genuine claim to fame. It is well known as a circus town.

Arriving in Sarasota in 1927, John Ringling settled his Ringling Brothers Circus there for the winter. Soon Barnum and Bailey's outfit joined him, making the city their permanent winter quarters. Ringling left the city he had adopted a substantial legacy. Today this is chiefly expressed by the attractions of the Ringling Residence, the Ringling Circus Museum, and most treasured of all, the Ringling Museum of Art, which houses the largest collection of Rubens' paintings in the United States. A reconstructed 18th-century Venetian Court Theatre, brought from Italy in 1949, presents plays, operas, films, lectures and concerts.

Near the southern point of the peninsula,

TAMPA

Hotels

CAUSEWAY INN: Campbell Causeway, tel 884 7561. 152 rooms. Moderate.

EXPRESSWAY INNS: 2 locations; 3693 Gandy Blvd, tel 837 1921. 60 rooms. 3688 Gandy Blvd, tel 837 1971. Inexpensive.

HOST INTERNATIONAL HOTEL: Tampa International Airport, tel 879 5151. 300 rooms. Expensive.

RAMADA INN: Tampa International Airport, tel 877 6181. 296 rooms. Moderate.

Restaurants

COLUMBIA RESTAURANT: 21st and Broadway, tel 248 4961. Award-winning Spanish restaurant with 11 dining rooms. Expensive-Moderate.

RISTORANTE MAMA MIA: at Holiday Inn West-Stadium, 4732 N Dale Mabry, tel 877 6061. Fun Italian restaurant. Moderate.

Places of Interest – See tour page 21.

FOR MORE INFORMATION: Greater Tampa Chamber of Commerce, PO Box 420, tel 228 7777.

FLORIDA

SARASOTA

Hotels

BEST WESTERN ROYAL PALMS: 1701 N Tamiami Trail, tel 365 1342. 37 rooms. Moderate.

CADILLAC MOTEL: 4021 N Tamiami Trail, tel 355 7108. 25 rooms. Inexpensive.

HYATT HOUSE HOTEL: 1000 Blvd of the Arts, tel 366 9000. 297 rooms. Expensive.

RAMADA INN: 700 Benjamin Franklin Dr, tel 355 7771. 110 rooms. Expensive.

Restaurants

CAFE L'EUROPE: 431 Harding Circle, tel 388 4415. Gourmet restaurant. Expensive.

MARINA JACK: 2 Marina Plaza, tel 958 3125. Delightful waterfront position. Moderate.

Places of Interest – See tour page 18.

FOR MORE INFORMATION: Sarasota County Chamber of Commerce, PO Box 308, tel 955 8187.

---

the Florida coastline breaks into thousands of island jewels – known as the Ten Thousand Islands – where the waters are packed with tarpon and snook. The angler, whether anchored on terra firma or in a boat gliding from island to island on a blue mirror of water, has about 600 varieties of fish to catch around Florida's coast, with red snapper, pompano, and marlin abundant both in the Atlantic and the Gulf of Mexico. At their southernmost extremes, the Ten Thousand Island range fringes Florida's 1,500 square miles of swampy wilderness, the Everglades. The Everglades National Park extends 45 miles from north to south, and about 30 miles across.

In the east, the swamps give way to the polyglot urban sprawl of Miami in the South-east Region, and its satellite cities, Coral Gables and Hialeah. Miami Beach, once the most fertile hunting ground of vacation-seeking millionaires, is now one of the least fashionable resorts in Florida. But further up, along a 50-mile stretch up to West Palm Beach, the shore is gilded with exclusive beaches. Fort Lauderdale, a city of islands where the boat rivals the motor car for transport, is a haven for residents with the money and the time to cruise on the 165 miles of channels, lakes, bays, inlets and canals. Tourists tend to pass through Fort Lauderdale merely to gawp at the mansions, but the city itself has one major conventional tourist attraction – Ocean World, where porpoises and sea lions perform each day, and there are displays of sharks and sea turtles in viewing tanks.

In this favoured South-east Region of Florida, the waters of the Atlantic, warmed by the Gulf Stream, lap endlessly on silver-gilt beaches. The glamorous resorts of Palm Beach, Lake Worth, Boynton Beach, Delray Beach, Deerfield Beach and Pompano Beach, offer a surfeit of hotels and bronzed bodies. Here, where the sun never seems to set, Florida has truly earned the title 'Sunshine State'.

High-speed airboats like this are an ideal way to explore the shallow creeks of the Everglades National Park, where many rare species of wildlife may be seen

Coastal Florida

Six days – 520 miles

Miami – Shark Valley – Everglades City – Marco Island – Naples – Bonita Springs – Estero – Cape Coral – Fort Myers – North Port – Sarasota – Bradenton – De Soto National Memorial – Ellenton – St Petersburg Beach – Treasure Island – Madeira Beach – North Redington Beach – Indian Rocks Beach – Clearwater – Tarpon Springs – Tampa – Lakeland – Winter Haven – Lake Wales – Davenport – Walt Disney World – Orlando – Winter Park – Titusville – Cape Canaveral – Cocoa Beach – Vero Beach – Fort Pierce – Stuart – Miami

From downtown Miami, head for US 41 – the Tamiami Trail. Drive for 18 miles through the Everglades to Shark Valley.

Shark Valley
An extraordinary slow-moving river, 50 miles wide and a few inches deep, the Everglades is fed by massive Lake Okeechobee to the north.

Everglades National Park, at 1.4 million acres is the largest sub-tropical wilderness in America, where the trees and flowers are much the same as those found in Cuba and the West Indies. In the Shark River area, mangroves grow to a towering 75 feet.

A tram tour begins at Shark Valley, off US 41, and two-hour scenic tours through the mangrove swamps are scheduled every day between Thanksgiving and Easter.

Continue west along US 41 for 20 miles, through Ochopee, then drive south on State Route 29 for 2 miles to Everglades City.

Everglades City
This popular departure point for fishing and sightseeing tours into the Everglades is at the north-west corner of the National Park. Boat trips and day excursions are also available. The Everglades City Ranger Station is open daily on the south side of town. No park entry fee is charged here.

Drive west on the Tamiami Trail for 16 miles to Royal Palm Hammock. Take State Route 92 and drive for 12 miles to Marco on Marco Island.

Marco Island
Once a fisherman's retreat, this island is now a thriving resort. At the northern tip of the Ten Thousand Islands on the southern gulf coast, it is a shell-gatherer's paradise.

Return to US 41 via State Route 951 and drive 8 miles north-west to Naples.

Naples
Back in 1885, when it was first developed, Naples was only accessible by water. Now it is the western terminus of the well-known Alligator Alley toll road which traverses the Big Cypress Swamp. There are over 40 miles of public beaches here, and shell-gathering and other beach front activities are available at Del-Nor Wiggins Pass State Recreational Area 11 miles north-west. Five miles south is Rookery Bay, an area of mangrove islands which are a haven for rare birds and marine life.

Regional history, including Indian relics, is on display at the Collier County Museum, 3301 Tamiami Trail. Admission is free.

At 1590 Goodlette Road, believe it or not, is Jungle Larry's African Safari at Caribbean Gardens. Hourly jeep rides whisk you through a 200-acre preserve to view wild animals in a jungle setting. Self-guided walking tours may be taken through the grounds, which are open daily.

Hotels

SHERATON EDGEWATER BEACH INN: 1901 Gulf Shore Blvd, tel 262 6511. 100 rooms. Expensive.

HOWARD JOHNSON'S MOTOR LODGE: 221 9th St S, tel 262 6181. 100 rooms. Moderate.

Restaurants

PICCADILLY PUB: 625 5th Av S, tel 262 7521. Old English atmosphere. Moderate.

ST GEORGE AND DRAGON: 936 5th Av S, tel 262 6547. Strict dress code, nautical surroundings. Moderate.

Drive north on US 41 for 13 miles to Bonita Springs.

Bonita Springs
Here you may catch a glimpse of Florida's past at the Everglades Wonder Gardens. Wildlife including bears, otters, panthers, deer, eagles, waders, alligators and even the endangered Everglades crocodile are on view.

Return to US 41 and drive for 7 miles north to Estero.

Estero
Right on your route on US 41 is the Koreshan State Historic Site. Over 300 acres occupy the site of a community established in the late

Many parts of the fascinating Everglades are accessible only by boat. Craft can be hired at Everglades City

COASTAL FLORIDA

19th century by a religious sect called the Koreshan Unity. A museum and park are open daily.

From Estero, continue north on US 41 for 8 miles, then take an unclassified road (College Parkway) for 3 miles west to its junction with State Route 867. Here, drive west across the Caloosahatchee River on State Route 867ALT to Cape Coral.

Cape Coral
North of the town, on State Route 78 is the Waltzing Waters Aquarama. An unusual blend of light, music and constantly changing fountains achieves the waltzing effect.
Continuous performances begin nightly at sundown. A unique water ski show, performing sealions and dolphins and other aquatic entertainments are on offer.

Drive east back across the Caloosahatchee River, then north along State Route 867 for 7 miles to Fort Myers.

Fort Myers
The streets of Fort Myers are lined with striking royal palms, and exotic flowers and tropical fruits create vivid splashes of colour. The Yacht Basin area is the amusement centre. From here, a tropical cruise leaves Lee Street to sail up the Caloosahatchee River. A must for every tourist is a visit to Thomas Edison's Winter Home at 2350 McGregor Boulevard. The house includes a museum, laboratory and 14 acres of botanic gardens with trees, shrubs and plants from all over the world. America's greatest inventor lived here from 1886 to 1931, the year of his death. The museum contains a large collection of his inventions, and his birthday is still celebrated here.

Hotels
BEST WESTERN ROBERT E LEE MOTOR INN: 6611 N US 41, tel 997 5511. 108 rooms. Moderate-Expensive.

ROCK LAKE MOTEL: 2930 Palm Beach Blvd, tel 334 3242. 18 rooms. Inexpensive.

Restaurants
EDISON CAFETERIA: 2480 Edwards Dr. Pleasant and inexpensive.

KENNY'S RESTAURANT: 8828 S Tamiami Trail, tel 936 6733. Extensive salad bar. Moderate.

Continue north on US 41 for 23 miles to Punta Gorda. Cross Peace River and drive another 19 miles to North Port.

The exterior and (inset) the parlour of Ca'd'Zan, the Venetian-style mansion in Sarasota built by John Ringling, master showman of Ringling Brothers Circus. The unusual name of the palace means 'House of John' in Venetian dialect

North Port
Drive two miles west of this small town on US 41, then drive north for a mile to Warm Mineral Springs. The springs produce nine million gallons of water daily and maintain a surface temperature of 87°F all year. A modern bathhouse and a white sandy beach are attractions, and picnicking is allowed.

Return to US 41 and drive west for about 11 miles to Venice, with its network of canals in the heart of town. Drive 18 miles north on the Tamiami Trail along the Sun Coast to Sarasota.

Sarasota
This leading resort of wide thoroughfares and parks is separated from the Gulf of Mexico by a chain of sandy keys. Now an active art centre, Sarasota was most famous as the winterhome of the Ringling Brothers and Barnum and Bailey Circus.
The Circus Hall of Fame exhibits fascinating circus memorabilia such as Tom Thumb's coach, presented by Queen Victoria.
The most distinguished man of the circus, John Ringling, spent his fortune partly on a fabulous art museum. The Ringling Museum, in addition to the Museum of Art, includes a Museum of the Circus, the Ringling Residence and the Asolo Theater. It takes about three hours to tour the whole complex. The Asolo Theater is a lavish 18th-century Venetian theatre, which features plays, operas, lectures and concerts. The recently renovated art museum is built in Italian Renaissance style with an inner courtyard peppered with reproductions of world-famous sculptures. The exhibition of masterpieces is dominated by an impressive Rubens collection, and other works represent European

COASTAL FLORIDA

Bradenton
Varied historical aspects of south-west Florida, ranging from Stone-Age relics to a Saturn rocket, may be seen at the South Florida Museum and Bishop Planetarium. A Space Transit Projector is featured in the planetarium.

Drive west across Bradenton along State Route 64 for 5 miles, then turn right on State Route 564 past Palma Solo to the De Soto National Memorial.

De Soto National Memorial
Close to the mouth of the Manatee River, the site commemorates the first significant European exploration of this corner of North America. In 1539, Hernando de Soto, together with about 600 pioneering Spaniards, landed somewhere between St Petersburg and Fort Myers in search of gold and the 'Fountain of Youth'. Battling with Indians all the way, the expedition covered over 4,000 miles. In 1541, de Soto discovered the Mississippi and was buried in it a year later. Only half the group survived the four-year ordeal. A film about the expeditions is shown hourly.

Return to Bradenton via State Routes 564 and 64, cross the Manatee River on the de Soto Bridge and turn right on US 301, driving 2 miles to Ellenton.

Ellenton
Gamble Plantation on US 301 is the site of the Judah P Benjamin National Confederate Memorial, built in the early 1840s. Benjamin was Secretary of State of the Confederacy and a fugitive from the US Government when he sought refuge here near the end of the Civil War. Picnicking areas are available and war relics are on display.

Return to US 19 and drive north for about 6 miles to Terra Ceia. Here join Interstate 275 and cross Tampa Bay for 11 miles across the spectacular Sunshine Skyway Bridge. Turn left on State Route A19A – the toll Pinellas Bayway, and drive for 3 miles across scenic Boca Ciega Bay to reach the resort of St Petersburg Beach.

St Petersburg Beach
This highly-developed resort centre on Long Key is one of a series of holiday havens on the Pinellas Suncoast, offering 38 miles of soft, white, sandy beaches. The city of St Petersburg, surrounded by water, presides over the peninsula.

Just north of St Petersburg Beach is the London Wax Museum at 5505 Gulf Boulevard, which displays over 100 life-size figures created by Tussauds. A chamber

A full-sized replica of HMS 'Bounty', built in Nova Scotia for the MGM film 'Mutiny on the Bounty', is moored at St Petersburg

painters between the 14th and 18th centuries. The circus museum displays gilded parade wagons, calliopes, costumes and a 'backyard' glimpse of circus life in the thirties. Ca' d' Zan, the Ringling residence, is a 30-room mansion built on the lines of a Venetian palace. Inevitably, the interior has a surfeit of marble, carved and gilded furniture and intricate tapestries.

South of the Ringling Museums are the Sarasota Jungle Gardens. Sixteen acres of jungles and ponds are the setting for over 5,000 varieties of tropical flora, with flamingos, macaws, cockatoos, alligators, monkeys and others thrown in for good measure. Biblical buildings are displayed in the Garden of Christ.

Bellm's Cars and Music of Yesterday has everything from the Gay Nineties and Roaring Twenties – over 170 antique cars and a unique collection of 1,400 mechanical music machines.

For peace and quiet try the Marie Selby Botanical Gardens, which overlook Sarasota Bay.

Continue north on the Tamiami Trail for about 9 miles to Bradenton.

COASTAL FLORIDA

of horrors adds spice and there are story-book characters for the children.

If you have time, there is much to see in St Petersburg itself, particularly around the downtown waterfront with its impressive Pier Place, shaped like an inverted pyramid. Boats of every size and description may be hired for fishing or sightseeing in the bay. A variety of tourist attractions, including museums and sunken gardens, are to be found on the waterfront.

Drive north on State Route 699 – the Gulf Boulevard – for 2 miles to Treasure Island.

A Buddha in the Oriental Garden, one of many theme areas at Florida Cypress Gardens

Treasure Island
A favoured resort, with a magnificent sandy beach, Treasure Island also boasts an auditorium where art exhibits, square and round dancing and other special events are held on 108th Avenue. Bogus pirates even launch invasions here to amuse visitors!

Continue north for 3 miles along this narrow peninsula on Gulf Boulevard to Madeira Beach.

Madeira, North Redington and Indian Rocks Beaches
A free causeway connects Madeira Beach to the mainland just north of St Petersburg. The favourite method of transport here is a sand-coloured minibus called a Dune Buggy. There are several marinas and good swimming and fishing in the Gulf. Drive north for 2 more miles on Gulf Boulevard to find North Redington Beach, otherwise known as the 'Million Dollar Mile' because of the luxury apartments and shops which characterise this residential area. Continue north on Gulf Boulevard for another 5 miles and you reach Indian Rocks Beach, a delightful seaside community, also connected to the mainland by a free causeway. Of particular interest at Indian Shores is Tiki Gardens and shops on State Route 699. The gardens are landscaped in a Polynesian style with tropical plants, birds, temples and statues. The life of the beachcomber looks very tempting along these shores.

Take the Gulf Boulevard north and drive for 7 miles to Clearwater Beach. Here, turn right over the landscaped Garden Memorial Causeway for 2 miles to Clearwater.

Clearwater
Perched on the highest coastal bluff along the Eastern Seaboard, this sparkling city is an all-year resort overlooking the Gulf of Mexico. Sunsets are spectacular, particularly with Clearwater Harbour in the foreground. Berthed in the harbour are fabulous craft such as the 30-foot Tahitian ketch called *The Sunchaser*. Captain Memo, dressed in pirate's garb, will take up to six people on an adventurous voyage. Clearwater Beach is part of the city, has dazzling white beaches and is home of many windsurfing competitions.

Hotels

THE DUNES MOTEL: 514 S Gulfview Blvd, tel 441 4939. 35 rooms. Moderate.

RED CARPET RESORT: 530 Gulfview Blvd, tel 447 6407. 27 rooms. Moderate.

SHERATON SAND KEY HOTEL: 1160 Gulf Blvd, tel 595 1611. 390 rooms. Expensive.

Restaurants

AUNT HATTIE'S TOWNE HOUSE: 416 Cleveland St, tel 446 6360. Family restaurant. Moderate.

FISH HOUSE: 1595 US 19 S, tel 531 3773. Popular and inexpensive.

THE KAPOK TREE INN: 923 McMullen Booth Rd, tel 726 4734. Beautiful tropical garden setting. Moderate.

Drive north along US 19 for 14 miles to Tarpon Springs.

Tarpon Springs
Steeped in Greek customs and folklore, this Old World community was an important sponge fishing centre at the turn of the century. Greek divers were encouraged to come here, and though the trade has diminished, their influence is everywhere – from sponge boats to the splendour of Greek Orthodox pageantry. St Nicholas Greek Orthodox Cathedral is a splendid example of neo-Byzantine architecture, with icons, stained glass and sculptured marble. A short drive away is Florida's Weeki Wachee Spring, where an underwater mermaid show can be viewed from a theatre 16 feet underwater and a cool, shady path along the river leads through a rain

Sleek yachts, palm trees and the warm waters of the Gulf of Mexico attract visitors to the popular resort of Clearwater throughout the year

forest with *performing* birds of prey!

Drive east for a mile along Tarpon Avenue (State Route 582), then turn right and drive 12 miles south on US 19 to the Courtney Campbell Causeway (State Route 60). This 10-mile causeway crosses a large expanse of busy Tampa Bay. The east shore of the bay is the site of the burgeoning city of Tampa.

Tampa

Tampa is the fastest-growing city in Florida, with an ultra-modern international airport. Its port is the eighth largest in the nation and has one of the largest shrimp-fishing fleets in the world.

Once in the city, pass the impressive Tampa International Airport on your left and join Interstate 275. Driving east along this highway, which is known here as the Tampa Expressway, the University in all its Moorish splendour lies to the right. Past the next interchange, Interstate 275 strikes north into the picturesque Latin Quarter. Also called Ybor City, this includes about two square miles of cobblestoned streets and antique stores. This city-within-a-city was founded in 1886 by Vincent Martinez Ybor, a Cuban cigar manufacturer who built the first cigar factory here. Paella and other Spanish and Cuban dishes are served in the picturesque restaurants nearby, where flamenco dancers and troubadours entertain.

Off Interstate 275, at North Boulevard and Sligh Avenue, is Lowry Park, landscaped with tropical flowers, shrubs and trees. Fairyland features life-size nursery characters and there is a small zoo. Continue for two miles north on Interstate 275 and turn right on Busch Boulevard (State Route 580). Just over two miles along this route is The Dark Continent at Busch Gardens. In this 300-acre adventure park, you may view wild animals of the African veldt from the Monorail Safari, the Skyride and from the Trans-Veldt Railway.

Continue east on State Route 580 and turn right on State Route 583 and drive for 2 miles south to US 92. Drive for about a mile east to join Interstate 4.

Continue east on Interstate 4 for 25 miles to Lakeland.

Lakeland

This citrus town turned resort is a well-groomed city embracing 13 lakes. Recreational opportunities are almost unlimited at the Lakeland Civic Center. Florida Southern College campus displays many examples of Frank Lloyd Wright's architecture.

Leave Lakeland on US 92 and drive east for about 14 miles to Winter Haven.

Winter Haven

This tropical centre of the citrus-growing region is surrounded by spring-fed lakes. A Citrus Showcase has displays and dioramas of the citrus industry. Slocum Water Gardens has over 100 varieties of aquatic plants in a beautifully landscaped setting. Just north, on US 17 is the Museum of Old Dolls and Toys, showing dolls spanning three centuries, dolls' houses, miniature furniture and old toys.

Two miles south-east on State Route 540 is the spectacular Florida Cypress Gardens. Footpaths or electric boats on winding waterways lead through 13 themed Gardens of the World, the Big Lagoon, Movie Isles and Oriental Gardens. The Living Forest offers a southern colonial theme and there are countless attractions for children.

From Cypress Gardens, drive east for 5 miles on State Route 540. Turn right and drive south on US 27 for 6 miles to State Route 60. Turn east and drive for 1 mile to Lake Wales.

Lake Wales

Famous for Spook Hill, where through an optical illusion, stationary cars appear to roll up hill, this town includes peninsular Florida's highest point. Devotees of another kind of transport will be fascinated by the Lake Wales Museum and Cultural Center on South Scenic Highway, housed in the former Seaboard Coastline Depot. Exhibited here are the original dispatcher's desk, telegraph set, a 1916 Pullman car and other antiques.

Most spectacular of the attractions lies to the east of town. One mile east of US 27A is the Singing Tower and Mountain Lake Sanctuary. Dead on the highest point of the peninsula is the Singing Tower Florida which contains 53 bells ranging in size from 17 pounds to more than 11 tons. They were all donated by author Edward Bok. Carillon recitals are given daily at 3pm and a selection is played every half hour. Surrounding the tower are the 128 acres of the scenic Mountain Lake Sanctuary, containing thousands of azaleas, camellias and magnolias. The nature reserve features a bird observatory. Picnicking is permitted. Facing Lake Pierce, seven miles north-east off US 27A, is Masterpiece Gardens, with a fine mosaic reproduction of Leonardo da Vinci's 'The Last Supper'

COASTAL FLORIDA

surrounded by tropical gardens. A miniature train and a skyride provide views of the jungle areas and there is the inevitable tropical bird show.

Just over a mile south-east, again off US 27A, is an outdoor amphitheatre which is the scene of the Black Hills Passion Play during the summer. Phone (813) 676 1495 for details of performances.

Hotels

EMERALD MOTEL: 530 S Scenic Hwy, tel 676 3310. 19 rooms. Inexpensive.

SANDS MOTEL: 830 Hwy 27 S, tel 676 3917. Inexpensive.

Restaurant

CHALET SUZANNE RESTAURANT: US 27A, tel 676 1477. Elegant, with antique furnishings. Expensive.

Return north along US 27 for 15 miles, then bear right on US 17 for 5 miles to Davenport.

Davenport
North of town, near the junctions of US 27 and Interstate 4, is the renowned Ringling Brothers and Barnum and Bailey Circus World. A participation circus allows visitors to fly on a trapeze, walk a tightrope and learn to juggle. You can also try your hand at clown face painting!

Drive north on US 17 for about 7 miles, then drive west on State Route 532 for 4 miles to Interstate 4. Drive north-east for 11 miles on Interstate 4 to Lake Buena Vista. Enter **Walt Disney World** via US 192. See page 13. Return to Interstate 4 and drive north-east for about 18 miles to the centre of Orlando.

Orlando
This beautiful city is reflected in dozens of lakes. Sightseeing boats glide through lush greenery and at night the Centennial Fountain glimmers in the moonlight. The transport hub of central Florida, visitors rarely stop to appreciate this face of the city, but hurtle on to Walt Disney World and other fun spots. Orlando itself has plenty to offer. The lakeside beach is fine for swimming and water sports. At night, historic Church Street Station vibrates with Dixie-land jazz at Rosie O'Grady's Good Time Emporium.

Just off the Beeline Expressway is Sea World of Florida, which features performances by trained sealions, dolphins and a killer whale, and where, in a giant aquarium, many other forms of sea life can be watched. Fountain Fantasy Theater presents a show based on water fountains and jets with coloured lights and music. Try the skytown ride.

Also off Beeline Expressway is the Stars Hall of Fame. Here more than 200 life-size wax figures of movie and television stars are recreated in over 100 displays of their best known scenes. Starway Theater presents highlights of the history of the film and television industries.

Head north-east for State Route 426 and Winter Park.

Winter Park
Impressive estates surround the numerous lakes of this area and scenic one-hour-long boat tours leave from the foot of Morse Boulevard. On the campus of Rollins College is the Beal-Maltbie Shell Museum.

Continue east on State Route 426 to its junction with State Route 436, then drive south to State Route 50. Follow this eastwards to Interstate 95. Join Interstate 95 and drive 4 miles north to the next exit. Turn right and drive 2 miles to Titusville.

Titusville
This town is flourishing as a result of the proximity of Cape Canaveral across the Indian River. Eight miles north-east off US 1, on State Route 402, is Merritt Island National Wildlife Refuge, accessible across the Titusville causeway. Hunting is permitted here in season and fishing is available all year.

Retrace your route to US 1 and drive south for 8 miles to the entrance to the Kennedy Space Center, then go east on Nasa Causeway to the visitors' centre.

Fairy-tales come true for many young visitors to Walt Disney World. The showpiece of the Magic Kingdom is Cinderella Castle, a glittering, fantastic palace that towers to a height of almost 200 feet

The Kennedy Space Center is the home of the reusable Space Shuttle

Cape Canaveral

The John F Kennedy Space Center and Cape Canaveral Air Force Station on Merritt Island are the hub of the nation's space activities. The 140,000-acre centre is the site of many historic launchings.

On the Cape Canaveral Air Force Station, east of the space centre, is a missile research and development test centre. Missile launchings may be viewed from a distance of eight to ten miles and from a pier one mile north of State Route 520 causeway. Drive-through tours are permitted on Sundays from 9am to 3pm when launchings are not imminent. A visitor centre on State Route 405 features various exhibitions, lectures and films explaining US space programmes, actual spacecraft and models. An escorted two-hour bus tour starts at the visitor centre and takes in the space centre and air force station. Stops include the Moon Launch Pad, the 525-foot Vehicle Assembly Building, the original Apollo launch site and the Air Force Space Museum.

Drive south from the visitor centre, through Courtenay to State Route 528. Turn left and drive towards State Route A1A. Continue southwards on State Route A1A for about 6 miles to Cocoa Beach.

Cocoa Beach

This splendid beach is popular for surfing and there is an annual Labor Day Surfing Contest at Canaveral Pier, an 800-foot finger projecting in to the Atlantic, which also offers fishing and dancing. A 218-acre recreation complex on Banana River offers all the fun-of-the-fair. Situated between Cape Canaveral and Patrick Air Force Base, landings are often viewed from the beach and a roadside missile exhibit fronts the technical laboratory of the airbase on State Route A1A.

Hotels

CROSSWAY INN MOTEL: 3901 N Atlantic Av, tel 783 2221. 94 rooms. Moderate.

HOLIDAY INN: N Atlantic Av, tel 783 2271. 313 rooms. Expensive.

WAKULLA MOTEL APARTMENTS: 3550 N Atlantic Av, tel 783 2230. 115 rooms. Expensive-Moderate.

Restaurant

BERNARD'S SURF: 2 S Atlantic Av, tel 783 2401. Large menu specialising in seafood. Moderate.

Continue south through narrow Cocoa Island on State Route A1A for 48 miles to Vero Beach.

Vero Beach

A favourite place for retirement, Vero Beach has style and comparative solitude. Of interest is the McLarty Museum of Sunken Treasure just north on State Route A1A, which exhibits scenes of the Spanish Silver Fleet of 1715.

Drive south on US 1 for 14 miles to Fort Pierce.

Fort Pierce

A 1,014-acre park, the Fort Pierce Inlet Recreation Area, is a favourite spot for family activities, with picnicking, swimming, fishing and boating facilities. Each winter an unusual celebration known as 'Sandy Shoes' highlights some lesser-known aspects of Florida life. Indian River Drive is a scenic road surrounded by a profusion of colourful trees, flowers and birds which leads to Jensen Beach. Visitors may became acquainted with Jai-Alai ("High-Lie"), the fast Basque handball game at the World Jai-Alai fronton on State 607.

Continue south on US 1 for 13 miles to Stuart.

Stuart

Apart from being one of Florida's leading chrysanthemum-growing centres, and a magnet for anglers, Stuart is connected to slender, nostalgic Hutchinson Island. In 1875, the US Coast Guard selected the southern position of this peaceful island as the site of a refuge for shipwrecked sailors. Today, the House of Refuge stands as a weathered monument to past memories and as a museum of seafaring memorabilia. Displays include an assortment of ship's logs, gear salvaged from wrecked ships and life-saving equipment. Nearby is Elliott Museum, housing a collection of Americana dating from 1750. Apothecary and clock shops, a collection of early bicycles, and an 1850 general store are among exhibits. A post office and nickelodeon are particularly fascinating reminders of yesterday. On a still, balmy night, a lonely stretch along Hutchinson Island is an ideal spot to watch the ritual of sea turtles laying their eggs.

Hotels

HOLIDAY INN: Center, on US 1, tel 287 6200. 120 rooms. Expensive.

HOWARD JOHNSON'S MOTOR LODGE: 950 S Federal Hwy, tel 287 3171. 82 rooms. Moderate-Expensive.

Continue south on US 1 for 22 miles to Jupiter – south from this point, the climate becomes subtropical. Drive west on State Route 706 for 5 miles and join State Route 821 – Florida's Turnpike – for the remaining 76 miles south to Miami.

Miami

The warmth of the welcome, the heat of the sun, and the convenience of the lifestyle often comes as a surprise to the first time visitor. The delight of finding a land dedicated to your pleasure and entertainment is for many a unique and unforgettable experience; and Miami, first and foremost, is out to please.

This is very much an American-style resort, full of razzmatazz; everywhere something shouts out for your attention. On Miami Beach alone stand a quarter of Florida's hotels, each one fiercely competing with its neighbour for custom; the result, a stunning assembly of fantastic, grandiose buildings and within them a standard of luxury hard to match anywhere else in the world.

But the American hard sell is tempered in Miami by a strong Latin influence, instilled into the city by the thousands of Cuban refugees who have settled here. Their culture and their food, the palm-lined streets and tropical flowers, together impart an almost Caribbean atmosphere to the streets.

Above all other attractions, however, it is the superb climate, the idyllic beaches and bright blue seas that have created this holiday paradise, and which attract people year after year back into Miami's lap of luxury. Among each year's influx can be counted greater numbers of Britons, for as Miami becomes more easily accessible to travellers from across the Atlantic, the stronger her spell grows.

▲ *The attractions of Miami do not end when the sun goes down. The city is packed with after-dark entertainments of all kinds, and the glittering lights of Downtown shine on across the bay until dawn*

MIAMI

Reliable sunshine, beaches spacious enough to allow peaceful sunbathing, and a warm sea – these are the ingredients which endear any seaside resort to the tourist. Miami has all three in plenty; no wonder it is the city most people think of first when they contemplate a holiday in the States. Certainly the British have adopted Miami as a kind of transatlantic Blackpool, although the American entrepreneurs have not always delivered the Blackpool-style welcome and entertainment in return. Miami is first and foremost an American resort for Americans.

The British seem to suffer from two particular illusions; that the tourist season is the same on both sides of the Atlantic, and that Miami itself is one vast beach. Miami's holiday season is not parallel to the summer season in Britain and Europe, for it occurs in the winter from late November until March. That is when families from the wintry northern states pack their bags and seek the sun in southern Florida. In summer when it is unbearably hot in the North, it is several substantial degrees hotter in Miami. Neither is Miami packed with beaches.

The real beach paradise lies across the Biscayne Bay, on an island connected to the mainland by five major causeways. This is Miami Beach, a separate community built along ten miles of coastline where over the last 50 years a phalanx of hotels has been erected capable of accommodating up to three times Miami Beach's permanent population of 90,000.

The road that runs almost the entire length of the island is named after its most resourceful pioneer, John Collins. He wanted to turn what was still at the turn of the century a wilderness infested by snakes and mosquitoes into arable land, but when two of his agricultural ventures failed, he turned his efforts to promoting the island as a residential community. His success is epitomised by Collins Avenue, a breathtaking extravaganza of massive hotels, ranging from the grand art deco of the 1930s to glittering modern-day monsters. From this bustling heart of the resort there is access to the wide, 10-mile-long shimmering white beach. The beach suffered from early development, becoming a polluted, unattractive tattered ribbon of sand, but in the early 1970s the United States Army Corps of Engineers moved in. More than 13 million cubic yards of sand was reclaimed from the ocean and laid on the beach at a cost of £30 million . . . a task colourfully described as 'the largest land movement in the history of the United States.'

Without one woman's aggressive confidence in the future of this Indian tribal land, Miami would probably never have been developed in time to benefit from the tourist boom of the 20th century. As the daughter of a member of the Florida state

Once a wasteland of palm trees and mangrove swamps, Miami Beach has developed into one of America's most famous resorts. A string of huge luxury hotels lines the golden sands, tempting the world's wealthy to spend their winters in Florida's subtropical climate.

MIAMI

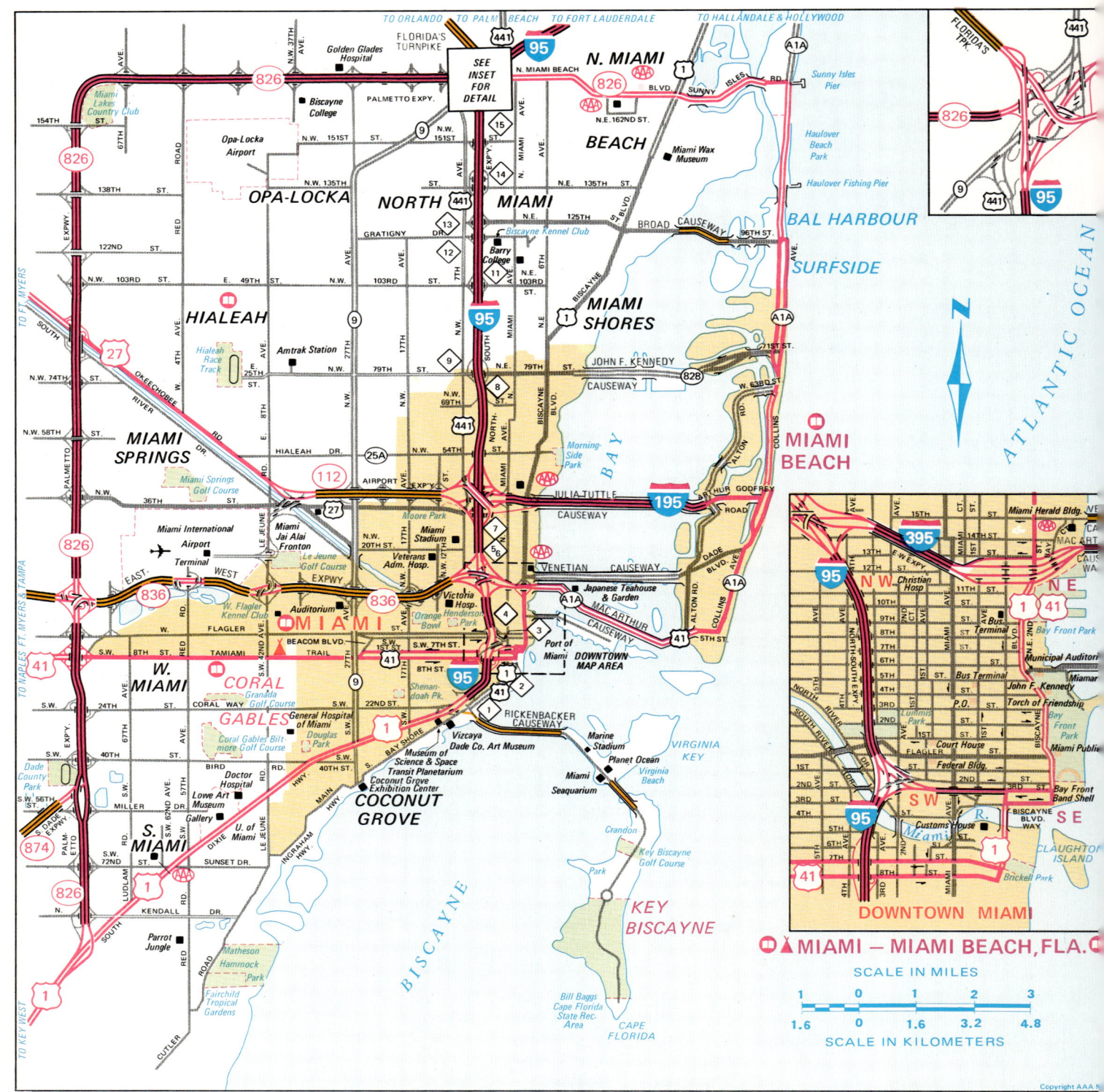

legislature, Julia Tuttle, in the latter half of the 19th century, was a frequent visitor to central Florida where her father had built a home. The widow of a Cleveland merchant, she used her charms to persuade railway tycoon Henry Flagler (he has Miami's main shopping street named after him; she, one of the causeways) not to abandon his ambitious plans to build a railway linking the already developing northern part of the state with the inhospitable mangroves and swamps further south. She did it by sending him a sprig of frost-free orange blossom as evidence that the sub-tropical climate she so enjoyed on her father's estate would make perfect conditions for attracting new settlers to the south. Her symbolic gesture paid off. Flagler travelled to Miami to meet this enterprising lady, and by the time he had to return home she had convinced him that not only should he continue laying the track to the tip of the

▶ *Miami offers excellent sports facilities. The city's many miles of waterfront make aquatic sports especially appealing. Marinas such as the Bayfront Miamarina, shown here, offer charter boats for pleasure trips or deep-sea fishing*

MIAMI

▲ *The culture and crafts of Indian tribes who have lived in Florida for hundreds of years are a source of great delight to modern tourists. Brightly coloured ethnic clothing, displayed on simple stalls, makes a refreshing change from the luxury goods on sale in Miami's exclusive stores, and the prices are attractive too*

peninsula and on to the end of the Keys, but that he should invest millions more developing the trading post there into a commercial port.

In April 1896 the track was completed and Flagler could begin bringing in the building materials to turn the village called Miami into a modern bustling metropolis. What Julia Tuttle and Flagler did not reckon with were the hurricanes and tidal waves, and the hordes of disease-ridden immigrants who landed at the port from the Caribbean islands. It was a constant battle against the elements. The building of a rail link all the way to Key West proved in the end to be too hazardous. In a spectacular hurricane in 1906, 200 men working on the track were killed.

For a time Flagler persisted. Despite constant damage from violent weather the railroad track was patched up over and over again. Then in June 1935 a massive 20-foot wall of water overwhelmed the Florida Keys and with it a train carrying 400 workers sent to repair the track. The tragedy spelt the end of Flagler's ambitions. Fortunately, by that time, the motor car had become a realistic alternative mode of transport. It made sense to rip up the track, and use the roadway across the 45 islands of the Keys as a motor highway. Since 1938, this overseas highway (US1) has been the artery nourishing the Keys and making Key West a bustling city, the most southerly in the United States.

Key West is a bizarre mixture of Caribbean and American influences. A popular draw for artists, it was also for many years after the Fidel Castro takeover in Cuba a temporary haven for his political exiles. Many of these refugees have settled in Miami – among them more than 200,000 Cubans who have created their own community within the city. A few streets around 8th Street in the south-east section of Miami are known as Little Havana, where the aroma of Cuban delicacies wafts from every doorway.

Close on half of the population of Dade County, the Metropolitan area of Miami and Miami Beach, are Latin immigrants. Spanish can be heard spoken in Miami's streets as naturally as English. Miami has other 'ethnic' conclaves, notably Indian reservations. The Tequesta tribe were believed to be the first to set up a Miami settlement, and a plaque marking the spot has been erected in Bayfront Park at the foot of Flagler Street. Another Indian tribe, the Cabusa, are credited with giving Miami its name by calling the river on which it stands Mayami. More recently, the Seminole Indians have settled in a reservation in the centre of Southern Florida, while the Micosukee have their tribal headquarters on the edge of the Everglades National Park to the west of Miami.

When the speculators arrived in their droves in the early part of the century, Miami was quickly and efficiently laid out in the familiar square patterns of so many American cities. Streets run horizontally and avenues at right angles. To make the going even easier Miami has divided its downtown area into four squares, identified by the diagonal points of the compass. Every address incorporates that information – useful to help pinpoint any house.

Miami and Miami Beach, and their satellite towns, have numerous high-quality high-priced shopping complexes which are worth visiting even if funds don't stretch to making purchases. You can pay between $10 and $100,000 for 'a little something

MIAMI

from Bal Harbour', a three-storey emporium dedicated to extravagance in one of the most exclusive parts of Miami Beach. The 'little something' could come from one of the 50 or more fashionable shops, many of them with world-famous names. Cartiers, Neiman-Marcus, Saks Fifth Avenue and Gucci are just some of the temples of extravagance and fine living that attract shoppers from as far afield as South America and Canada.

Another shopping treat is at the Mayfair shopping centre at Coconut Grove, a Miami neighbourhood notable for its art colony, and for an architectural style that ranges from Tudor cottages to 20th-century farmhouses. It is housed in a pretentious castle-like building with elegant wrought-iron staircases and fountains. The decor perhaps induces the right conditions of make-believe to persuade shoppers to throw caution to the wind. The merchandise is top class, and so, of course, are the prices. There are other massive shopping conglomerates. On Biscayne Boulevard, Omni houses 165 stores, 21 restaurants, six cinemas and a 556 room luxury hotel all under one roof.

The Falls, off South Dixie Highway, at south-west 136 Street, is even bigger. Claimed to be the largest environmental shopping, dining and entertainment complex in the United States, it is really a village set in a simulated tropical forest, but imaginatively designed to provide speciality shops and restaurants appealing particularly to the tourist.

As diverse and imaginative as the shops, hotels can cater for the £100 a night client or for the £10 overnight motorist at one of the numerous motels. Luxury hotels are fun to visit just for a drink. At the 1,200 room Fontainebleau Hilton, guests can swim under a waterfall, dip into a salt-water pool or take their pick from seven tennis courts. The smaller hotels, many of them survivors of a more select era, are busy finding a new role for themselves serving the package tour holiday maker. Like the Marina Park Hotel on Biscayne Boulevard which overlooks the yachting centre, many hotels have modernised, put on a new face and got on with the job of catering for a year-round clientele.

The restaurants, too, range from the fast-food chains (including one that specialises in British-style fish and chips), to the old-established eateries catering still for the same client whose support first brought them into being nearly 50 years ago. Joe's Stone Crab Restaurant is said to be the oldest restaurant on Miami Beach. It still flourishes, thanks to a reputation for superbly prepared fresh crustaceans, harvested by its owner, Joe Weiss, from his own fishing grounds off the coast. The place was

◀ *The carefully preserved 'Art Deco' area of Miami Beach makes a welcome change from the architecture of the later 20th century with its great expanses of plate glass, steel and concrete. Buildings like the St Moritz sprang up in the 1930s, in one of Miami's first building booms, some 30 years after the building of the railway began to open up the tourist potential of the area*

▶ *Ten acres of formal gardens are the setting for Villa Vizcaya, a mansion built in the Italian Renaissance style by James Deering. The tycoon had the mansion designed to house the many priceless works of art he had collected on his travels overseas. The villa is said to have cost him some $10 million and involved 1,000 craftsmen*

MIAMI

◀ *Performing dolphins are a star attraction at the 60 acre Miami Seaquarium. Porpoises, sealions and killer whales have also been specially trained to entertain visitors, while many other forms of aquatic life, both small and large, are on display in tanks*

immortalised by American short-story writer Damon Runyon in a tribute which is printed on the menu. The decor has virtually remained unchanged since 1913. Open only between October and April when the stone crabs are in season, the restaurant is always full. As booking a table is not allowed, it's a case of arriving early (that means soon after 5pm for dinner) and waiting in a long queue for your turn. A city with such a strong Spanish and Caribbean influence naturally offers enormous choices of ethnic foods. Apart from the Cuban and Hiatian dishes, Miami also enjoys a sizeable cuisine from its indigenous Chinese, French and Dutch-South African villages.

Miami's neighbouring city of Coral Gables was built in the Spanish Colonial style at the turn of the century. It is attractively laid out in tree-lined boulevards, with numerous fountains, and, in pride of place a Venetian pool built out of coral rock in the 1920s, modelled to the design of a Venetian lagoon. More than 200,000 visitors a year come either to swim in it or just to wander around the grotto and shady porticoes surrounding it.

Around Miami and attached to it are other self-contained cities. Hialeah, with a population of 121,000 is basically residential with its houses set among lush tropical greenery. Hollywood, though very different from its famous counterpart on the west coast, is worth visiting for its fine harbour.

Miami has more zoos and jungles and marine displays on its doorstep than any city really needs. The Metro Zoo, already covering 260 acres, is planned to grow into the largest zoo in America. It plays host to Bengal tigers, gibbons, gazelles, zebras, wildebeeste, ibexes and orang-utans, among many other exotic animals, which roam among temple ruins and jungle clearings in film-set style locations.

Key Biscayne, reached via the Rickenbacker causeway, lies four miles off the mainland and is almost totally dedicated to the pursuit of pleasure. Its two-mile long coastline is divided into seven specialised beach areas – one even for nude bathing. Apart from the usual outdoor activity sports, the island boasts the world's largest tropical marine aquarium. The Seaquarium has killer whales, sharks, sealions, seals, and dolphins performing daily. For more educational purposes Planet Ocean traces the role of oceans. It offers visitors an underwater display, and the opportunity to touch a real iceberg. It can also whip up a hurricane to order, bring on an indoor cloud and

MIAMI DIRECTORY

rainstorm, and recreate conditions aboard a submarine and the bridge of an oil tanker.

At the southern tip of the island Bill Bagg's Cape Florida State Recreation Area, named after the city's most prominent conservationist, covers 900 acres of natural ocean, with a museum to point out the phenomena.

Although Miami and Miami Beach have enough attractions to hold the interest of any visitor flying in for two weeks or more, a car is essential if other parts of Florida are on the itinerary. Car rental firms are numerous, and the arrangements for hire are easy and quick. But beware of the parking regulations. It is always wiser to park in a parking lot. There are also ample train and bus connections with many parts of Florida and beyond, and from the airport, there are frequent flights to Palm Beach and Orlando.

◀ Many of the world's most unusual and colourful tropical birds can be seen at Parrot Jungle. One popular attraction is Flamingo Lake, home of almost 100 of these graceful long-legged birds. The lake is reached by winding trails through lush jungle foliage

Miami Directory

HOTELS

Unless otherwise stated, all the hotels listed here are on the Miami Beach seafront, and have rooms with private bathrooms and colour television. Hotels and restaurants are classified as either inexpensive, moderate or expensive as a guide to cost.

AMERICANA OF BAL HARBOUR: 9701 Collins Av, tel 865 7511. 715 rooms, outdoor saltwater pool, health club. Expensive.

BEST WESTERN SAHARA MOTEL: 18335 Collins Av, tel 931 8335. 144 rooms, pool, coin laundry. Dining room, coffee shop. Closed Sep. Moderate.

DEAUVILLE HOTEL: 6701 Collins Av, tel 865 8511. 542 rooms, saltwater and wading pools, 3 tennis courts, exercise room (free) and sauna, children's entertainment, night club. Expensive.

DI LIDO HOTEL: 155 Lincoln Rd, tel 538 0611. 351 rooms, swimming pools, night club, coffee shop, room refrigerators. Moderate.

DORAL-ON-THE-OCEAN HOTEL: 4833 Collins Av, tel 532 3600. 425 rooms each with refrigerator. Cocktail lounges, rooftop dining room, sports courts. Expensive.

EDEN ROC: 4525 Collins Av, tel 327 8337. 350 rooms, unique views of beach, famous-name cabaret, solarium, dance lessons. Expensive.

FONTAINEBLEAU HILTON: 4441 Collins Av, tel 327 8367. 1200 rooms, golf course, bowling alleys, tennis courts, pool tables, Jacuzzi baths, two nightclubs, cocktail lounges. Expensive.

HADDON HALL HOTEL: 1500 Collins Av, tel 531 1251. 126 rooms, across the street from beach. No TV in rooms. Inexpensive.

KONOVER HOTEL: 5445 Collins Av, tel 327 0555. 465 rooms, all with refrigerators and extra-large beds. Famous-name cabaret and dancing. 2 swimming pools, sports and recreation rooms. Expensive.

MARINA PARK HOTEL: 340 Biscayne Blvd, Miami, tel 371 4400. 210 rooms. Near marina and port area, restaurant, bar and lobby on three levels form attractive garden terrace. Moderate.

OMNI INTERNATIONAL HOTEL: At 16th St, Biscayne Blvd, Miami, tel 374 0000. 556 rooms. Pool, sauna. Fee for health spa, lighted tennis. Large shopping and entertainment complex. Expensive.

RALEIGH HOTEL: 1777 Collins Av, tel 531 0792. 126 rooms, coffee shop, swimming pool. Inexpensive.

SHERATON BEACH RESORT: 19400 Collins Av, tel 325 3535. 498 rooms, many with private terraces. Tennis courts, swimming pools. Moderate.

WELWORTH HOTEL: 7326 Collins Av, tel 861 2426. 35 rooms each with refrigerator. Budget rate apartments available. Inexpensive.

RESTAURANTS

Miami can boast eating places ranging from sandwich shops to gourmet restaurants, as well as some of the finest Kosher and Cuban restaurants to be found anywhere in the world. Gold Coast specialities include sea food such as crawfish or Florida Lobster, stone crabs from south Florida or Everglades frogs' legs.

EMBERS: 245 22nd St, tel 538 4345. Order prime ribs of beef, duck, chicken or pheasant and watch it grill over hickory charcoal, but seafood such as Icelandic flounder and Maine lobster is a speciality. Open evenings only. Moderate.

FAMOUS RESTAURANT: 671 Washington Av, tel 531 3981. A well established restaurant with an enormous menu offering Jewish-American, Romanian, Ukrainian, Hungarian and Polish specialities. Open evenings only. Moderate.

FORGE RESTAURANT: 432 Arthur Godfrey Rd, tel 538 8533. A high class steak house illuminated by crystal chandeliers that once adorned the White House. Open evenings only. Expensive.

JOE'S STONE CRAB RESTAURANT: 227 Biscayne St, tel 673 0365. Splendid seafood menu in this popular restaurant. Stone crabs are a speciality and portions are generous. Moderate.

LE PARISIEN: 474 Arthur Godfrey Rd, tel 534 2770. Intimate restaurant with splendid French cuisine and adept service. Reservation recommended. Expensive.

PIETRO'S RESTAURANT: 1233 Lincoln Rd, tel 673 8722. Top quality Italian cooking with specialities such as linguine with clam sauce and saltimbocca. Moderate.

PUMPERNIK'S: 6700 Collins Av, tel 866 0242. Interesting meats and cheeses form part of a full delicatessen menu; there are also imaginative sweets. Breakfast here too. Inexpensive.

RED COACH GRILL: 1455 Biscayne Blvd, tel 379 4008. Generous portions are served at this popular restaurant which has an inviting, rustic decor, there is also a children's menu. Inexpensive.

RONEY PUB: 2305 Collins Av, tel 532 3353. Take your pick from a selection of seafood dishes or try New York-cut sirloin, cooked on an open-hearthed charcoal fire. There is also a stunning array of sweets. Open evenings only. Moderate.

SONNY'S ITALIAN RESTAURANT AND PIZZERIA: 247 23rd St, tel 538 1196. Almost every Italian dish ever thought of is on the large menu, but pizzas are the speciality here. Open evenings only. Moderate.

WOLFIE'S: 195 Lincoln Rd, tel 538 0326 and 2038 Collins Av, tel 538 6626. Both locations feature delicatessen menus with interesting soups, imaginative sandwiches and delicious pastries. Good coffee too. Reasonable.

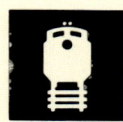

TRANSPORT

BUSES: Downtown Miami is served by The Metro Transit Agency which links with routes to Miami Beach and Coral Gables. Throughout the day, a special shuttle bus covers the City Centre in a continuous loop.

CAR HIRE: Rental rates can vary a lot between agencies and according to season. The major companies are: Airways, 3590 NW 36th St, tel 635 6444; Avis, 244 NE 1st St, tel 377 2531; Dollar, 300 Biscayne Blvd, Miami Beach, tel 358 2541; Hertz, 666 Biscayne Blvd, tel 377 4601; National, Miami International Airport, tel 526 5645.

MIAMI INTERNATIONAL AIRPORT: Le Jeune Rd and NW 36th St. One of the world's busiest airports, with flights direct from Britain and all major American cities. There are also 750 flights a week from 48 Latin American cities.

TAXIS: It is usually easy to hail one of the numerous taxis on the street or pick one up at the entrance of a large hotel. The major companies are: Yellow Cab Company, tel 634 4444; Diamond Cab Company, tel 545 7575. Other companies are listed in the telephone directory.

TRAIN: Details of train services from the Amtrak's Miami station at 8303 NW 37th Av, tel 691 0125. Fort Lauderdale

MIAMI DIRECTORY

station is at 200 SW 21st Terrace. There is no train service to Miami Beach.

TOURING INFORMATION

AAA: The East Florida Division of the AAA is at 4300 Biscayne Blvd, tel 573 5611. Open Monday to Friday during office hours. There are also branch offices in Miami, Jordan Marsh, 1501 Biscayne Blvd, tel 377 1911; South Miami, 7000 SW 62nd Av, tel 661 6131; North Miami Beach, 1435 NE 162nd St, tel 949 1421 and Jordan Marsh, 1475 NE 163rd St, tel 944 5161.

METROPOLITAN DADE COUNTY BUREAU OF TOURISM: 24 W Flagler St, tel 579 4694.

MIAMI BEACH VISITOR AND CONVENTION AUTHORITY: 555 17th St, Miami Beach, tel 673 7070.

PLACES TO SEE

CRANDON PARK ZOO: 4000 Crandon Blvd, Key Biscayne, tel 361 5421. Bengal tigers are among the 1,200 animals at this well-stocked zoo. Children are welcome at the 'petting zoo'.

MARINE STADIUM: 3601 Rickenbacker Causeway. With 6,500 covered seats, this is the place to see powerboat races and water shows. A 9-hour endurance race is usually held in mid-January.

METROZOO: SW 152nd St. Already covering a 260-acre site, Metrozoo is destined to become the largest zoo in America. Many of the animals here roam in locations that look like film-sets – Asian jungles and temple ruins, for example.

MIAMI HERALD BUILDING: NE 1 Herald Plaza, 2 blks E of US 1 via MacArthur Causeway. Reputedly one of the finest newspaper plants in the country. There are 45-minute tours, by appointment, on Monday, Wednesday and Friday at 10am and 2pm.

MONKEY JUNGLE: 14805 SW 216th St, Goulds (22 miles S off US 1), tel 235 1611. Watch out for chimpanzees, gibbons and orang-utans swinging through the trees at head level. South American monkeys can be seen in an Amazonian rain forest – their natural habitat.

SEAQUARIUM: Rickenbacker Causeway, tel 361 5703. This is the largest tropical marine aquarium in the world. Sharks, killer whales, dolphins and sea lions perform here daily.

MUSEUMS AND GALLERIES

BACARDI ART GALLERY: 2100 Biscayne Blvd. Exhibited here are works by local, national and international artists.

BASS MUSEUM: Collins Av at 21st and 22nd Sts, tel 673 7530. As well as displays of Renaissance, Baroque, Rococo and modern painting there are sculpture, tapestries and prints.

THE CLOISTERS OF THE MONASTERY OF ST BERNARD: 16711 W Dixie Hwy in North Miami Beach. Originally constructed in the province of Segovia, Spain, in the 12th century, they were occupied by Cistercian monks. In 1925 they were shipped to the United States and reconstructed on the present site in 1964. Ancient artwork, paintings and furniture are on display.

GROVE HOUSE: 3496 Main Hwy, tel 445 5633. A non-profit cooperative for craftsmen and artists which exhibits the work of award-winning artists from Florida.

LOWE ART MUSEUM: 1301 Miller Dr, tel 284 3535. One of the finest galleries in the South, this museum is part of the University of Miami at Coral Gables. It specialises in oriental porcelain and bronze and Indian tribal art.

MIAMI WAX MUSEUM: 13899 Biscayne Blvd, tel 945 3641. More than 40 scenes of America's past and present depicted in wax. Life-size statues of Columbus and President Carter are among the exhibits.

MUSEUM OF SCIENCE AND SPACE TRANSIT PLANETARIUM: 3280 S Miami Av, tel 845 4242. Part of the Historical Museum of South Florida, its displays cover Florida culture and wild-life from Indian times through to the Space Age. The exhibits include a live iguana, tarantula spider and a baby alligator. A planetarium offers shows daily.

PLANET OCEAN: 3979 Rickenbacker Causeway, Key Biscayne, tel 361 9455. Headquarters of the International Oceanographic Foundation, it is an educational ocean science centre offering the thrills of an indoor cloud and rainstorm, and a hurricane. The history of the world's oceans is told in seven cinemas, and there are over 100 exhibits.

VIZCAYA-DADE COUNTY MUSEUM: 3251 S Miami Av, tel 579 2708. In 35 ornate rooms, the European treasures of this former millionaire's home span 18 centuries. In the grounds, sculptures from France and Italy are shown off beside pools and fountains.

PARKS AND GARDENS

BAYFRONT PARK: Biscayne Bay, NE 5th St to SE 2nd St. Outdoor amphitheatre fringed by stately palms where concerts, operas and pageants are held. The park also contains the Civic Auditorium, library, and the John F Kennedy Memorial Torch of Friendship.

BILL BAGGS CAPE FLORIDA STATE RECREATION AREA: Key Biscayne. The Cape Florida lighthouse and a reconstructed keeper's home and office are some of the features of a museum complex on 900 acres of this huge park on the southern tip of the island. Museum and lighthouse tours daily.

FAIRCHILD TROPICAL GARDENS: 10901 Old Cutler Rd, tel 667 1651. A rain forest is one of the attractions of the reputedly 'largest tropical botanical garden' in the United States on 83 acres of rolling greenery. Guided motor tours are available.

GARDEN OF OUR LORD: St James Lutheran Church, 110 Phonetia, Coral Gables. Many plants mentioned in the Bible are sown and grown here.

JAPANESE TEAHOUSE AND GARDEN: Watson Park, MacArthur Causeway. Landscaped garden setting is dominated by a ceremonial Japanese teahouse. Features include stone lanterns, a pagoda, an arbur, rock gardens and a lagoon. Admission free.

MATHESON HAMMOCK PARK: Old Cutler Rd. The park has a beach beside Biscayne Bay, with a boat ramp. Trails cut through native shrubs and virgin forest.

MIAMI BEACH GARDEN CENTER AND CONSERVATORY: Washington Av, north of Lincoln Road Mall. See the Cloud Forest, a jungle environment under a dome generating intense heat that allows all manner of exotic plants to thrive. The Garden Center is a municipal enterprise to which admission is free.

ORCHID JUNGLE: 26715 SW 157th Av, Homestead, tel 247 4824. Though 25 miles out of the city, this is worth a visit for the bonus of the ladies receiving an orchid and for the breath-taking sight of orchids growing naturally.

REDLAND FRUIT AND SPICE PARK: junc Coconut Palm Dr and Redland Rd, Homestead, tel 247 5727. More than 250 species of fruit, nut and spice trees and plants on show on 20 acres. The fruit can be sampled.

SPORT

BOATING: With room for more than 4000 boats in Miami, the marine facility at Miamarina on Biscayne Bay caters for sightseeing and charter boat customers from its 178 slips. The choice includes water skiing.

FISHING: The Gulf Stream brings gamefish like marlin, dolphin and tuna within reach of deep-sea fishermen on chartered boats. The 50-mile-long Tamiami Canal, along the western boundary of Miami, is well stocked with fish. Licences can be obtained from County Judge Office, in Dade County Courthouse. Bridge Fishing is fun from MacArthur, Rickenbacker, 79th St and Sunny Isles causeways.

GOLF: With more than 35 golf courses in the Greater Miami area, the opportunities are wide. Choose from Le Jeune, an 18-hole course on rolling fairways at 1802 NW 37th Av; the championship course (18 holes) at Key Biscayne, 6200 Crandon Blvd; the Biltmore (18 holes) at 1210 Anastasia Av, Coral Gables; and the Miami Springs (18 holes), at 650 Curtis Pkwy, Miami Springs. Your hotel may have special arrangements.

ICE SKATING: This is available in the luxurious Fontainebleau Hotel on Collins Av, Miami Beach's leading hotel. There is also an ice rink at the Polar Palace, 3685 NW 36th St.

TENNIS: Many parks and several hotels have tennis courts. Among those with at least four courts are Douglas Park, 2755 SW 37th Av; Curtis Park, 1901, NW 24th Av; Henderson Park, 971 NW 2nd St; Moore Park, 765 NW 36th St; Morningside Park, 750 NE 55th Ter; Shenandoah Park, 1800 SW 21st Av.

THEATRES

DADE COUNTY AUDITORIUM: 2901 W Flagler St, tel 642 9061. Opportunities for all year round theatrical and cultural events.

GUSMAN CULTURAL CENTER: 174 E Flagler St, tel 358 3430. 40-week season of dramas and musicals of all kinds.

MIAMI BEACH THEATER OF THE PERFORMING ARTS: 1700 Washington Av. Home of the Miami Beach Symphony Orchestra, it also houses pre- and post-Broadway shows, seasons by the Miami Ballet, the Florida Philharmonic Orchestra and the Greater Miami Opera Association.

PLAYERS STATE THEATER AT THE COCONUT GROVE PLAYHOUSE: 3500 Main Hwy, Coconut Grove, tel 442 4000. This is an ideal holiday theatre venue, with visiting star-studded shows and a resident repertory company.

The Mid-Atlantic States
Delaware, Maryland, Pennsylvania, Virginia and West Virginia

Pennsylvania played a central role in the War of Independence, and from its forges came the cannon for Washington's Continental Army. The guns seen here are being fired at Valley Forge, where Washington's army spent a terrible winter in 1777-8, as part of celebrations staged by the Valley Forge Historical Society every December.

These five states all lie within easy reach of America's capital, Washington DC, and each one is inextricably bound up with the events of history which heralded the birth of the United States.

Here, to the eastern seaboard, came the early European settlers: the Dutch and the Swedes sought the flatlands of coastal Delaware and the deep wooded valleys to the north; in 1634 persecuted Catholics from England settled in Maryland, the state that bore the brunt of the 1812 war with England which gave the nation its national anthem.

To Pennsylvania came the *Deutsch*, religious refugees from the Palatinate of Germany in the late 1600s, later to be known as the Pennsylvania Dutch. Charles II granted what is now Pennsylvania to William Penn after it was wrested from the Dutch in 1664, and here he founded his new Quaker society, based on ideas of tolerance and sobriety which he instilled in the settlers. Many sects still practice the simple lifestyle of these early founders.

Colonial Virginia thrived on tobacco, which meant the labour of slaves. The state provided the first Presidents after Independence was won in 1783. In 1861, however, it seceded from the Union, declared Richmond the Confederate capital, and became the central arena for the battles of the Civil War. In turn, West Virginia separated from her parent state in 1863 – the 'hillbillies' of the west had little in common with the colonial society of the east – and joined the Union.

These mid-Atlantic states were the nation's richest agricultural area in colonial times, and with the passing of the War of Independence and the Civil War, are now rich in the historic beginnings of what is today the most powerful nation on earth.

THE MID-ATLANTIC STATES

You don't need to be a student of American history to know that in this corner of the United States the American colonies were lost to Britain 200 years ago.

Certainly they have much to tell in Pennsylvania, Maryland, Virginia, West Virginia and Delaware about battles won and lost, not only in the American Revolutionary War, but also a century later in the Civil War, which rent the country apart as effectively as the British defeat 100 years earlier had united it.

It is not their geographical proximity to power alone that makes these five states so exciting and stimulating to visit; it is that no states come closer to the heart of what the United States is all about than those that surround Washington.

The part of Virginia which matters to the Washington visitor is bounded by the familiar names of American history, such as Harrisonburg in the west, Fredericksburg in the centre, Richmond, the state capital, 50 miles south, and Norfolk on the coast.

Norfolk's harbour, one of the finest in the world, is home to more than 100 ships of the Atlantic and Mediterranean fleets, and together with the naval shipyard in neighbouring Portsmouth, is the largest naval base in the world. Both the naval station, with its submarine piers, and the air station under US Naval command, can be toured by coach.

At the mouth of the James River a few miles away, Newport News, its breezy name catching the salty tang of a seafarer's town, has a comprehensively stocked Mariner's Museum and Library on Museum Drive, and a Victory Arch on 25th Street and West Avenue, which, though built in 1919 after World War I, is a memorial to American servicemen and women of all wars.

It was the sea around the coast of Virginia (the state was named after the virgin Queen Elizabeth I) that made history for the New World. Despite several previous attempts to land along the coast, the first permanent English colony was established on the continent on 13 May, 1607, when a London expedition of three ships sailed up the James River.

Susan Constant, *Godspeed* and *Discovery* landed their cargo of settlers and supplies on Jamestown Island. The immigrants spent the next years grappling with a hostile environment and trying to survive disease, fire and hunger. Then, fortunately, a new influx of settlers and supplies arrived to sustain the surviving 60 pioneers. Lasting prosperity, however only came much later, when the tobacco leaf brought the world's traders to these shores. Replicas of the three vessels are moored in the James River near James Fort, and *Susan Constant*'s tiny quarters have been carefully reconstructed for the tourist. The first permanent English settlement is recreated in wattle and daub in the Jamestown Festival Park.

NORFOLK

Hotels

ECONO LODGE: 1850 Little Creek Rd, tel 583 1561. 59 rooms. Restaurant. Inexpensive.

HOLIDAY INN: 930 Virginia Beach Blvd, tel 622 2361. 169 rooms. Moderate.

OMNI INTERNATIONAL HOTEL: 777 Waterfront Dr, tel 622 6664. 461 rooms. Expensive.

Restaurant

THE ESPLANADE: in Omni International Hotel, tel 622 6664. À la carte menu, refined atmosphere. Expensive.

SHIPS CABIN: 4110 Ocean view Av. Overlooking Chesapeake Bay. Delicious seafood kebabs of skewered oysters, shrimp, scallops, lobster, fish, tomatoes, onions and peppers. Expensive.

Places to See

CHRYSLER MUSEUM: 3 blks W of Virginia Beach Blvd. Paintings, sculpture and glassware from four continents.

GENERAL DOUGLAS MACARTHUR MEMORIAL: City Hall Av. Impressive range of MacArthur memorabilia plus film show, all housed in 1847 courthouse.

HERMITAGE FOUNDATION MUSEUM: 7637 North Shore Rd. Large collection, specialising in both Oriental and Western Art.

MYERS HOUSE: corner of Freemason and Bank Sts. Restored, late 18th-century example of Federal architecture. All original furniture.

NORFOLK GARDENS-BY-THE-SEA: adjacent to municipal airport. Mature azalea, camellia and rhododendron gardens. Native pine, laurel and dogwood in lakeland setting.

Part of the first permanent English colony in America, James Fort has been realistically reconstructed for visitors to the Jamestown Festival Park

THE MID-ATLANTIC STATES

Yorktown battlefield, scene of the British surrender at the end of the Revolutionary War in 1782

NEWPORT NEWS

Hotels

COLONIAL COURTS MOTEL: 10451 Jefferson Av, tel 599 3345. 46 rooms. Moderate.

ECONO-TRAVEL MOTOR HOTEL: 11845 Jefferson Av, tel 599 3237. 72 rooms. Inexpensive.

TRAVELERS INN MOTEL: 14747 Warwick Blvd, tel 874 0201. 119 rooms. Restaurant. Expensive.

WARWICK MOTEL: 12304 Warwick Blvd, tel 599 4444. 31 rooms. Restaurant. Inexpensive.

Places of Interest

MARINERS MUSEUM AND LIBRARY: exit 9 from 1-64 at Museum Dr. Houses an extensive and varied collection of nautical artefacts.

NEWPORT NEWS HARBOR CRUISE: departs Jefferson and 12th St. 1½hr trip takes in shipyards and the Naval HQ for the US fleets.

PENINSULA NATURE AND SCIENCE CENTER: in deer park off J Clyde Morris Blvd. Includes zoo, aquarium, observatory and many natural history exhibits.

WAR MEMORIAL MUSEUM OF VIRGINIA: ½ mile N of James River Bridge on US 60. International exhibits from World Wars I and II, plus SE Asian campaigns.

Jamestown's pride is the Old Church Tower which is the only genuine remaining structure of the 17th-century to be preserved. But many other souvenirs of the town's 300 years of history have been lovingly recreated. Paintings depicting the completed buildings from the remains that have been excavated are on show, and the foundations of the first statehouse, the scene of the first attempt at representative government in America, can also be viewed.

Further up the coast, another river later gave birth to another historic town. In the 18th-century Yorktown became a busy seaport near the estuary of the York River. It was here that on 5 September 1781, after a decisive naval battle of the War of Independence, the French forced the British fleet to retire. As a consequence, British troops surrendered, bringing the American Revolution virtually to an end.

Capturing the excitement of these stirring

JAMESTOWN

Place of Interest

JAMESTOWN FESTIVAL PARK: Glasshouse Point. Amusement park opened in 1957 to celebrate the town's 350th anniversary. Theme buildings explain early American life.

times are nine buildings in the town which were standing at the time of the siege and surrender of 19 October. There is also a well-ordered tour of the Battlefield in the Colonial National Historical Park, with all the important sites of the great battles marked.

But it was not to be the only time Yorktown earned a place in the history books. In the Civil War, in which the southern states of the Confederacy fought the northern states for the right to secede from the Union, it was besieged by Union forces and subsequently was the scene of a humiliating surrender by the Confederates.

Nearby Williamsburg (to which the besieged Confederate armies at Yorktown retreated) is now a picturesque, but bustling town of more than 11,000 inhabitants. It was used as an outpost of Jamestown in 1633 when the settlers first tried to gain a foothold on the peninsula.

'That the future may learn from the past' is the motto by which Williamsburg has tackled its restoration programme throughout the mile-long and half-mile wide colonial area of the city. Known as Colonial Williamsburg, it is a harmonious blend of houses, shops and public buildings

THE MID-ATLANTIC STATES

YORKTOWN

Hotels

DUKE OF YORK MOTOR HOTEL: 2 blks E of US 17, Water and Ballard Sts, tel 898 3232. 57 rooms. Expensive.

YORKTOWN MOTOR LODGE: 3¼ miles S of Yorktown Bridge on US 17, tel 898 5451. 42 rooms. Moderate.

Restaurant

NICK'S SEAFOOD PAVILION: off US 17 under Yorktown Bridge on Water St, tel 887 5269. À la carte and children's menus. Inexpensive.

Places of Interest

BATTLEFIELD: within Colonial National Park. A tour road follows encampment sites and fortifications.

GRACE CHURCH: built in 1697 and partially rebuilt following the fire damage of 1814. Used as a magazine during the Yorktown siege. 500-year-old Communion silver still in use.

NATIONAL PARK SERVICE VISITOR CENTER: at the end of Colonial Parkway. Various nautical exhibits, self-guided battlefield tours and film.

WILLIAMSBURG

Hotels

ECONO LODGE II: 1408 Richmond Rd, tel 229 2981. 56 rooms. Inexpensive.

HOWARD JOHNSON'S MOTOR LODGE: 1800 Richmond Rd, tel 229 2781. 77 rooms. Moderate.

QUALITY INN – FORT MAGRUDER: 1660 Pocohontas Trail, tel 220 2250. 244 rooms. Expensive.

Restaurants

ABERDEEN BARN: 1601 Richmond Rd, tel 229 6661. Good food in rustic atmosphere. Moderate.

CHRISTINA CAMPBELL'S TAVERN: Waller St, tel 229 2141. 18th-century tavern. Moderate.

YORKSHIRE INN: 700 York St, tel 229 9790. Good food, pleasant atmosphere. Moderate.

Places of Interest

ABBY ALDRICH ROCKEFELLER FOLK ART CENTER: between Williamsburg Inn and the lodge. One of America's finest folk art collections.

BRUSH-EVERARD HOUSE: on NE side of Palace Green. 18th-century middle-class home with period furnishings, antiques and a library.

CAPITOL: E end of Duke of Gloucester St. Twice rebuilt following fire damage, but refurnished according to original records. Rare portraits of early American presidents.

GOVERNOR'S PALACE: facing Palace Green. Once used by the 18th-century royal governors. Large courtyard, gardens and nearby canal.

WILLIAMSBURG NATIONAL WAX MUSEUM: 2¾ miles NW on US 60. 33 life-size tableaux, depicting colonial history up to the Battle of Yorktown.

Replicas of 18th-century buildings bring the past to life in Colonial Williamsburg

set in nearly 100 beautifully kept gardens. More than 80 18th-early-19th-century buildings have survived, and many more have been faithfully rebuilt on their original sites. With a passion for pageantry and a devotion to detail, Williamsburg lays on the past with style and enthusiasm. The city's calendar offers events all year round, notably around Christmas and in mid-August to commemorate the birthday of King William III, after whom the town was named.

A few miles out of the city are two major tourist attractions. One is Carter's Grove (no relation!) which has been described as the most beautiful house in America. It was built in the middle of the 18th century, as a memorial to an entrepreneur called Robert 'King' Carter, who owned more than 300,000 acres and over 1,000 slaves. In the grounds is the site of a British plantation colony, believed to be the first planned in British America, but destroyed by Indians in 1622.

The other large-scale attraction is Busch Gardens, which, known as 'The Old Country', reproduces the national characteristics of European cultures; costumed 'extras' appear as Beefeaters from the Tower of London, burgomasters raise frothing Steins in German-style beer cellars, and other imported national costumes from France and Italy are dramatically illustrated.

Virginia is undoubtedly best known throughout the world for its most enduring export, the tobacco leaf. Whether a smoker or not, don't miss the opportunity to see for yourself how important this fascinating industry has been to the prosperity of Virginia. In Petersburg, about 30 miles east of Williamsburg, the Brown and Williamson Tobacco Corporation holds open house during weekdays, and in Richmond, the capital of Virginia, two factories allow visitors: the American Tobacco Company at 26th and Cary Streets, and Phillip Morris and Company at the junction of Commerce and Bells Roads.

Most of the sights in Richmond com-

RICHMOND

Hotels

AMERICAN HOUSE MOTOR INN: 515 W Franklin St at Belvidere, tel 643 2831. 192 rooms. Inexpensive.

EXECUTIVE MOTOR HOTEL: 5215 W Broad St, tel 288 4011. 142 rooms. Moderate.

RICHMOND HYATT HOUSE: 6624 W Broad St, tel 285 8666. 400 rooms. Expensive.

Restaurants

CAPRI RESTAURANT: 1 E Grace St, tel 644 5813. À la carte Italian food. Inexpensive.

LA PETITE FRANCE: 2912 Maywill St, tel 353 8729. Excellent French cuisine. Moderate.

TOP OF THE TOWER: 104 W Franklin St, tel 649 0000. Good food and panoramic views. Moderate.

Places of Interest

CAPITOL: Capitol Sq. Designed by Jefferson in style of Roman temple. Construction began in 1788. Two central halls formerly the seat of the General Assembly.

POE MUSEUM AND RICHMOND'S OLDEST HOUSE: 1914 E Main St. Memorial Building, Old Stone House (the town's oldest house, built in the 1680s) and a converted carriage house. Edgar Allan Poe memorabilia.

RICHMOND NATIONAL BATTLEFIELD PARK: site of the struggle for possession of the Confederate capital. Individual battlefields landmarked.

VIRGINIA MUSEUM OF FINE ARTS: Grove Av. Wide-ranging collection from ancient to contemporary art. Notable Fabergé jewelled objects. Plays and music productions staged in winter.

THE MID-ATLANTIC STATES

memorate the political and military battles of the great internal wars. Many of the giant figures of early America lived, worked, or came to debate here. Among the numerous places worth visiting, St John's, a modest 18th-century church, is where the early decisions were taken by luminaries like George Washington and Thomas Jefferson, the author of the Declaration of Independence. Jefferson himself designed the Capitol building in the town after the Maison Carrée, a Roman temple at Nîmes. Although the central part was completed in 1788, the wings were not added until the beginning of this century.

Fredericksburg, about 60 miles north of Richmond on Interstate 95, is where George Washington's mother, Mary, lived until her death in 1789. There is a monument engraved to her memory on Washington Avenue at the end of Pitt Street. The great President's birthplace, located on the borders of Maryland and on the southern side of the Potomac River, is a national shrine. Thirty-eight miles east of Fredericksburg, it includes 538 acres of plantation. The house, finished in 1726, was destroyed by fire on Christmas Day in 1779, but a memorial house has been built on the site, a reconstruction based on information gleaned from excavations of five original foundations which is furnished with antiques reflecting the period of Washington's early life.

As in so many other parts of America, motoring can be very rewarding. Along the Blue Ridge Mountains to the west of the state, a 469 mile scenic motorway called the Blue Ridge Parkway connects the Shenandoah National Park with the Great Smoky Mountains National Park in North Carolina and Tennessee. It follows the crest of the Blue Ridge at times rising to more than 6,000 feet, and numerous stopping off places are provided from which to admire the Southern Highlands – a stunning view. There is overnight accommodation on the mountains, particularly at Doughton Park and Rocky Knob.

Though only slightly smaller than Pennsylvania – the largest among all the states in the vicinity of Washington – Virginia might have been more than half as big again if West Virginia had not seceded and set up on its own. The mountain people of the western areas of Virginia became disenchanted with the way the legislative powers in the richer east, who created wealth through slave-worked plantations, controlled the state. Also their trade interests differed, the east was oriented around the coast, the west turned more towards New Orleans. So on 20 June, 1863, West Virginia joined the Union as the 35th state. Today West Virginia has one of the finest park systems in the USA, and offers some of the most dramatic scenery east of the Rockies.

Maryland's territorial problems were different. It had to make do with the 12,000 square miles it was left after a small but significant acreage had been appropriated for the creation of the District of Colombia, the patch of land at the confluence of the Anacostra and Potomac Rivers on which Washington stands. But despite the state's size, the lush terrain, extending from the rugged Allegheny Mountains to languid Chesapeake Bay, is surprisingly varied. Maryland's highest point is 3,360-feet-high Backbone Mountain, while at sea level the state's 7,000 miles of shoreline is only 1,000 miles less than the endless beaches around Florida. Neither has lack of size prevented Maryland from scoring a number of firsts, for its people have always taken pride in being pioneers. Here the first commercial railroad ran on the continent of America, here the first telegraph line was laid, here the first linotype machine was operated, the first friction matches were struck and the first dental college opened.

The timbered hillsides of the Shenandoah National Park, which extends 80 miles along one of the highest and most beautiful parts of the Blue Ridge, harbour a remarkable variety of wildlife, including groundhogs and bears

FREDERICKSBURG

Hotels

BEST WESTERN-THUNDERBIRD INN: 3000 Plank Rd, tel 786 7404. 48 rooms. Expensive.

DAYS INN: on US 17 at junc I-95, tel 373 5340. 120 rooms. Moderate.

THR-RIFT INN MOTEL: 1031 Warrenton Rd, tel 371 6000. 100 rooms. Moderate.

Restaurant

P.K.'S RESTAURANT: in Westward Shopping Centre 2051 Plank Rd, tel 371 3344. Victorian atmosphere. Inexpensive.

Places of Interest

FREDERICKSBURG NATIONAL MILITARY PARK: 5,000-acre park on outskirts of town, the site of four Civil War battlefields. Exhibitions, paintings and historic markers.

HISTORIC FREDERICKSBURG MUSEUM: 623 Caroline St. Built around 1772 by John Glassell, a Scot. Exhibits record town life, supplemented by a short film.

RISING SUN TAVERN: 1306 Caroline St. Built by Charles Washington, brother of George, in 1760. Formerly a meeting place for pre-revolutionary sympathisers. Restored with period furnishings.

VISITOR CENTER: 706 Caroline St. Information for visitors and guidance on self-organised tours.

THE MID-ATLANTIC STATES

Chesapeake Bay, 30 miles at its widest point, helps to cut much of Maryland off from the bustle of commercial America, and here people live simply in the bayside island communities of Deal, Hoopars, Kent, Tangier or Tilghman's.

The most northern port in the bay is Chesapeake City, an important transportation point for traffic on the Chesapeake and Delaware Canal, which permits waterborne craft direct access to Philadelphia, so shortening the route between Baltimore and Philadelphia by more than 275 miles.

Boat building is one of the important Maryland industries, and tobacco, too, makes a significant contribution to its economy.

At its narrowest point near the town of Hancock, Maryland is eaten away by the bulbous protrusion of West Virginia, and cut off by the uncompromising straight-line border of Pennsylvania to the north. The largest town in this area, in the heart of the Appalachian Mountains, is Cumberland,

Many craft connected with Chesapeake Bay are on display at the museum at St Michaels

where the Chesapeake and Ohio Canal has its western terminal. It is also the western terminal of the Cumberland Trail, the first road built to cut through the Appalachian Mountains through the gateway known as the Cumberland Narrows. (Not to be confused with Cumberland Gap, the pass in the south-western tip of Virginia, first explored in 1750, which played a crucial role in the fighting of the Civil War). The pass is now part of the 22,000-acre National Historical Park. From Cumberland all the way to Washington, along that 200-mile-long border with West Virginia, the Chesapeake and Ohio Canal National Historical Park follows the course of the Potomac River from Georgetown, the prestigious Washington suburb. Along its route the 184-mile-long canal takes in the spectacular Great Falls of the Potomac, the most popular tourist attraction in the park.

Annapolis, now the state capital, played a decisive role in the protest against British rule, and staged its own version of the Boston Tea-party (see page 91) by burning the tea ship *Peggy Stewart* in the harbour. One of the oldest cities in the United States, it has the only 18th-century waterfront still existing on America's Atlantic coast.

But Maryland's commercial heart is at Baltimore, the fifth largest city on the East Coast. With a population of 827,000 and as cosmopolitan as any great city, Baltimore suffers from an inferiority complex in that it has to live in the shadow of Washington less than 40 miles away to the south. So many

---

ANNAPOLIS

Hotels

ANNAPOLIS HILTON INN: at city dock, tel 268 7555. 140 rooms. Moderate.

THR-RIFT INN MOTEL: 2¼ miles SW on US 50, 2542 Riva Rd, tel 224 2800. 150 rooms. Inexpensive.

Restaurants

HARBOUR HOUSE: on city dock, 87 Prince George St, tel 268 0771. Popular restaurant. Children's menu. Moderate.

WHITEHALL INN: 1½ miles W of Chesapeake Bay Bridge, tel 757 3737. Rustic restaurant. Moderate.

Places of Interest – see page 41

THE MID-ATLANTIC STATES

Washingtonians have taken Baltimore into their lives that the army of commuters between the cities has made it almost a suburb of the nation's capital. Even Baltimore-Washington International Airport, as its name implies, is as much at the service of the Washington jet-setter as it is for its own visitors. There is, nevertheless, much to see and enjoy in Baltimore. America's oldest warship, the United States Frigate *Constellation*, has been preserved in Constellation Dock. Launched in 1797, it was used against pirates in 1802, the British in 1812 and against the Confederate forces in the Civil War. As recently as World War II, it was an auxiliary flagship of the Atlantic Fleet. The harbour – Baltimore is still a major Atlantic port – was once surrounded by decaying factories and warehouses, but is now the showplace of the city. The Charles Center, Baltimore's business area, includes a 12,000-seater civic centre where conventions, exhibitions and sports events are held. The interior of the city hall, built in 1875, was renovated for its centenary at a cost of 11 million dollars.

Baltimore also offers the visitor the chance to see the place where a young Georgetown lawyer called Francis Scott Key was inspired to write the words of the 'Star-Spangled Banner', America's national anthem set to an old English drinking tune. Key was witness to the British attempt to seize Baltimore during the Forgotten War of 1812. To take Baltimore the British fleet had to capture Fort McHenry, guardian of Baltimore's inner harbour. This they failed to do, and the sight of the American flag flying triumphantly above the fort after surviving 25 hours of bombardment prompted Key to set pen to paper. The full story is told in the Fort McHenry National Monument and Historic Shrine. If such patriotic nostalgia is not enough, tourists can visit the Star-Spangled Banner Flaghouse at 844, East Pratt Street, at Albemarle, where a seamstress called Mary Pickersgill made the very fifteen star and fifteen stripe American flag flown at Fort McHenry during the bombardment. A replica, measuring 30 foot by 42 foot, is on display, and there is a museum next door.

The Stars and Stripes also played a significant part in the history of Delaware, the diminutive state on the Eastern seaboard, which cuts a 2,000-square-mile chunk of territory out of the peninsula between Chesapeake Bay and the Atlantic. Ranking 49th in the pecking order of American states, it can look back for its moment of glory to 3 September 1777. In the only battle on its soil during the Revolutionary War, the Stars and Stripes were said to have been exposed to enemy fire for the first time at Cooch's Bridge. Delaware was also the first state to declare itself loyal to the new union and constitution.

The people of Delaware are known as 'Blue Hen Chickens', a nickname earned for them by their soldiers during the Revolution. Cockfighting was a popular pastime among the troops, and in Delaware a few especially successful birds were rumoured to be the offspring of a blue hen – 'Blue Hen Chickens' became the tag by which the soldiers became known, eventually to be inherited by all the citizens of Delaware. Ironically, the state's largest agricultural industry today is the raising of broilers, which bring in half the total farm income of nearly 150 million dollars a year.

Delaware possesses one of America's oldest and smallest state capitals, the pleasant colonial city of Dover. William Penn suggested that a county courthouse and prison be built here in 1683, and by 1777 the beautiful Old State House, formerly the courthouse, had been made the state capitol. But Dover today is overshadowed by the giant commercial city of Wilmington. Although founded in 1638, it remained a quiet Quaker town until the early 19th-century, when E I du Pont de Nemours and his two sons founded their modest gunpowder factory (see also page 45). The first barrel of Du Pont gunpowder was produced in 1803. Since then the company has become the ninth largest conglomerate in the world with interests in a vast range of chemical and oil industries. The Henry Francis du Pont Winterthur Museum and the Hagley Museum encapsulate the Du Pont story and their effect on Wilmington's prosperity. In the 200-acre complex of museums and mills which constitutes the Hagley Museum – some restored to their original 19th-century

Launched in 1797, the US Frigate 'Constellation' was in service as a warship for more than 150 years. It is now in retirement at Constellation Dock, Baltimore

BALTIMORE

Hotels

BALTIMORE HILTON: at Charles Center, tel 752 1100. 510 rooms. Expensive.

QUALITY INN-NORTHWEST: on US 140 at I-695, 10 Wooded Way, tel 484 7700. Moderate.

Restaurants

CAFE DES ARTISTES: in Mechanic Theatre Bldg, 9 Hopkins Plaza, tel 837 6600. French cooking, cocktails. Expensive.

PIMLICO HOTEL RESTAURANT: 5301 Park Heights Av, tel 664 8014. Extensive menu including Chinese dishes. Moderate.

Places of Interest

BABE RUTH BIRTHPLACE AND MUSEUM: 216 Emory St. Numerous photos, paintings and other memorabilia of America's legendary baseball player.

DRUID HILL PARK: NW of Baltimore via Eutaw Pl or Pennsylvania Av. 674-acre park criss-crossed with scenic drives. Features include children's zoo, conservatory and gardens.

SHERWOOD GARDENS: Highfield Rd. Thousands of azaleas and tulips. English boxwood, cherry and many other shrubs and plants. Peak bloom time early May.

WALTERS ART GALLERY: N Charles and Centre Sts. Paintings, sculpture, illuminated MSS and decorative art spanning 5,000 years.

THE MID-ATLANTIC STATES

appearance – there is a reconstruction of the first office that Du Pont used. Visitors can also see the restored 19th-century family garden and a library of company records.

Parts of Pennsylvania, however, shun such commercial and industrial activity. Around the city of Lancaster is a region inhabited by the 'plain people' (see page 45) descendants of German and Swiss people who came here some 300 years ago in search of religious freedom. The communities those early settlers established, swelled in later years by other sects of similar beliefs, are still flourishing, their inhabitants living the same simple, religious lives.

Great moments of history have been enacted on Pennsylvanian soil, and none greater than in Philadelphia, a metropolis of more than 1,700,000 population. For it was in Philadelphia on 4 July 1776, that the Declaration of Independence was agreed. And thanks to William Penn a century earlier, whose vision of a land where religious tolerance could be protected by law, where a prisoner was given the right to be heard, a tax payer the right to vote, and an accused man the right to be heard by jury, the city became a mecca for scholarly and enlightened people. As a cultural centre, it appealed to leading artists, statesmen, writers and politicians. Today the city is an urbane sprawl of urban communities, and something of a tourist curiosity shop. It was the seat of government only until 1800 when Washington, dug out of the muddy banks of the Potomac, was ready to function as the capital of the new nation.

Though it no longer plays such a significant role in the affairs of the country, Philadelphia, despite its proximity to Washington DC, is the focal point of a territory where the foundations of modern America were laid. To capture the essence of the struggle for unification, visit Valley Forge and Gettysburg, both within easy motoring distance of the city. Valley Forge National Historical Park (see page 44) stages a reconstruction of the huts and headquarters the Revolutionary Army used before laying siege to the British in Philadelphia, and Gettysburg is where Abraham Lincoln delivered his momentous Address on November 19, 1863, a few months after the bloodiest battle of the Civil War had been fought between 97,000 Union troops and a Confederate army of about 75,000 men. Over 50,000 casualties resulted from this engagement. Today, over 1300 monuments, statues and markers, three observation towers, and 31 miles of marked paved avenues can be toured in the Gettysburg National Military Park on the battlefield.

The replica of the blacksmith's hut at the Valley Forge National Historic Park

Annapolis and Chesapeake Bay

1 day – 82 miles

Washington DC – Annapolis/Chesapeake Bay

Take the Baltimore-Washington Parkway for 8 miles, then continue east on US 50. After 2 miles turn south on State Route 202. Turn west after 5 miles at Largo on to State Route 214 and cross the Patuxent river. From State Route 214, take State Route 2 and State Route 450 into Annapolis.

Annapolis

Set on the western shore of Chesapeake Bay, at the mouth of the River Severn, Annapolis is one of the oldest cities in the United States.

The town was first established in 1649 by a group of Puritan families from Virginia, who called their early settlement Providence. By 1694 the settlement had become a prosperous port, and in that year was made the state capital of Maryland under the title Anne Arundel Town. The following year the community renamed their town Annapolis, in honour of Princess Anne, later Queen of England.

In 1708 Annapolis received its charter, and preserved from those days is the 18th-century waterfront, the only one to survive along the Atlantic coast. Many fine old colonial buildings still grace the city and there is much to exemplify the life and architecture of pre-Revolutionary America. Among the many famous buildings is the State House of 1779, where the American Revolution was officially ended in 1783. State House was the Capitol of the USA from 26 November 1783 to 13 August 1784. This, the oldest state capitol building in continuous use, and which still serves as the local parliament building is also notable for its remarkable domed roof, constructed of wood, entirely without the use of nails. Free guided tours show you the sights, among them the Old Senate Chamber where Washington resigned his commission as Commander-in-Chief of the Continental Army. If ecclesiastical architecture is one of your delights, St Anne's Church at Church Circle has an exquisite memorial window which should not be missed. It won first prize for ecclesiastical art at the Chicago World Fair in 1893.

A Chippendale bridge and a 'wilderness garden' are attractive features of the carefully restored William Paca House and Gardens at 186 Prince George Street. This mid 18th-century property is furnished in period style. A previous owner was a governor of Maryland whose claim to fame was as a signatory to the Declaration of Independence. Standing on the site of Old Fort Severn and covering over 300 acres on the south side of the River Severn is the US Naval Academy, which boasts a museum displaying ship models, battle flags, weapons and memorabilia of Navy-trained astronauts. The Chapel houses the crypt of John Paul Jones, America's most famous naval hero of the American Revolution. The Old Treasury Building on State Circle offers information on guided walking tours of the city, but you may prefer to spend your time exploring Chesapeake Bay, America's largest estuary.

Annapolis' marketplace on the waterfront. Still in the catering business is Middleton's Tavern (centre), which dates from 1750

Perhaps the best way of seeing the bay is aboard the *Annapolitan*, which will take you on a relaxed cruise across the bay to the picturesque fishing village of St Michael's, where passengers are allowed three hours for lunch. Before settling down to an unforgettable meal of fresh oysters, crabs, clams or terrapin, visit the Chesapeake Maritime Museum and the unusual six-sided 19th-century lighthouse raised on stilts. One of the largest floating exhibitions in the USA – the 'In the Water Boat Show' is held in Chesapeake Bay in October.

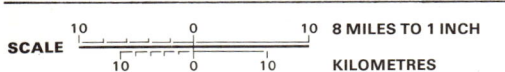

Return to Washington on US 50 and the Baltimore-Washington Parkway.

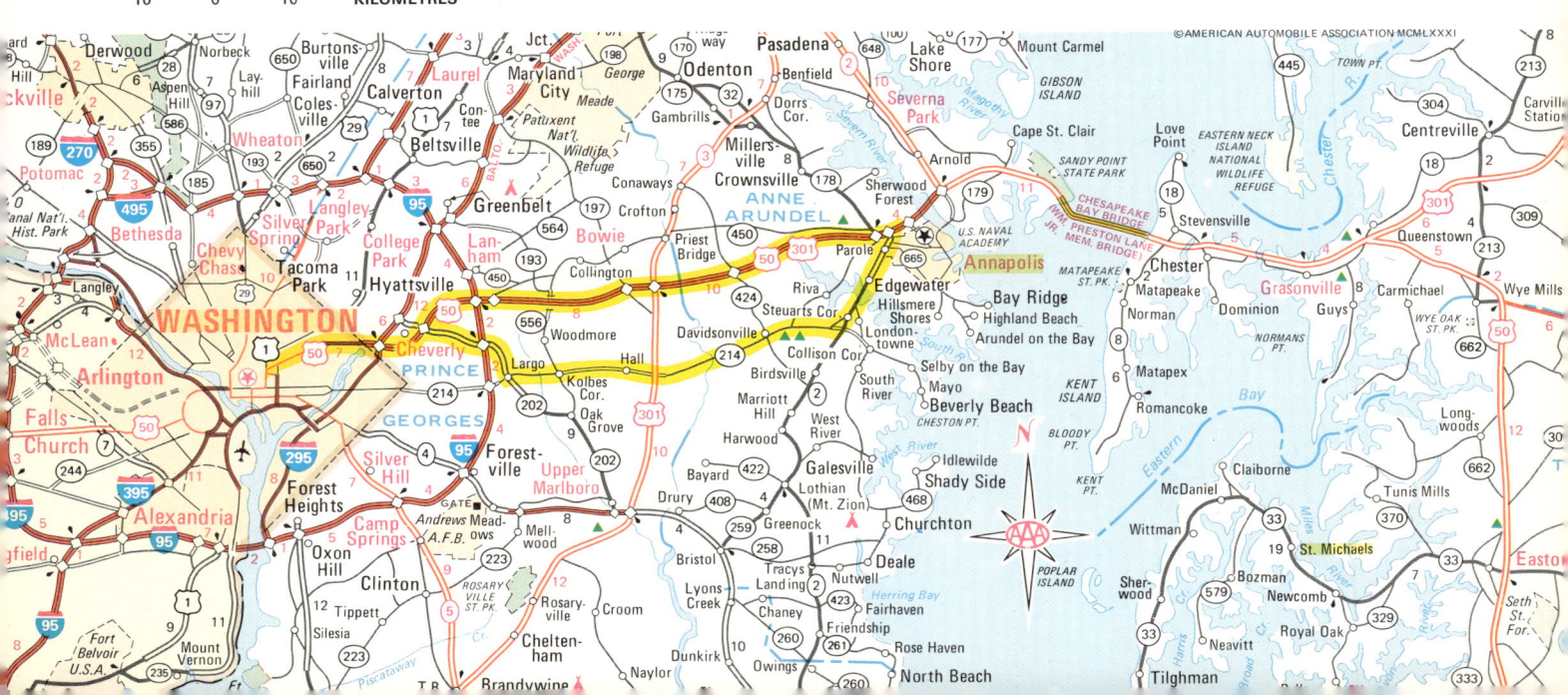

HARRISBURG
READING
LANCASTER
YORK
BALTIMORE
Lebanon
Hershey
Palmyra
Carlisle
Camp Hill
Middletown
Elizabethtown
Ephrata
Denver
Akron
Lititz
Manheim
Mt. Joy
Marietta
Columbia
Wrightsville
Hanover
Westminster
Towson
Cockeysville
Hunt Valley
Bel Air
Aberdeen
Havre de Grace
Elkton
Edgewood
Ellicott City
Columbia
Laurel
Annapolis
Bowie
Glen Burnie
Essex
Gaithersburg
Wheaton
Silver Spring
College Park
Bethesda
Arlington
Chevy Chase
Hyattsville
Lanham
Cheverly
Newark
West Chester
Middletown
Chestertown
Grasonville
DAUPHIN
PERRY
LEBANON
BERKS
LANCASTER
CHESTER
YORK
PA.
MD.
DEL.
Susquehanna River
Patapsco River
Magothy R.
Severn R.
South R.
Chester R.
Elk R.
Sassafras R.
Bush R.
Eastern Bay
Liberty Res.
Loch Raven Res.
Prettyboy Reservoir
Triadelphia Reservoir
Baltimore Washington International Airport
CHESAPEAKE BAY BRIDGE
EASTERN NECK I.
WASHINGTON

The Pennsylvania Dutch Country

Three days – 330 miles

Washington DC – York – Harrisburg – Hershey – Lancaster – Ephrata – Hopewell Village – Valley Forge – Longwood – Wilmington – Baltimore – Washington DC

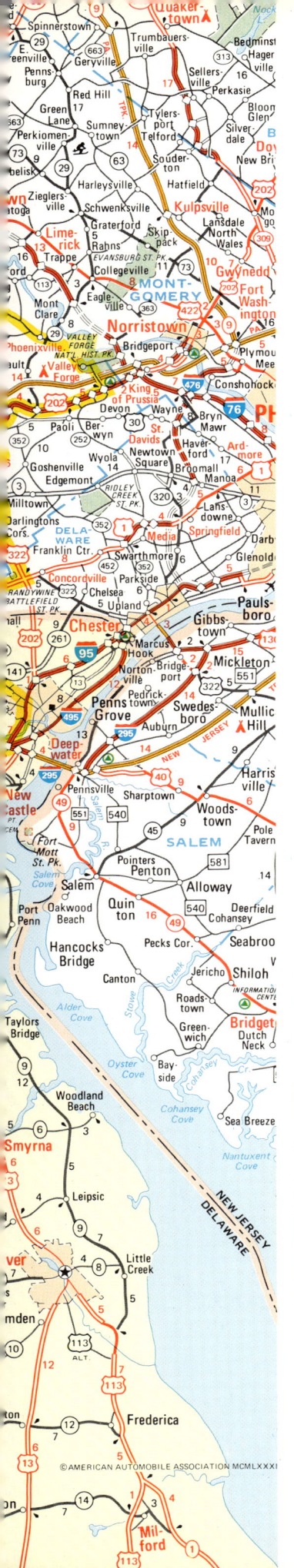

Leave Washington on the Baltimore-Washington Parkway, bypassing Baltimore on Interstate 695 and rejoining Interstate 83 at exit 24 for York.

York

York is today an important industrial city, but in the latter half of the 18th century, when the British occupied Philadelphia, the town served briefly as the capital of the American colonies. The early days of York are recalled at Lauck's Farm and Craft Museum, and by the Historical Society of York County, whose reconstruction of York Village Square as it stood in 1776, with taproom and old apothecary shop, gives a special insight into early American history.

The Rodney C Gott Museum, on the other hand, is devoted to motor-cycling memorabilia, including the original 1903 Harley-Davidson motorbike. Attached to the museum is an actual Harley-Davidson assembly plant, where visitors can see a modern motorcycle assembled every 90 seconds.

If your taste is more physical than mechanical you might enjoy the free exhibition at the Weightlifter's Hall of Fame, at 26-52 N Ridge Avenue, where some of the world's greatest exponents of the sport have trained.

What you must not miss are the famous farmer's markets on Tuesdays, Fridays and Saturdays, where you can buy genuine Pennsylvania-Dutch delicacies.

Hotels

HOLIDAY INN: 2600 E Market St. Expensive.

HOWARD JOHNSON'S: I-83 at Arsenal Rd. Moderate.

MODERNAIRE: 3311 E Market St. Inexpensive.

Restaurants

LINCOLN WOODS INN: 2510 E Market St. Merrie England theme, with steak and seafood specialities. Expensive.

SEVEN COUSINS: 2400 E Market St. Pleasant surroundings, Italian and American menus. Expensive.

Leave York on Interstate 83 for Harrisburg 18 miles away. The route passes rolling, wooded farm country which is especially beautiful in the autumn.

Harrisburg

One John Harris first established a trading post here in 1710, a fact which made his son proud enough to insist that the city be called after the family name. His bid for immortality paid off, for 100 years later Harrisburg was chosen as the state capital and the name duly entered the history books.

The magnificent Italian Renaissance State Capitol, which was completed in 1906, stands in 13 acres of parkland and takes up two acres for itself and the 650 rooms it contains. Look for the bronze doors, the mural paintings and the marble grand staircase modelled after the one in the Paris Opera House – all under a 272-feet-high dome.

The new William Penn Memorial Museum should also be visited. Here are exhibits of natural history, an art gallery and a planetarium. The Archives Tower next door holds records dating back to 1681.

If you can manage to be in Harrisburg in January, February or October, you can see some of the most impressive countryside outdoor events in the Pennsylvania Farm Show Building which takes up 13 acres on Cameron and Maclay Streets.

Journey for 5 miles on US 322 to Hummelstown. Before reaching Hummelstown look for the Indian Echo Caverns. Visitors can take a guided tour through spectacular limestone formations and view the prettily-named Crystal Lake. Continue through Hummelstown on US 322 and in 5 miles stop at Hershey.

Hotels

CONGRESS INN: 1350 Eisenhower Blvd. 62 rooms. Moderate.

NATIONWIDE INN: 525 S Front St. 125 rooms. Expensive.

SHERATON MOTOR INN: I-83 at Turnpike exit 18A. 200 rooms. Expensive.

Restaurants

AUJOUR LE JOUR: 540 Race St. Continental cuisine in an intimate, rustic setting. Moderate.

CASTIGLIA'S: 706 N 3rd St. Pasta and American dishes. Inexpensive.

INN 22: 5 miles E of US 22. Baked stuffed shrimp a speciality in this pleasant Early American establishment. Expensive.

Hershey

The aroma of chocolate will allow you to nose in on what this community of 7,500 is all about. Since the turn of the century, when Milton S Hershey founded the factory, the Hershey Foods Corporation has turned it into the largest chocolate and cocoa plant in the world.

Hershey's Chocolate World on Park Boulevard is a Disney-style extravaganza which has been described as an automated ride into a simulated world of chocolate. The place shows how the cocoa bean is gathered and how it all ends up as a succulent morsel in the mouth. Hershey Park offers 36 amusement rides, including a 1930s carrousel.

If that is not enough, the Founders Hall has a visitor's programme of maps, slides, models and a 30-minute film on the beginnings of Hershey, and the founding of the Milton Hershey School.

Away from confectionery, the Hershey Museum of American Life features artefacts of American-Indian and Eskimo origins and exhibits of Pennsylvania German folk art.

Continue east on US 322 to State Route 72, take State Route 72 south for Manheim. Here, a red rose is given each year to the heir of Baron Steigel, the town's founder, in lieu of rent.

From Manheim drive for 9 miles on State Route 72 to Lancaster.

43

PENNSYLVANIA

Lancaster

Lancaster lies in the heart of Pennsylvania Dutch country, where prosperous farmlands yield healthy crops, old-country style foods and flowers – all of which are on sale in Lancaster's popular Farmers' Markets. It is where the best of Pennsylvania-Dutch tradition lingers and where, for the price of an admission ticket, the tourist can take his pick of any number of period spectacles. And if you really want to know, it is also the city that started F W Woolworth off on his penny bazaar bonanza.

Although much of this land reflects the simplicity of the 'plain people' (see opposite), Wheatlands, on Mariettea Avenue, is a little more sumptuous. This is a handsome Federal mansion where President James Buchanan lived until his death in 1868. The house contains original furnishings and many of the President's personal belongings.

Also rather contrary to the philosophy of the 'plain people' is Dutch Wonderland, four and a half miles east on US 30, which is a 44-acre 'familyland' of storybook characters and scenes, dolphin and sealion shows, and numerous amusement rides.

To understand the people who have given Pennsylvania so much of its unique character visit the farms of one of the sects – the Amish. Amish Homestead is a working farm preserved by descendants of the original sect, three miles east on State Route 462, where you can join conducted tours through the house and farm buildings.

Amish Farm and House, six miles east on US 30, is furnished in the old Amish style, and here also 'respectfully lectured tours' are offered. For further information the Mennonite Information Center at Millstream Road will explain the 'plain people's' objectives and the differences between each of the sects.

Mill Bridge Village, eight miles out of town on US 30, is a cherished restoration of an original Pennsylvania Dutch village, including the market place, bakeries and a village store. You can take carriage rides and watch arts and crafts being demonstrated.

Leave Lancaster on US 222; after 9 miles take US 322 for 2 miles north-west to reach Ephrata.

Ephrata

Ephrata Cloisters is where a Seventh Day German Baptist sect lived in semi-monastic seclusion until 1934. They left behind them ten buildings filled with evidence of their love of music, calligraphy and fine printing.

In July and August of each year the Vorspiel, a performance of music two centuries old, is given. Beforehand visitors are taken on a tour of the Cloisters, and are able to watch the crafts of these people being demonstrated.

Return to US 322 and continue to Blue Ball. Take State Route 23. At Warwick, turn 10 miles north-east on State Route 345 to Hopewell Village.

Hopewell Village

Hopewell National Historic Site commemorates one of the most successful iron-making villages of the early 19th century. It was founded by Englishman William Bird who started Hopewell forge in 1740, which subsequently gave employment to a village community and produced cannons and shot during the American Revolution. The furnace operated until 1883, and careful restoration of much of the village has made it a popular tourist attraction. Visitors can see the old water wheel, blast machinery, bridge house, cooling shed, barn store and cast house. Also on display are original castings and the tools used by the craftsmen who worked here.

Continue along State Route 23 for 15 miles. Stop at Valley Forge.

Valley Forge

The National Historic Park of 2,500 acres marks the site where Washington's tattered and hungry army camped through the bitter winter of 1777–8, with the loss of many troops through illness and exposure, after the British had occupied Philadelphia. Here can be seen restorations of the cabins used, including Washington's headquarters, the remains of entrenchments and fortifications and many state and national monuments. The small museum houses relics of several bloody battles fought in the area by Washington's Revolutionary Army.

From Valley Forge join US 202 on its southwards swoop to Chadds Ford 20 miles away, where the Brandywine Battlefield Park marks the spot where American forces under Washington were defeated in 1777. Join up with US 1 to reach Longwood 5 miles south.

The 18th-century iron-working settlement of Hopewell Village is preserved as a National Historic site, where many of the buildings are restored to their original condition

PENNSYLVANIA

Longwood

Longwood Gardens near Kennet Square are 1,000 acres of the former estate of Pierre du Pont, and are now one of the most outstanding display gardens in America. Apart from the outdoor gardens, there is a large indoor conservatory, an open-air theatre complete with stage fountains and a water curtain, and an Italian water garden. Especially spectacular are the coloured fountains, the finest in the world.

Take US 1 north, then State Route 52 south-east to Wilmington.

Wilmington

Wilmington is where E I du Pont de Nemours and his two sons came, originally to finance a colonisation project, but eventually to open mills devoted to the manufacture of gunpowder – a commodity in demand at the time.

There is much evidence in Wilmington today to show that the Du Pont business was highly profitable. The Hagley Museum, a few miles out of town on State Route 141, stands on the 200-acre site of the original Du Pont black powder works. Here is where you can learn how the stuff is made. The museum itself traces the growth of industry in the area, and there is a tour of the Du Ponts' home, Eleutherian Mills.

Somewhat different in character and content is the Henry Francis du Pont Winterthur Museum, six miles north-west on State Route 52. This is for the furniture and antiques buff. In more than 175 rooms representing the years between 1640 and 1840 the largest and richest collection of Early American interior architecture, furniture and knick-knacks has been assembled. Exquisite European antiques, Aubusson tapestries and Dutch landscapes dominate five of the rooms. The Winterthur Gardens specialise in plants and which flower in spring.

Continue the antiques trail at the Nemours Mansion and Gardens three miles out in Rockland Road, where the 77-room modified Louis XVI chateau on a 300-acre estate contains a fine collection of rare tapestries, furniture and objets d'art. The gardens are a third of a mile long, so expect the tour to last at least two hours.

Hotels

BRANDYWINE HILTON INN: 1–95 at Naamans Rd, tel 792 2701. 196 rooms. Expensive.

HOTEL DU PONT: 11th and Market Sts, tel 656 8121. 300 rooms. Expensive.

TALLY HO MOTOR LODGE: 5209 Concord Pike, tel 478 0300. 106 rooms. Expensive.

Restaurants

COLUMBUS INN: 2216 Pennsylvania Av, tel 571 1492. Very good food in Early American atmosphere. Expensive.

HOTEL DU PONT'S BRANDYWINE AND GREEN ROOM: 11th and Market Sts, tel 656 8121. Tasteful surroundings, strict dress code. Expensive.

CHARCOAL PITT: 2600 Concord Pike. Hamburgers and ice-cream. Inexpensive.

Return on Interstate 95 to Baltimore.

Baltimore

Baltimore is known as the economic and educational centre of Maryland (see page 38) – a truly cosmopolitan city where harbourside ethnic festivals fill the summer months.

You must find time to stop for a meal here. Or two. Or more. Crab, locally caught, is the speciality and many restaurants serve them on a newspaper on the table. Often a mallet provided in lieu of a knife and fork.

Return on Interstate 95 to Washington.

Once surrounded by decaying factories and warehouses, Baltimore's Inner Harbour is now one of the city's showplaces

The Plain People

Every now and again, on this tour, you will forget that you are in America. For here in Pennsylvania the influence of the European immigrants of the 17th century has survived, along with the religious ideals which they brought with them in their search for freedom.

Under the leadership of William Penn, who founded the state in 1680, Quakers and other Presbyterian and Protestant sects were able to settle and practise their faith without fear of persecution. These people were mainly English, Swedish and German; it is the latter two races who formed the Pennsylvania Dutch, and who still practise their special life-style in the lands around Lancaster.

Whole communities of these people shun modern life – no cars, electricity or television – and often still ride in horse-drawn buggies wearing the clothes of 100 years ago – broad black hats and sombre costume for the men, bonnets and full-skirted long dresses for the women.

They may not have the advantages of modern machinery, but the 'plain people' are master farmers, and are proud of their produce and food. Pennsylvania Dutch cooking is a treat. It is based on seven sweet and seven sour dishes, and the combinations produce such foods as pickles, relishes, apple and egg dishes, pretzels and the famous molasses shoo-fly pie.

Although collectively named the 'plain people', there are a number of different sects, including the Amish, the Brethren or Dunkards, and the Mennonites. They vary in beliefs and customs to a certain extent, but all follow the concept of simplicity, are deeply religious, and all can be seen in the towns on market day. In Lancaster at the 244-year-old market, visitors can sample such delicacies as Lebanon bologna, scrapple and smierkase – a local cheese.

A visit to the Pennsylvania Farm Museum at Landis Valley, three miles north of Lancaster on US 222, gives an idea of early rural life in America, with 250,000 items on display. A visit to one of the Amish farms open to the public shows you that history is alive today.

Washington

The centre of the free world, a city of high-flying politics, Washington DC makes history every day, spreading its influence almost imperceptibly from the White House and the Capitol to every corner on earth – and these days, even to the moon and beyond.

Washington is a cosmopolitan city, 132 nations are represented here by an army of diplomats, and as host, the capital knows how to make visitors feel welcome.

For the tourist, Washington has plenty to offer – it is one of America's leading tourist attractions. It is a clean, spacious city, characterised by stately avenues, streets and squares, interspersed with well-planned parks. Gleaming white buildings of marble, monuments and museums, many of which are free of charge, commemorate, display and exhibit America's history. Most of what any visitor will want to see is found in the easily accessible north-western sector of the city.

Alternatively, the tourist can drink in the political atmosphere of this exciting city by sitting in on a Senate committee meeting, attending a foreign policy briefing, or witnessing the Supreme Court at its deliberations.

Above all else Washington is one of the most freely open cities in the world – even the President can only have his home to himself two days of the week.

Washington at dusk. Floodlit against the evening sky is the United States Capitol, the city's most famous landmark. The dome is surmounted by a bronze statue of Freedom

WASHINGTON

Across the Potomac River from Washington DC (the DC stands for District of Columbia), lies Arlington National Cemetery, the resting place of many famous Americans, including John F Kennedy and his assassinated brother Robert. Here also is the tomb of Pierre L'Enfant, the brilliant French engineer who, at George Washington's invitation, drew up a revolutionary plan to build the capital city of a new nation.

When George Washington's troops finally overwhelmed the British Army at Yorktown in 1781, and in that victory assured the birth of the United States, the problem arose as to where to build the nation's capital. Congress had set up a temporary home in Philadelphia, and for seven years it argued about the siting of their new 'federal' town. When Washington picked a mosquito-infested fen on the banks of the Potomac River, he diplomatically fulfilled the aspirations of both the northerners and the southerners. He extracted a donation of land for the city from Maryland on the north bank and Virginia on the south bank; between them the two states provided a hundred square miles.

Rivalling Paris in elegance and splendour, Pierre L'Enfant's vision of the city was to create a series of spacious circles from which radiated broad avenues, flanked by impressive monuments and buildings. Central to this pattern was to be the Capitol building. Begun in 1793, the north wing of the Capitol was completed seven years later, allowing Congress to move to its new home. Unfortunately, George Washington had died a year earlier, which left L'Enfant's dream without a champion. In due course Congress rejected his plan on the grounds of cost. His drawings are today on show at the Library of Congress.

Work on the new capital almost came to a standstill. Virginia, dismayed at the slow rate of progress, claimed her share of land back, and for decades Washington remained a rough, backward town. In the 1812–15 war with Britain Washington was thought not to be important enough to defend; the British duly sacked the town, burning the President's house, the Capitol (which had still not been completed) and many other public buildings. As fires raged, the President's house was engulfed, but saved in the nick of time by a torrential thunderstorm.

After the war had ended, the blackened walls of the President's house were repainted white, earning it the name of the White House. The refurbishing of the mansion seemed to signal a new turn of events. Trade developed, the city at last seemed set on the road to prosperity. Even the ravages of the American Civil War left Washington largely untouched. Yet still the capital was by no means a comfortable place to live in. The streets were unlit and unpaved, every rainfall turned them into an impassable quagmire. But with the election of President Ulysses Grant in 1869, L'Enfant's dream was resurrected. The Chief of Works chosen by Grant was 'Boss' Shepherd, who paved and lit the streets, and had laid on main services within three years. L'Enfant's plans were dug out of the archives, and many of his ideas implemented, among them the system of parks he had envisaged.

By the turn of the century, Washington had become of age. Along the newly created Mall, which today stretches from the Lincoln Memorial to the Capitol, great marble, columned buildings rose up to house the machinery of government, and with their coming, the city gained the dignity it had always sought as its birthright.

Among its many fine buildings Washington has more that are famous, and more monuments to the famous, than any other American city. It also commemorates its heroes in some unusual, although highly practical ways, for while Washington does not identify its streets with the names of the country's great leaders, many of its bridges are called after them;

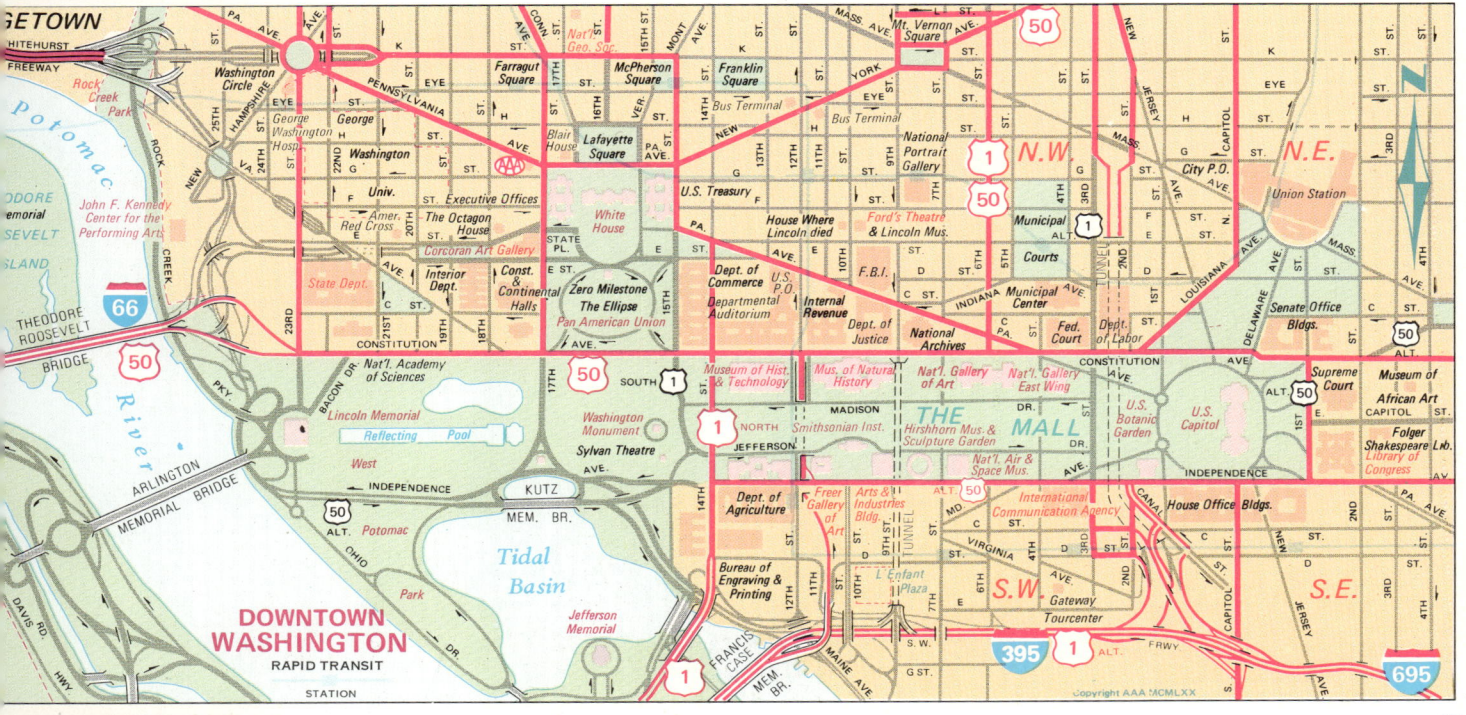

WASHINGTON

WASHINGTON

Theodore Roosevelt has one in his name, and so has march composer John Philip Sousa and even Francis Scott Key, the man who wrote the words to the 'Star Spangled Banner' (see page 39). To make room for his bridge they first had to knock down his house!

Along more traditional lines is the magnificent Jefferson Memorial, named after the author of the Declaration of Independence and third president. A circular domed building, surrounded by Ionic columns, it is situated on the south-east side of the Tidal Basin. Inside, in the Central Memorial Room, is Jefferson's effigy cast in bronze surrounded by panels inscribed with extracts from his writings.

At the west end of the Mall is the shrine built in honour of America's martyred Civil War president, Abraham Lincoln. Built along the lines of a Greek temple, there are 36 columns, one for each state in Lincoln's time, to symbolise the Union. Within, the 19-foot-high figure of the president, seated on a simple throne, gazes out towards the Washington Monument.

In contrast, Franklin D Roosevelt who died just before the end of World War II after 12 years in office, is remembered by a small, unassuming monument in white marble. It stands on Pennsylvania Avenue. Although there is no monument to the memory of President John F Kennedy, who was the 34th president and who died at the hands of an assassin on 22 November, 1963, aged 46, the John F Kennedy Center for the Performing Arts, opened in 1971 at the foot of New Hampshire Avenue, has become one of the world's great cultural havens, staging drama, opera, concerts, films and many other popular musical and theatrical events.

Two of the most interesting national treasure houses are the National Archives in Constitution Avenue, and the Federal Bureau of Investigation building on Pennsylvania Avenue (see Directory).

Neither London nor Leningrad can compete with the profusion and variety of America's greatest treasure trove, the Smithsonian Institution. Housed in 12 separate buildings scattered throughout the city (see Directory) the Institution is administered from its original building in the Mall, a medieval castle-like building, purpose-built in 1846 to house a collection amassed 'for the increase and diffusion of knowledge among men'.

To feel the pulse of power which is at the heart of Washington, visits to the White House, the Capitol and the Supreme Court should be at the top of your list of places to see.

Every president except George Washington has lived in the White House, originally designed by James Hoban in 1792. The mansion stands in 18 acres of gardens surrounded by elegant railings, and

Originally financed by the bequest of English scientist James Smithson, the Smithsonian Institution has preserved important American memorabilia since 1846. At first the entire collection was housed in an ornate building in the Mall (above). Now the Institution occupies 12 buildings throughout the city, among them the National Air and Space Museum (left). Exhibits here span the entire history of aviation, with one of the best aircraft collections in the world. Among the more unusual sights is the 'walk through' Skylab Orbital Workshop, a striking contrast to the Balloons and Airship Gallery and the traditional monoplanes seen here

WASHINGTON

is the most popular tourist draw in Washington. During the summer, 10,000 people a day queue at the East Gate on East Executive Avenue for the two hour guided tour of ground-floor public rooms. These include the State Dining Room, which can seat up to 140 people, the Red, Blue and Green rooms and the East Room, the largest, where the President appears to an invited public from time to time.

The Capitol, at the east end of the Mall, is where the country's politics are played out. Both the Senate and the House can be visited and Congress watched at work. Walk up the steps of the East Front, where all the presidents since Andrew Jackson have been inaugurated; visit the massive central Rotunda, entered through huge bronze doors, and see the historic paintings, statues, frescoes and friezes among which 25 leading Americans, including Abraham Lincoln and John F Kennedy, have lain in state.

Across the street from the East Front of the Capitol is the magnificent Supreme Court building, built of gleaming white marble. The ground floor is open to the public, and so is the courtroom of marble, mahogany and velour, where the highest court in the land sits. There are about 150 seats allotted to the general public when the Court is in session, and it is well worth trying to secure one. When the Court is out of session, lectures are given in the courtroom about the building and the history of the Supreme Court by young law students.

When tired of visiting the shrines of the powerful, the great and the famous, there is no better way of regaining a little calm than to walk in one of Washington DC's many parks. It is said there is more parkland in Washington than in any other city.

▲ *At the edge of the northern boundary of Arlington Cemetery stands the world-famous US Marine Corps War Memorial, above which the American flag flies 24 hours a day in tribute to 'the courage and valor of the American fighting forces'*

WASHINGTON

Houses dating from the 18th century lend a period atmosphere to the tree-lined streets of Georgetown, an old city that is now a chic suburb of Washington

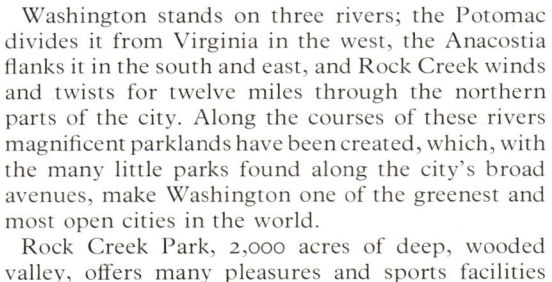

Washington stands on three rivers; the Potomac divides it from Virginia in the west, the Anacostia flanks it in the south and east, and Rock Creek winds and twists for twelve miles through the northern parts of the city. Along the courses of these rivers magnificent parklands have been created, which, with the many little parks found along the city's broad avenues, make Washington one of the greenest and most open cities in the world.

Rock Creek Park, 2,000 acres of deep, wooded valley, offers many pleasures and sports facilities within easy reach of downtown Washington. It is an ideal place to picnic, perhaps on the banks of the rushing creek itself, or you can either visit the superb National Zoological Park or the Rock Creek Nature Centre.

In Potomac Park, divided into east and west by the waters of the tidal basin, 3,000 Japanese cherry trees present a breathtaking spectacle in spring, and is the scene of the week-long Cherry Blossom Festival, a festival planner's nightmare – for the blooms may only last a week or two, and the time of their blooming is hard to predict. Opposite West Potomac Park, across the river, is Ladybird Johnson Park on a 121-acre man-made island created in 1916. On Columbia island, the park was named after the wife of the 35th president, Lyndon Johnson, in 1968, in recognition of her national campaign to beautify America. A memorial to her husband there is in a 15-acre grove of several hundred white pines, dogwoods, rhododendrons and azaleas.

Anacostia Park lies on both sides of the Anacostia River. Here, where 400 years ago stood the Indian Village of Nacotchtank, are a bird sanctuary, tennis courts, a swimming pool and a skating rink. These 750 acres are a favourite lunchtime refuge for city workers and exhausted tourists.

Perhaps the most visited open space of Washington and Virginia are the 500 acres of Arlington Cemetery, just across the Potomac River from the capital on land which one belonged to the latter state. At one end, overlooking the dignified rows of simple white headstones (among them the tomb of President Kennedy upon which an eternal flame flickers), rises the 78-feet-high Marine Corps War Memorial. The statue, showing a group of four soldiers raising the American flag on Mount Suribachi, is the largest monument ever to be cast out of a single piece of bronze, and is based on a famous press photograph of World War II taken when the American Marine Corps was fighting for possession of the Japanese Island of Iwo Jima in 1945.

At the south-east corner of the cemetery stands the forbidding bulk of the Pentagon, one of the largest office buildings in the world, from where America's leaders direct the defence of their country.

Two suburbs of Washington well worth a visit are Georgetown and Alexandria, where many houses and streets of the 18th and 19th centuries survive, lovingly restored by the fashionable of today.

Once proud of its own charter, Georgetown lost its independence and became part of the city in 1871. Here is a colony of antique shops and art galleries, patronised by the smart social set who moved in since the 1950s and made Georgetown a leader of style and fashion.

In Alexandria which, unlike Georgetown, has managed to retain its autonomy, the houses, shops and restaurants are also much in demand – as much by the visiting diplomatic community as by the residents and passing tourists.

Shopping in Washington itself is a treat. Look at the hundreds of smart small shops or wander through the large department stores like Garfinkle's, Hecht's and Bloomingdale's. At Woodward and Lothrop, they have built an underground station inside the store.

A word of warning. Washington is an exciting city to walk in, but certain sections should be avoided. Always stick to busy, well lit streets, and when in doubt, ask for advice.

Washington Directory

HOTELS

Hotels and restaurants shown here are either recommended by the American Automobile Association (AAA), or are chosen because they are particularly appealing to tourists. To give an approximate guide to cost they have been rated as either expensive, moderate or inexpensive. All the hotels have private bathrooms and colour television unless otherwise stated.

DUPONT PLAZA HOTEL: Dupont Circle, Connecticut and Massachusetts Avs NW. 1500 New Hampshire Av, tel 483 6000, 310 rooms all with refrigerator and telephone. Entertainment provided. Moderate.

HARRINGTON HOTEL: 11th and E Sts NW, tel 628 8140. 600 rooms all with air-conditioning and telephone. Cafeteria and garage. Within walking distance of White House and Capitol. Inexpensive.

HOTEL WASHINGTON: 15th and Pennsylvania Av NW, tel 638 5900. 370 rooms and a rooftop restaurant. Centrally located. Moderate.

LOMBARDY TOWERS: 2019 Eye St NW, tel 828 2600. 127 rooms. Kitchenettes, walk-in closets, desks in all rooms. Laundry facilities. Moderate.

PARK CENTRAL HOTEL: 705 18th St NW, tel 393 4700, 250 rooms. Roof garden and restaurant. Coin laundry and pay garage. Centrally situated. Moderate.

QUALITY INN – CAPITOL HILL: 415 New Jersey Av NW, tel 638 1616. 314 rooms. Restaurant and cocktail lounge, films, rooftop pool, sauna and gymnasium. Moderate.

WATERGATE HOTEL: 2650 Virginia Av NW, tel 965 2300. 240 rooms. Heated indoor pool, health club and sauna. Restaurant and cocktail lounge. Shopping mall. Expensive.

RESTAURANTS

Washington offers a wide variety of excellent restaurants in which it is possible to eat well in pleasant surroundings. Eat European style if you wish but it is also possible to sample a wide and tempting variety of authentic dishes from Asia and Latin America.

THE BREAD OVEN: 1220 19th St NW, tel 466 4264. Eat at this bright, bustling French restaurant from breakfast to dinner time. The French bread tastes as good as it smells and lunch is particularly good, with five main dishes. Lamb couscous and veau Niçoise are specialities here. Inexpensive.

CAFE RONDO: 1900 Q St, Corner of Connecticut Av, tel 232 1885. In a busy area of town, but you can still enjoy an outdoor lunch or dinner under colourful awnings. Lots of egg dishes, soups and salads are available, but the original beef Rondo, meat and vegetables in wine sauce, is particularly good. Inexpensive.

EL CARIBE: 1828 Columbia Rd NW, tel 234 6969. A small restaurant which deserves its many awards. Warm atmosphere with lantern lit wooden wall and beamed ceiling. Specialities here are Latin-American, Mexican and Spanish dishes, and the seafood, poultry and meat is served in traditional style. Inexpensive.

THE DELLY ON CAPITOL HILL: 332 Pennsylvania Av SE, tel 547 8668. This modern-looking restaurant close to the Capitol (and attracting many of its staff) serves food in the old-fashioned way: hot pastrami and corned beef thick sandwiches on rye bread and tasty home-made chicken soup. Creamy cheesecake is just one of the rich desserts. Inexpensive.

K STREET SALOON AND STEAKERY: 1511 K St NW, tel 659 8170. An intimate, elegant Victorian-style restaurant where you can dine in style on delicious steaks or roast beef. Having chosen your main course, help yourself from an awesome salad bar. Service is pleasant and there are bargain meals to be had, especially at lunchtime. Moderate.

MARTIN'S TAVERN: 1264 Wisconsin Av NW, tel FE3 7370. A dark-walled tavern famous for lots of no-nonsense food served by lighthearted waiters in mid-1930s movie surroundings. Speciality is cabbage and corned beef, or try the roast duck. Inexpensive.

MIKADO: 4707 Wisconsin Av NW, tel 244 1740. Delightfully authentic Japanese restaurant where the waitresses wear traditional costumes. Either try unusual dishes such as sashimi (raw fish) or donburi (shrimps, eggs or meat on rice), or feast on a ten-course dinner, but leave room for one of the tempting desserts. Moderate-expensive.

PIER 7: 7th St and Main Av, SW, tel 554 2500. Waterfront restaurant with superb seafood and a wide assortment of meat and poultry dishes served in a warm and convivial atmosphere. Inexpensive-moderate.

TRANSPORT

AIRPORTS: 22 airlines and three airports serve Washington, two of the airports are international, the other is domestic. Most international flights come to Dulles International, located in Virginia, 50 minutes away from the city. Baltimore – Washington International Airport is 34 miles north-east of the city, reached in 45 minutes by bus. Washington National is for domestic internal flights only, and is across the Potomac River just $3\frac{1}{2}$ miles from the downtown area. It is much used by commuting senators and congressmen. There is a regular bus service to all the airports; times can be checked by telephoning 393 3060.

BUSES: The entire District of Columbia (the area occupied by the city of Washington itself) is covered by the Metro bus system. So, too, is the metropolitan area, including parts of Maryland and Northern Virginia. The express buses operate in rush hours and have only limited stops. No change is given so the correct money or tokens are needed. Greyhound and Trailways buses pull in at New York Av.

CAR HIRE: There are many car hire firms to choose from. The largest with numerous location points are: American Rental Systems, 2600 Jefferson Davis Hwy, Arlington, tel 684 7500; Avis, 1722 M St NW, tel 467 6585; Dollar Rent-a-Car Systems, 2400 Jefferson Davis Hwy, Arlington, tel 979 4200; Hertz, 1622 L St NW, tel 800 654 3131; National, 12th and K Sts NW, tel 842 1000.

METRO RAPID RAIL SYSTEM: This architecturally striking subway is an efficient and economical way of visiting most of the city's major attractions. $32\frac{3}{4}$ miles of the new system are now open – altogether 101 miles are planned. Maps and information kiosks assist passengers in planning their routes. For information telephone 637 2437.

TAXIS: Taxis within the District charge by the zone and work out a relatively expensive means of transport. The major companies are: Capitol, tel 546 2400. Eastern Imperial, tel 829 4222 and Yellow Cab tel 544 1212.

TRAINS: From Union Station near the city centre (1st St and Massachusetts Av NE), rail connections with all parts of the States are very good, and the Metroliner whisks passengers to New York in about three hours.

TOURING INFORMATION

AAA: The offices of the Potomac Division of the American Automobile Association are at 1730 Pennsylvania Av NW, Suite 300, tel 393 3300. There are other offices in Alexandria and Falls Church, Virginia, and in Wheaton, Maryland. Open during office hours, Monday to Friday; Washington office, Saturday.

NATIONAL VISITOR CENTER: Located at Union Station, Massachusetts Av at E St NE, tel 523 5300, the center is open from 9am to 5.30pm, Monday to Friday. In addition, kiosks are to be found at the Lincoln Memorial, Washington Monument, the Ellipse, Jefferson Memorial, Lafayette Park, the Museums of Air and Space, Natural History, History and Technology and the National Gallery of Art.

PLACES TO SEE

FEDERAL BUREAU OF INVESTIGATION: E St between 9th and 10th Sts NW, tel 324 3447. Fascinating 75-minute conducted tours show what the FBI is really like. Featured are; a brief history of the Bureau, biographies of gangsters, fire-arm demonstrations, the 'ten most wanted fugitives' board, as well as a tour of the laboratories.

LIBRARY OF CONGRESS: 1st St between E, E Capital St, and Independence Av, tel 287 5000. Completed in 1897, the building is of richly ornamented, modified Italian Renaissance architecture. It is the largest and richest library in the world, designed originally as a research base for Congress. The library contains more than 19 million books and pamphlets, and over 33 million manuscripts, maps, music, motion pictures and photographs. The collection of fine prints and rare books includes one of the three existing copies of the Gutenberg Bible.

JEFFERSON MEMORIAL: East Potomac Park, tel 426 6841. This white-domed colonnaded edifice is a tribute to the author of the Declaration of Independence, founder of the Democratic Party and third President of the United States. A handsome, bronze statue of Jefferson stands in the memorial room, where extracts from his writings are inscribed on four panels.

WASHINGTON DIRECTORY

NATIONAL ARCHIVES: Constitution Av, between 7th and 9th Sts NW, tel 523 3000. This handsome building preserves and makes available all the most important American historical records. The records date from 1744 and include the Declaration of Independence and the Bill of Rights which are kept in helium-filled glass and bronze cases in order to protect these priceless charters. A semi-circular gallery surrounds the Exhibition Hall, which houses changing exhibitions.

ROOSEVELT MEMORIAL: ROOSEVELT ISLAND: A memorial to Theodore Roosevelt, America's 26th President, this 88-acre island, lies in the Potomac River opposite the mouth of Rock Creek and is reached by a bridge. It contains nearly two miles of footpaths winding through picturesque woods containing over 50 species of tree and 200 varieties of wild flower. The highlight is a massive granite monument incorporating a 17-feet-high bronze statue of Roosevelt. Guided tours are available.

TREASURY DEPARTMENT EXHIBIT HALL: 15th and Pennsylvania Av NW, tel 566 5221. The displays in the Exhibit Hall and Mint Salesroom reflect all the activities under the jurisdiction of the Treasury Department, and include counterfeit and real money as well as solid gold bars and uncirculated coins.

WASHINGTON CATHEDRAL: Wisconsin, Massachusetts and Woodley Avs NW, tel 537 6200. Begun in 1907, but still not completed this 14th century Gothic-style cathedral is the sixth largest church in the world. Its central tower is the highest point in Washington. The cathedral contains some remarkable stained-glass windows (don't miss the Rose Window) including the Space Window, which contains a piece of moon rock brought back by Apollo 11's astronauts.

WASHINGTON MONUMENT: On the Mall at 15th St. Soaring 555ft up into the sky, this shaft of white marble was erected to commemorate George Washington, the first president of the United States. The view from the top (reached by lift) is magnificent. The Monument dominates the Mall – a two mile avenue of green leading from the Lincoln Memorial to the Capitol and one of the oldest of the Federal parks.

MUSEUMS AND GALLERIES

ARTS AND INDUSTRIES: (Smithsonian) 900 Jefferson Dr SW, tel 357 2700. Exhibits from the 1876 Centennial exhibition in Philadelphia are housed here. Items include memorabilia from the US Navy and US Army, and manufactured goods and machinery of the period.

FORD'S THEATER: 511 10th St, NW, tel 347 4833. Where President Lincoln was shot by John Wilkes Booth on 14 April 1865. After having been occupied by government offices, the theatre has now been restored to look much as it did in the 19th century. Daily mini-plays are staged depicting life in the 1850s and tell Lincoln's life story and the history of the Civil War. There is also an excellent Lincoln museum in the basement.

HILLWOOD MUSEUM: 4155 Linnean Av NW, tel 686 5807 is a mansion once owned by Marjorie Merriweather Post, whose father founded the Postum Cereal Company. On display is china used by Catherine the Great and a bejewelled Easter Egg made by Carl Faberge for the Russian Imperial Court. Other exhibits include 18th-century French furniture and a collection of Wedgwood.

HIRSHHORN MUSEUM AND SCULPTURE GARDEN: (Smithsonian) Independence Av and 8th St SW. The works of artists such as Degas, Matisse and Picasso are on display in this completely circular building, together with paintings and sculptures from the late 19th century to the present. Adjacent to the building is a multi-terraced sunken garden containing a rectangular pool.

NATIONAL AIR AND SPACE MUSEUM: (Smithsonian) Independence Av, between 4th and 7th St SW, tel 357 2700. This is the largest of the Smithsonian museums and is all about the story of man's conquest of aviation and space flight. There are many superb exhibits including the Wright Brothers' 1903 Flyer, Lindbergh's Spirit of St Louis, a Bell x-1 and the Apollo 11 Command module. Children will be fascinated by the filmed aerial journey of five continents and the Spacearium.

NATIONAL GALLERY OF ART: 6th St at Constitution Av NW, tel 737 4215. Here is to be found the country's greatest collection of fine art. The gallery offers examples of Italian painting and sculpture and rooms full of Rembrandts, Leonardo da Vinci, Vermeer, Goya, Degas, Renoir, van Gogh and Dali. In the striking new East Building, one of the most striking of Washington's buildings, there are examples of 20th-century art, as well as old master sculpture.

NATIONAL MUSEUM OF AMERICAN ART: (Smithsonian) 8th and G Sts NW, tel 357 2700. Two special galleries help to appreciate and explore the sensory aspects of art in this museum which houses American works of art from the 18th century to the present day.

NATIONAL MUSEUM OF AMERICAN HISTORY: (Smithsonian). Constitution Av at 12th and 14th Sts NW, tel 357 2700. Exhibits here embrace art, stamps, ceramics and many other subjects representing the history of invention. Highlights range from inventions, such as Bell's telephone, Edison's light bulb and Whitney's model of the original cotton gin, to domestic – for example George Washington's false teeth, his uniform and tent and the gowns of numerous 'First Ladies'.

NATIONAL MUSEUM OF NATURAL HISTORY: (Smithsonian Constitution Av at 10th St NW, tel 357 2700. Fascinating exhibits and displays feature items such as archaeology and fossils, birds of the world, primitive peoples, marine life, pre-historic creatures and gems – including the Hope Diamond.

NATIONAL PORTRAIT GALLERY: (Smithsonian) 8th and F St. Included here are over 500 paintings (not all of them great works of art) depicting some of the people who have helped to shape America's development in politics, science, art and warfare.

RENWICK GALLERY: (Smithsonian) Pennsylvania Av at 17th St NW, tel 357 2700. The gallery display continually changing exhibitions featuring the achievements of American designers and craftsmen. The principal rooms have been redecorated and furnished in 19th-century style.

WASHINGTON DOLLS' HOUSE AND TOY MUSEUM: 5236 44th St NW, tel 244 0024. Featured here is a collection of authentically furnished dolls' houses, toys and games, mostly from the Victorian period, owned by Flora Gill Jacobs, an authority on miniature antiques.

WOODROW WILSON HOUSE: 2340 S St NW, tel 673 4034. The Georgian-style house that was President Wilson's retirement home after he left the White House in 1921. The house is filled with artefacts from the President's administration, a permanent display of needlework and lace from World War I and a restored 1920s kitchen.

THEATRES AND CINEMAS

ARENA STAGE AND KREEGER THEATER: 6th and M St, SW, tel 488 3300. A resident repertory company presents works of classical and modern playwrights during the autumn and winter seasons.

FOLGER LIBRARY'S ELIZABETHAN THEATER: 201 E Capitol St, SE, tel 546 4800. This Elizabethan-style theatre specialises in Shakespearian productions, but also stages contemporary plays.

NATIONAL THEATER: 1321 E St, NW, tel 628 3393. Major productions are staged here all the year round.

CIRCLE CINEMA: Near Washington Circle on Pennsylvania Av NW, tel 331 7480. A popular downtown neighbourhood movie theatre which carries re-runs of classic and foreign films. These are often presented as a festival series.

AMERICAN FILM INSTITUTE: In the Kennedy Center. Here films are also shown in a series format quite often on the works of one particular director or on one particular type of film.

WOLF TRAP FARMPARK FOR THE PERFORMING ARTS: Rt 7 near Vienna, accessible via Dulles Airport access highway, tel 703 938 3800. A beautiful outdoor setting for musicals and ballet, pop concerts and symphony music.

SPORT

GOLF: Public courses in this area include East Potomac Park, Hains Point, tel 554 9813 which has four, 9 hole courses, and Rock Creek Park, Military Road NW, tel 723 9832, which has two 9 hole courses but can be played as one 18 hole course.

SWIMMING: Washington has no beaches for swimming but the District's Department of Recreation operates 41 free entry swimming pools (34 outdoor and seven indoor). One of the best is Capitol East Natatorium, 635 North Carolina Av SE.

TENNIS: There are about 115 tennis courts in the city. The Recreational Department, 3149 16th St NW, tel 637 7646, issues free permits to use them. National Park Service courts, which charge a fee, are at Hains Point, 16th and Kennedy Sts NW, and Pierce Mill, in Rock Creek Park.

CLIMATE

Washington has four distinct seasons: spring, made all the more attractive by tender shades of green and pastel flowers, is mild, with warm days and cool evenings. Summer is hot (around 90°F) and humid, but sudden thunderstorms often clear the air. Autumn is the time when the city is alive with bright colours – perhaps the best time for beauty and the best weather. Winters are not especially cold – reaching a low of 27°F but at least one snowstorm is guaranteed. By the end of February, spring is not far away. Autumn, when it is cool and the summer crowds have long gone, is perhaps the best time to visit the capital.

The Empire State – New York

Why Empire State? Because even prior to the American Civil War (1861–5) New York state had the largest population, the greatest foreign trade, the best transportation, the richest agriculture and the swiftest rate of growth of any state in the country.

Empire State – rich, industrially powerful, holding close to its heart the United States' greatest and most American town, New York City. Yet it also has a wealth of another kind – here you can climb or merely admire gaunt and majestic mountains, sail or swim in giant lakes, fish or canoe in fast-flowing rivers, explore thousands of inland islands at leisure or enjoy select stretches of golden coastal beaches. New York state is as exciting and varied as its cities and people.

Winter sports are especially popular; in the Adirondack and Catskill Mountains skiing and ice-skating attract thousands to luxurious resorts –

famous Lake Placid is one – which are popular among the international skiing fraternity. Of course, outdoor pursuits of all kinds have a place here: fishing, golf, hiking, and where there is water (and there are 1,745 square miles of it) there is boating.

Everyone who visits New York expects to see two things – the Empire State Building in New York City, and, 450 miles away, Niagara Falls, the 'Thunderer of the Waters'. The magnificent falls, partly in the USA and partly in Canada, are comfortably accessible and yet provide a spine-tingling and exhilarating experience few other of the world's great natural phenomena can match.

From the beaches of well-heeled Long Island, to the wilderness of the Adirondacks, from quiet lakeside villages to vibrant, bustling cities, New York state is always colourful, vivid, surprising – like its people. They are a mix of nationalities, whose forebears came here 200 years ago in search of fame or fortune or merely freedom. Their spirit is evident wherever you go, encapsulated by the state's motto, Excelsior – ever upward.

The thin, clear air of the Catskill Mountains, in the south-east of New York state, imparts a stunning vibrancy to the glowing colours of autumn. This farm, in the foothills near Lexington, lies near the edge of the Catskill Forest Preserve

NEW YORK STATE

For many people the name New York is instantly associated with that high-rise city of steel, stone, concrete and glass at the mouth of the Hudson River. But it is also the name of a massive state.

New York state is virtually the same size as England, with barely a third of the population. It is the second most populous state in the Union, the second wealthiest, and was one of the original 13 to rise against the British and declare themselves 'free and independent'.

Its fertile lands lie south of the St Lawrence River and Canadian border, north of Pennsylvania, and have access to the Atlantic where the Hudson River flows into New York Bay. In the west, the state border includes Lake Erie and Lake Ontario of the Great Lakes. The Erie Canal, which joins the Great Lakes in the west with the Hudson in the east, and the St Lawrence Seaway, a mighty gateway from Lake Ontario to the Atlantic Ocean, supplement the natural trade routes of sea and river to ensure the growth and continued prosperity of the state, now America's leading industrial centre.

The first industries here were farming and fur trading, and although clothing and printing are the major concerns today, the countryside which fostered those early industries is still important; both in terms of agriculture and recreation. New York boasts the greatest dairy herds in the nation, for example. But perhaps more important, the quiet valley farmland, the wooded mountains, the ocean and the lakes provide breathing space for the millions who live most of their lives in the great industrial cities or in the 'Big Apple' itself, New York.

The central and western districts are low-lying, fertile farm land; also in the west are a number of lakes, established summertime resorts, such as Lake Chautauqua – although the largest are Lake Seneca and Lake Cayuga. Parts of Lake Erie and Lake Ontario are also under New York jurisdiction. In the east of the state are the Adirondack and Catskill Mountains. Lying in the north-east, the Adirondacks are dotted with ski-resorts (winter sports are one of New York's great attractions – no city is more than a few hours from a winter resort), set in a countryside often rugged and wild. The Catskills in the south-east, although higher, are noted for luxurious resorts, golf courses, and an elaborate social round. Along the eastern border are Lakes George and Champlain, in the north the Thousand Islands of the St Lawrence are an international holiday spot, and of course the beaches of Long Island and Fire Island on the Atlantic coast off New York City are favourite summertime retreats.

The largest cities in the state are Buffalo, Rochester, and Niagara Falls in the west, Watertown to the north, Syracuse and Utica in the central area, and the greatest of them all, New York City, in the south-east.

Although most of New York state's cities have a staggeringly diverse industry, many have become synonymous with one product. Rochester is one such town. Despite its nickname, Flower City, earned because of the numerous nurseries and parks, the city is dominated by the Eastman Kodak works, the largest film and camera plant in the world. Rochester is the state's third largest city after New York and Buffalo, and lies amid America's richest fruit-growing and gardening region – the rose gardens at Maplewood Park are especially magnificent. In Upper Falls Park, on the Genesee River, you can see a 100-foot-high waterfall. Once used to drive the city's mills, it now generates electricity.

Another town which unwittingly nurtured a commercial empire is Watertown, about 75 miles north-east of Rochester and almost on the shores of Lake Ontario. Just over 100 years ago, when they held a fair here, a young trader took over part of a local department store because he had an idea that people would flock to his counters if he could sell a whole range of merchandise all for the same low price. His name was F W Woolworth.

Buffalo, on the north-eastern tip of Lake Erie, is New York state's leading inland port. Great Lakes steamers and seagoing

ROCHESTER

Hotels

MARRIOTT AIRPORT INN: 3½ miles N of I-490, 1890 Ridge Rd W, tel 225 6880. 211 rooms. Expensive.

TRAVELODGE: 390 South Av, tel 454 3550. 103 rooms. Inexpensive.

Restaurants

CHEZ JEAN-PIERRE: ½ mile on East Av, 295 Alexander St, tel 325 3329. Delightful French decor. Fine continental entrees. Moderate.

ROYAL SCOT STEAK HOUSE: 657 East Ridge Rd, tel 342 4220. Popular, informal dining-room. Children's menu. Inexpensive.

Places of Interest

EASTMAN-KODAK: Kodak Pk, 200 Ridge Rd W. 90-minute tours of huge film, paper and chemical factories.

INTERNATIONAL MUSEUM OF PHOTOGRAPHY: George Eastman House, 1 mile E at 900 East Av. Comprehensive collection of pictures, cameras and films charting the history of photography.

ROCHESTER MUSEUM AND SCIENCE CENTER: 657 East Av. Regional museum featuring natural history, science, industry and technology. Strasenburgh Planetarium adjoins the building.

SENECA PARK AND ZOO: 2222 St Paul St. Smallish zoo in pleasant grounds. Outdoor swimming pool.

Rochester at night – a great commercial city which never seems to sleep

NEW YORK STATE

The city of Buffalo, a leading inland port set in 3,000 acres of parks and gardens

BUFFALO

Hotels

BEST WESTERN MOTOR INN: 510 Delaware Av, tel 886 8331. 61 rooms. Moderate.

BLUE DOLPHIN MOTOR LODGE: 1951 Niagara Blvd, tel 691 9392. 21 rooms. Moderate.

THE EXECUTIVE MOTOR INN: opposite Buffalo Int Airport, tel 634 2300. 283 rooms. Expensive.

Restaurants

LORD CHUMLEY'S: 481 Delaware Av, tel 886 9158. Excellent food. Children's menu. Moderate.

PLAZA SUITE: on Main St, 1 M & T Plaza, tel 842 5555. Good food. Fine views of the city. Moderate.

ALBRIGHT-KNOX ART GALLERY: at junc SR 198 and Elmwood Av. Good example of Greek Revival architecture. Excellent art collection. Interesting Mirrored Room.

BUFFALO MUSEUM OF SCIENCE: Humboldt Pkwy at Northampton St. Featuring many aspects of science including zoology, botany and geology, plus a children's discovery room.

NAVAL AND SERVICEMEN'S PARK: on waterfront at Main St and S Park Av. Self-guided tours available on a destroyer and cruiser.

THEODORE ROOSEVELT INAUGURAL NATIONAL HISTORIC SITE: 641 Delaware Av. Restored with period furniture. Library was the site of Roosevelt's inauguration. Slide show.

---

ships dock here; the Erie Canal, which has its western terminal here, provides access to the eastern seaboard. Buffalo's most enduring historical event (other than the burning of the town by the British during the 1812–15 war) occurred on 14 September 1901, when President William McKinley, the 24th President of the Union, became the third incumbent of that precarious office to be assassinated. His successor, Theodore Roosevelt, took his oath of office in a house in Delaware Avenue later the same day.

To the north of Buffalo, on the Niagara River separating Canada from the United States, one of the greatest shows on earth is relentlessly doing its natural best to attract the thousands of tourists who swell the 80,000 population all year round. This is Niagara Falls – a phenomenon New York state shares with Canada's Ontario.

The massive cascade of water is caused by a dramatic drop of nearly 200 feet in the bed of the Niagara River, about half-way along its 37-mile course between Lake Erie and Lake Ontario. Altogether there are three falls; one on the Canadian side, the curved Horseshoe Falls, 176 feet high and 2,000 feet wide, and two on the American side, American Falls, 1,075 feet wide and 184 feet high, and Bridal Veil Falls, separated from the latter by Luna Island. On each side of the river a township serving mainly the tourist trade has grown up, but with the harnessing of the tremendous hydro-electric power of the falls, the town on the New York side has also attracted an industrial community. Both sides of the river are easily reached via the Rainbow Bridge.

The production of hydro-electricity has, unfortunately, slightly reduced the awesomeness of the falls. Instead of showing off its mighty freeflow of one and a half million gallons per second, the falls have been reduced to 748,000 gallons per second, and outside the main tourist season, even less.

Further along the river, Whirlpool Rapid Bridge leads to another phenomenon – the whirlpool created at a point where the river makes a 90 degree turn. Though the whirlpool is on the Canadian side, a 109-acre state park in New York is the best place to view it.

The Canadian falls, perhaps because they give the most dramatic performance, provide a much wider variety of entertainments than the New York side. A ride in the whirlpool aero car high over the Niagara Gorge and back is an unforgettable experience. The falls are also accessible, sometimes uncomfortably so, by boat. There are lifts to tunnels where the fury of the falls can be seen at close quarters; a twin cable rail car system, called the Horseshoe Falls Incline Railway; a Great Falls Trip, which includes a journey to river level just north of the Whirlpool Rapids Bridge; and an official Niagara Falls Museum in which the most popular exhibition is the 'Daredevil Hall of Fame', a tribute to the foolhardy who tried to navigate the falls.

WATERTOWN

Hotels

HOLIDAY INN: 300 Washington St, tel 782 8000. 172 rooms. Expensive.

HOWARD JOHNSON'S MOTOR LODGE: 1190 Arsenal St, tel 788 6800. 96 rooms. Expensive.

REDWOOD MOTOR LODGE: exit 45 or 47 off I-81, Gifford St Rd, tel 788 2850. 24 rooms. Moderate.

Restaurants

THE GOLDEN LION RESTAURANT: 1116 Arsenal St, tel 782 1440. Relaxed atmosphere and good food. Children's menu. Moderate.

PARTRIDGE BERRY INN: 4¼ miles E on SR 3, Black River Garden Center, tel 788 4610. Excellent food, country inn style restaurant. Moderate.

Places of Interest

GARDEN VILLAGE: 4¼ miles E on SR 3, at Black River Garden Center. Historic buildings from Jefferson County, including reconstructed inn, schoolhouse, blacksmith shop and weigh station. Landscaped grounds.

JEFFERSON COUNTY HISTORICAL SOCIETY: 228 Washington St. 19th-century costumes, portraits, furniture, Indian artefacts.

NEW YORK STATE

NIAGARA FALLS

Hotels

ANCHOR MOTEL: 2332 River Rd, tel 693 0850. 21 rooms. Inexpensive.

NIAGARA HILTON: 300 Third St, tel 285 3361. 398 rooms. Expensive.

SANDS MOTEL: 6 miles S of US 62, 9393 Pine Av, tel 297 3797. 17 rooms. Moderate.

Restaurant

JOHN'S FLAMING HEARTH: $5\frac{1}{2}$ miles S on US 62, 1965 Military Rd, tel 297 1414. Limited menu featuring steak. Moderate.

Places of Interest

AQUARIUM OF NIAGARA FALLS: Whirlpool St at Pine Av. Sea-life exhibits including penguins and dolphins.

GOAT ISLAND: between Canadian and American Falls. Mid-river wooded island affording splendid views.

NIAGARA VIEWMOBILES: board at Goat Is or Prospect Pt. 30-minute trips allowing fine close-up views of the falls.

POWER VISTA: $4\frac{1}{2}$ miles N of falls on SR 104. Theme building featuring energy production. Models, movies and dioramas illustrate how Niagara's power was harnessed.

SCHOELLKOPF GEOLOGICAL MUSEUM: $\frac{1}{4}$ mile N of Rainbow Bridge, from Main St. Audio-visual display charting local geological history. Garden and nature trail.

From the American side of the river, Goat Island, which separates the American Falls from the Canadian falls, can be reached by a pedestrian bridge. A particularly attractive feature are the wooden walkways which take visitors to within 25 feet of the base of the falls.

At night, the stunning spectacle is enhanced by the equivalent of four billion candlepower of light from both sides of the river – the electricity, of course, powered by the falls themselves. Commercialised though it is, Niagara Falls as an entertainment centre has benefited from the razzamatazz, for this natural wonder could never be seen in such glorious detail without the money to pay for the facilities. Although officially customs regulations still apply between the two countries, the amenities on both sides are accessible to visitors with little or no formalities.

The Erie Canal, linking the Hudson River with the Great Lakes, has, since it opened in 1825, brought prosperity to cities like Rochester, Syracuse, Utica and Rome.

Rome was originally called De-O-Wain-Sta by the Indians. Roughly translated it means 'The carrying place' – an appropriate name for a town in which the predominant feature is the canal. A village restored to resemble an 1840 community is one of the major tourist draws here. Syracuse can also thank the Erie Canal for its growth. Now the fourth largest city in the state, with a population of more than 180,000, it had the good fortune of finding a rich source of salt in Lake Onondaga. For many years after Syracuse was founded in 1805, the bulk of the salt used in America came from here and was processed in the city. A canal museum at the corner of Erie Boulevard and Montgomery Street tells how the canal was built, used and administered. At Utica, one of the highlights of a visit is to see the West End Brewing Company's works at Court and Varick Streets. Here the entire process of beer-making is demonstrated and there are trolley rides to a tavern built in 1888, where visitors can taste the beer.

A similar prosperity has come to another lakeland area, known as the Finger Lakes, in western New York state. It is not only the centre of a rich agricultural industry, but also the heart of America's central wine-growing regions. The most fertile vineyards (or wineries as the Americans call them) lie between the lakes of Canadaigua and Keuka, two of the Finger Lakes (the latter is shaped like a thumb and forefinger). Hammondsport, a 1,200-strong community on Keuka lakeside is where winery tours are conducted. Naturally, they include wine-

ROME

Hotel

BEST WESTERN AMERICAN HERITAGE INN: Lawrence St exit off US 49, Erie Blvd W, tel 339 3610. 28 rooms. Inexpensive.

Restaurant

SAVOY RESTAURANT: 255 East Dominick St, tel 336 9932. Good American and Italian fare. Inexpensive.

Places of Interest

ERIE CANAL VILLAGE: 3 miles W on SR 49. Rural community including farm and canal, just as it was in the 1840s.

ORISKANY BATTLEFIELD: 6 miles E marked by granite pole. Scene of the goriest battle of the Revolution. Dioramas and tours.

---

tasting sessions. Near the southern end of Canadaigua Lake is the village of Naples, which is known for its wine cellars, breathtaking scenery, numerous waterfalls, and rivers packed with rainbow trout.

Alexandria Bay, at the source of the St Lawrence, is the gateway to the Thousand Islands. Not all of them are habitable, and only a few are large enough to house a sizeable community. Dotting the river for about 15 miles all the way to Chippewa Bay,

NEW YORK STATE

lake are 155 islands, among them 48 that have been developed for camping, and lakeside facilities include steamboat rides, a lake shore drive and a memorial highway to a spectacular viewpoint overlooking the picturesque lake.

A resort which attracts weary 'townies' as much as tourists is Saratoga Springs. Originally a health spa, it now has year-round entertainment and sports facilities. Set in beautiful countryside to the north of the Catskill Mountains, it hosts important motor-car race meetings and skating championships during the winter sports festivals. On 2,000 acres of the Saratoga Spa State Park, the Performing Arts Center is home of the New York City Ballet during July, and the famous Philadelphia Symphony Orchestra in August. Nearby is also a private estate, called Yaddo, where artists, writers and composers are drawn into a free-wheeling working community.

Way up north on the eastern corner of the state is one of America's most durable public sights. Over a hundred years ago, Ausable Chasm, a one-and-a-half-mile-long gorge with many waterfalls and rapids, was first made available for sightseeing. Here the Ausable River winds and twists beneath sheer rock walls 200 feet high. There are boat trips and a three-quarter-mile walkway with many steps, requiring stout shoes and lots of energy.

The brave among visitors to Niagara Falls may enjoy a ride in the 'Maid of the Mist'

the islands are ideal for swimming, boating, fishing and camping. Such simple waterside pleasures as these islands afford contrast sharply with the sophisticated and organised entertainment of the most famous lakeside resort of all – Lake Placid. Deep in the Adirondack Mountains, in a region of numerous beautiful lakes – Mirror Lake, Silver Lake, and Flower Lake – Lake Placid lies in the shadows of the 4,800-foot-high Whiteface Mountain. This is where the 1980 Winter Olympics were held, leaving the resort a legacy of outdoor and indoor stadia, and Olympic bobsled course.

Equally popular in summer, Lake Placid has a historical fascination, too. For here is where John Brown's body lies-a-mouldering in the grave since the great slavery abolitionist was hanged in December 1859, and became a folk hero. His grave is preserved at the John Brown Farm, two miles south of the village.

On the shores of Lake George, at the southern tip of the 32-mile-long lake, is the holiday village of the same name. On the

---

UTICA

Hotels

GATEWAY MOTOR INN: 175 N Genesee St, tel 732 4121. 90 rooms. Moderate–expensive.

QUALITY INN DOWNTOWN: 267 Genesee St, tel 724 8161. 105 rooms. Moderate–expensive.

TRINKAUS MANOR MOTOR LODGE: 311 Utica St, tel 736 5205. 40 rooms. Moderate.

Restaurants

HART'S HILL INN: 4 miles W via SR 69 and ½ mile S on Clinton St, tel 736 3011. Fine regional dishes. Views over valley.

TRINKAUS MANOR: As above, tel 736 5205. 150-year-old mansion where the speciality of the house is Cornish game hen. Expensive.

Places of Interest

MUNSON-WILLIAMS-PROCTOR INSTITUTE: 310 Genesee St. Includes a museum of American art from the colonial period to the present. Adjoining is Fountain Elms, a house dating from 1850, furnished in period.

ONEIDA COUNTY HISTORICAL SOCIETY: 318 Genesee St. Exhibitions about Utica, Oneida and Mohawk Valley history.

SYRACUSE

Hotels

BEST WESTERN-NORTHWAY INN: 400 7th North St, tel 451 1511. 128 rooms. Expensive.

RODEWAY INN: at Thompson Rd and SR 298, tel 463 6601. 120 rooms. Moderate.

SYRACUSE HILTON INN: 1308 Buckley Rd, tel 451 1212. 150 rooms. Expensive.

Restaurants

BARBUTO'S: 50 Presidential Plaza, tel 474 3000. Seven-course continental meals, intimate atmosphere. Expensive.

GLEN LOCH MILL: 4226 North St, tel 469 6969. Delightful restored mill by stream. À la carte and children's menus. Moderate.

VALLE'S STEAKHOUSE: 2803 Erie Blvd, tel 446 8330. Pleasant and very popular restaurant with an extensive menu. Inexpensive–moderate.

Places of Interest

EVERSON MUSEUM OF ART: 401 Harrison St. Exhibits art from the 18th century to the present, including American paintings, sculpture, ceramics and Oriental art.

ONONDAGA LAKE PARK: NW via SR 57 .6 miles of east shore. Picnic sites, marine, boating harbour and reproduction of Jesuit Fort Ste Marie de Gannentaha (originally founded here in 1656) are among the attractions and facilities here.

NEW YORK STATE

LAKE PLACID

Hotels

ADIRONDACK INN: 217 Main St, tel 523 2424. 44 rooms. Moderate.

HOLIDAY INN: 1 Olympic Dr, tel 523 2556. 131 rooms. Expensive.

THE NORTHWAY MOTEL: 5 Wilmington Rd, tel 523 3500. 12 rooms. Inexpensive.

Restaurant

THE STEAK AND STINGER: 15 Cascade Rd, tel 523 9927. Pleasant dining areas. Comprehensive menu. Moderate.

Places of Interest

HOME OF 1,000 ANIMALS: 1½ miles W on SR 86. A specialist zoo featuring fur-bearing and game animals. Llama rides and chimpanzee entertainment.

JOHN BROWN'S FARM STATE HISTORIC SITE AND GRAVE: 2 miles S on SR 73. Restored farmhouse and burial monument. Free entry.

LAKE PLACID BOAT RIDES FROM HOLIDAY HARBOR: 1 mile N on Mirror Lake Dr. Daily 1-hour cruises. Excellent scenery.

At the eastern end of the Erie Canal, is Albany, the capital of New York. This was the destination of the first successful steamboat run on the Hudson River from New York in 1807. The city prospered when the Erie Canal opened in 1825 to water traffic from the western reaches of the state, and today the city is an important inland port. It has also benefited from Governor Nelson A Rockefeller. A large section of the town between Madison and State Streets has been turned into a complex of offices and cultural facilities known as the Governor Nelson A Rockefeller Empire State Plaza, dominated by the 44-storey State Office Tower, which has an observation deck at the top. In contrast to these modern structures, the New York State Capitol between State Street and Washington Avenue, and Swan and Eagle Streets, was built in the late 19th century, a blend of classical styles in granite. The New York State Museum in the Cultural Education Center, apart from exhibiting artefacts to trace geological and human progress in various parts of the state, also recently put together an exhibition on the development of New York City.

Albany was first settled by 18 Dutch families in 1624 15 years after Henry Hudson sailed into Albany on the river that was to be named after him and claimed the region for the Dutch. They established important trading posts along much of that eastern coastal area, and called the township on Manhattan Island New Amsterdam. Later, in 1664, the English took possession and renamed it New York.

For many years, the province was at the heart of a power struggle between the two colonial nations. After 1664, when the issue of the control of the province had been settled in favour of the English (the aspirations of the French had also to be taken into account), the real balance of power was found to be in none of these countries' hands. Instead, it belonged to the five powerful Indian tribes in the area, the Cayuga, the Mohawk, the Oneida, the Onondaga and the Seneca.

These tribes formed into a confederacy in 1570, and used their considerable united strength against the European intruders. The battles that ensued traversed the entire territory, raging from as far north as Montreal down to Manhattan Island. Ultimately, the superior armoury and numbers of the white man's troops triumphed over the Indians and spectacular victories such as the fall of Montreal and the seizure of Niagara helped to break the Indians' hold over the territory.

Yet these battles were nothing compared to those fought on that same soil during the Revolutionary War of the 18th century. Nearly a third of all the battles in that war took place in what was to become New York state. The first occurred with the occupa-

ALBANY

Hotels

AMERICANA INN: 660 Albany Shaker Rd, tel 869 9271. 188 rooms. Expensive.

BEST WESTERN-INN TOWNE: on US 9 and 20, 300 Broadway, tel 434 4111. 137 rooms. Inexpensive.

HOLIDAY INN OF LATHAM: 946 New Loudon Rd, tel 783 6161. 120 rooms. Moderate

Restaurants

BAVARIAN CHALET: center of Guildezland on US 20, Western Av, tel 355 8005. Good German and American food. Inexpensive.

STONE ENDS: on US 9 W, ¾ mile S of exit 23, tel 465 3178. Continental menu. Reservation advised. Moderate.

Places of Interest

ALBANY INSTITUTE OF HISTORY AND ART: 125 Washington Av. Houses many American antiques, specialising in Dutch culture, regional painting and sculpture. Oldest museum in New York state.

FIRST CHURCH IN ALBANY (REFORMED): N Pearl at Clinton. Dating from 1642, has MSS and old silver on display. Both the weathervane and pulpit were built in 1656.

GOVERNOR NELSON A ROCKEFELLER EMPIRE STATE PLAZA: between Madison and State Sts. Complex of ten buildings including shops, offices, auditorium and a tower block.

HISTORIC CHERRY HILL: on S Pearl St near junc of First Av. A Georgian-style house displaying the possessions of the Van Rensselaer family.

---

tion of New York City by the British, and General Washington's retreat to New Jersey after his defeat at the battle of Long Island. The British launched a three-pronged attack on Albany. Two of them failed, though a southern attack managed to get through to Kingston, which was burnt. But without support from the north, the British troops withdrew again to New York City. This resounding colonial victory persuaded the French to support the revolutionaries – a move which signalled the end of British rule in North America.

One of the most momentous battles of the Revolutionary War took place at White Plains on Manhattan Island. Three monuments to the battle, fought on 28 October 1776, have been erected at the White Plains Battlefield Site. It was here three months earlier that New York state was born, when the provincial congress first met.

The following year, the state constitution was drafted at Kingston, which then became the state's first capital. The Senate House at Clinton Avenue and Fair Street was where the first New York Senate met. After the British surrendered at Yorktown in 1781, General Washington established his headquarters in Hasbrouck House in

Franklin D. Roosevelt's father bought this mansion at Hyde Park in 1867. It is kept as it was left when the President died in 1945

New York's State Capitol, built in the 1800s, is surrounded by the futuristic buildings of Albany's Empire State Plaza

NEW YORK STATE

from Europe in vast numbers between 1830 and 1930, New York became an exciting, if somewhat chaotic, state. It was also a breeding ground for new ideas in politics and art. Women's rights, prohibition and penal reforms were often under debate. Writers such as Mark Twain, Herman Melville, Walt Whitman and James Fenimore Cooper were drawn by the stimulating ideas of the late 19th-century reformers. At Palmyra, in the west of the state, Joseph Smith founded the Mormon religion. On Hill Cumorah, four miles out of the village, a 40-foot monument topped by a statue, symbolises the miracle of Angel Moroni from whom Smith is said to have received the gold plates inscribed with the history of ancient America. This led him to translate the inscription into the Book of Mormon for publication in 1830. To Judge William Cooper, the father of writer James Fenimore Cooper, is attributed the founding of Cooperstown in 1786. His son was inspired by the nine-mile-long Otsego Lake to create 'Glimmerglass', the fictional lake of so many of his stories. Just a mile out of town a museum at Fenimore House celebrates the writer's life.

When the Civil War broke out, the tide of mass immigration had permitted nearly half a million New Yorkers to join up and fight for the Union cause. Although the Civil War nearly destroyed the economy of New York state for the rest of the 19th century, giving rise to political corruption on a massive scale, the national leaders who emerged at the beginning of this century put the state on a more secure footing.

For many years enjoying a self-imposed exile from the rest of the world, America abandoned its isolationist attitudes towards Europe in the 1930s, thanks to the liberal policies of Franklin Delano Roosevelt, who for 12 years ruled skilfully and benignly from the White House. He died just before the end of World War II. He and his wife, Eleanor, are buried in the 187-acre estate at Hyde Park, about 30 miles from New York, bought by Roosevelt's father for the family home in 1867. Now a national historic site, the house built in about 1826, was remodelled in 1915, and has since been preserved in the condition it was in when Roosevelt died in April 1945. His grave, marked by a plain white marble monument, can be seen in the rose garden; the house itself is too small to accommodate more than a few visitors at a time. Attached to the house is a library and museum, containing manuscripts, books, paintings, prints, historical material and public and personal papers belonging to the president and his wife. In the gift room is a display of unusual presents sent to the White House during Roosevelt's term of office. The estate includes a coach-house, ice-houses and a walking trail.

ITHACA

Hotels

HOLIDAY INN: 310 N Triphammer Rd, tel 257 3100. 120 rooms. Moderate.

MEADOW COURT MOTEL: 529 S Meadow St, tel 273 3885. 58 rooms. Inexpensive.

Restaurants

ODYSSEY RESTAURANT: 1654 Trumansburg Rd, tel 272 2422. Seafood plus some Greek specialities. Inexpensive.

TAUGHANNOCK FARMS INN: 10 miles N on SR 89, tel 387 7711. Well-prepared meals. Overlooking Cayuga Lake. Moderate.

Places of Interest

CORNELL UNIVERSITY: NE side of town. Beautifully set hilltop campus encompassing 13,000 acres of buildings and farms. Conducted tours available.

STEWART PARK: around Cayuga Lake. Rose gardens and picknicking areas. Adjacent to wildfowl preserve and bird sanctuary.

TAUGHANNOCK FALLS STATE PARK: 10 miles N on SR 89. 825-acre park featuring 215-foot waterfall situated in steep-sided glen.

Newburgh on the banks of the Hudson while the army was being disbanded. Today the house where he worked from April 1782 to August 1783 contains paintings, furnishings and a museum of the period, carefully restored and preserved. Having furnished so many convenient battlefields in the Revolutionary War, New York state became fertile ground, too, for the political struggles which followed, and which, in one form or another, raged throughout much of the 19th century. The emergence of America's two powerful political parties, the Republicans and the Democrats, can be traced to the titanic problems confronting the Americans after their victory. Made up of representatives of many disparate nations, with different ambitions for, and visions of, the new nation's role, the future legislators had, for instance, first to choose between state or federal rule.

The 1812–15 war with Britain temporarily united the factions again, but with the defeat of the British Fleet on Lake Champlain, the peacetime problems of the new state intensified. Meanwhile the population was growing fast, as more and more merchants settled in the New World.

Nourished by the arrival of immigrants

Around Long Island

2–3 days – 265 miles

New York City – Kings Point – Oyster Bay – Huntington – Centerport – Stony Brook – Setauket – East Setauket – Ridge – Riverhead – Cutchogue – Greenport – Montauk – Amagansett – East Hampton – Bridgehampton – Southampton – Sayville – Old Bethpage – New York City

Leave New York City on the Long Island Expressway (Interstate 495). At exit 30 join Cross Island Parkway North and after one mile join State Route 25A, then Great Neck Road and Bayview Avenue to King's Point on Little Neck Bay.

Kings Point
Grounds totalling 75 acres house the United States Merchant Marine Academy. Over 1,000 midshipmen with aspirations to a commission and a university degree are accommodated in what used to include the estate of Walter Chrysler, the motor car tycoon. The academy was founded during World War I.

Drive out of Kings Point on an unclassified road to Thomaston. Here, take State Route 25A and drive 10 miles east to East Norwich. Head north on State Route 106 to Oyster Bay.

Oyster Bay
Two separate main streets a block apart testify to the dual 'settling' of this village in the 17th century by both Dutch and English. West Main Street is well known for Raynham Hall, farmhouse home of Samuel Townsend and his son Robert. Townsend junior was an intelligence agent who was involved in the capture of the 18th-century British spy Major John André, and the subsequent exposure of Benedict Arnold's plan to betray West Point.

Cove Road houses the Roosevelt Bird Sanctuary and Trailside Museum. This was once the summer home of Theodore Roosevelt, and examples of local fauna and flora are on show as a memorial to the conservationist president.

Another of Theodore Roosevelt's homes, known until his death in 1919 as the 'Summer White House', is four miles east of Oyster Bay at Sagamore Hill National Historic Site. An Indian Chief named Sagamore Mohannes once owned the land. The Roosevelt furnishings have been preserved in the house and numerous fascinating gifts from foreign rulers, such as elephant tusks from the Emperor of Ethiopia, are on display.

Leave Oyster Bay eastwards on East Main Street, then Oyster Bay Cove Road. Pick up State Route 25A 2 miles south, turn left and drive 6 miles east to Huntington.

Huntington
No fewer than 17 communities and five harbours are contained in the 50 miles of coastline which make up Huntington. The town's most famous son is the distinguished poet and journalist, Walt Whitman, whose birthplace, a period-style farmhouse, is a State Historic Site. Pictures, manuscripts and books are on display, and it is a fascinating place to visit.

Heckscher Park on Main Street has a fine museum which contains a permanent collection of American and European paintings and sculpture.

You will probably be content to while away the time here watching the fabulous yachts and cruisers in one of the many prosperous boating clubs in the area.

Continue east along State Route 25A for 5 miles to Centerport.

Centerport
Overlooking Northport Bay are the magnificent Spanish–Moroccan-style mansion and beautifully tended gardens of a 43-acre estate which was once the home of William Vanderbilt, son of the renowned 19th-century financier and railway magnate, Cornelius Vanderbilt.

Portuguese works of art, such as a 13th-century Aubusson tapestry, and rare antiques, such as 17th-century carved Florentine walnut furniture, are on display.

Hour-long shows are held in the planetarium in the mansion grounds which contains astronomy and science exhibits, telescopes and an observatory. The chief attraction is the 60-foot diameter screen onto which the night sky is projected. The Vanderbilt Museum, and the Hall of Fishes (in a separate building), contain marine and wildlife specimens, souvenirs and trophies.

Follow State Route 25A eastwards for about 15 miles through Fort Salonga, Kings Park, San Remo and Smithtown, then turn left on to Ridgeway Avenue to Stony Brook.

Stony Brook
Time has virtually ignored this old colonial-style village since the early 19th century. Cleverly conceived buildings allow a very modern shopping centre to retain an old world air. The museum complex on Main Street displays 19 old buildings, including a one-room schoolhouse, a reconstructed blacksmith's forge and a carriage shed. In the carriage museum on the south side of the town, about 100 horse-drawn vehicles, some dating back to the late 17th century, are well worth a visit. The 19th-century painter of rural scenes, William Sidney Mount, who once lived in Stony Brook, is well represented in the local art gallery.

Continue east on Ridgeway Avenue and State Route 25A for 2½ miles to Setauket.

Setauket
Named after Queen Caroline, wife of George IV of England, who donated a silver communion service, the Caroline Church of Brookhaven, in the main street at Setauket Green, was built in 1729 and restored in 1937. As well as the queen's gift, many features of the interior date from the early 18th century.

Continue east along an unclassified road and State Route 25A for about one mile to East Setauket.

East Setauket
Unusual painted walls in Thompson House, a typical 18th-century English-style home, may be seen on North Country Road one mile north-east of Stony Brook station.

Drive south for 7 miles on State Route 112 to Coram, then eastwards for 6 miles along State Route 25 to Ridge.

Ridge
Research into the peaceful uses of atomic energy is carried out at the Brookhaven National Laboratory on the William Floyd Parkway. It was established in 1946, and some parts of this enormous top-secret centre can be visited, including the first atomic reactor ever built for peace-time study.

Continue eastwards along State Route 25 for 13 miles to Riverhead.

Riverhead
Renowned for its excellent potato and market garden crops, Riverhead is set at the point where the North and South Forks of Long Island meet.

Long Island's past is recalled in the premises of the Suffolk County Historical Society, where a large collection of historical objects of all kinds are on view.

Captain Kidd is reputed to have buried treasure near here in one of the many sheltered coves or inlets.

Hotels
BEST WESTERN CIRCLE MOTOR INN: 30 E Moriches Rd, tel 727 6200. 68 rooms. Moderate.

HOLIDAY INN: On SR 25 exit 72, Long Island Expwy, tel 369 2200. 100 rooms. Expensive.

WADING RIVER MOTEL: 9 miles W on SR 25, tel 727 8000. 32 rooms. Moderate.

Continue east on State Route 25 for 12 miles to Cutchogue.

Cutchogue
The finest example of English architecture in the United States is considered to be Old House, built in 1649. It was once the home of a sailing captain. Exposed sections inside the house show intriguing features of its construction.

Drive eastwards along State Route 25 for 11 miles to Greenport.

Greenport
Some of the best oysters in the world may be sampled in this port, which was the centre of Long Island's oyster industry at the turn of the century. The town is most exciting in September during the Oyster Festival.

A hand-carved Swiss model village and antique dolls may be viewed at the Museum of Childhood on Broad Street.

Leave the North Fork and take the car ferry to Shelter Island, well known for golfing and yachting. On the far side of the island, take the ferry to Sag Harbour. Drive south-east for 7 miles along State Route 114 to East Hampton, then travel 21 miles east along State Route 27, which traverses the spectacular Montauk Peninsula, to Montauk.

Montauk
Woodlands, cliffs, sparkling freshwater lakes and white beaches surround this liveliest of the fishing villages of Long Island, famous for its 'cod ledge', where the sport of deep-sea fishing is unrivalled. Bluefish and tuna are among many prized species caught here. Surfing, swimming, sailing and birdwatching are other interesting leisure activities well-favoured in this refuge for jaded city-dwellers.

The eastern headland of Long Island is dominated by Montauk Lighthouse, built in 1796 by order of George Washington. From this point, Block Island Sound may be viewed in one direction, whilst in other directions the Atlantic stretches out for hundreds of miles.

The Montauk Lighthouse, a landmark older than the Statue of Liberty

Hotels
DRIFTWOOD MOTEL & COTTAGES: 5 miles W on SR 27, tel 668 5744. 50 rooms. Moderate.

GURNEY'S INN: 3 miles W on Old Montauk Hwy, tel 668 2345. 125 rooms. Expensive.

RONJO RESORT MOTEL: centre, tel 668 2112. 33 rooms. Moderate.

SEA CREST MOTEL: 5 miles W on SR 27, tel 267 3159. Moderate–inexpensive.

Restaurants
GURNEY'S INN: As hotel above. Attractive dining rooms overlooking ocean, excellent food. Strict dress code. Moderate–expensive.

THE INN AT NAPEAGUE: 5½ miles W on SR 27, tel 267 8103. Continental and American food. Moderate.

THE LITTLE PARK RESTAURANT: centre on US 27, tel 668 3131. Limited menu, but fine continental cuisine emphasising seafood. Moderate.

Return westwards along State Route 27 for 11 miles to Amagansett.

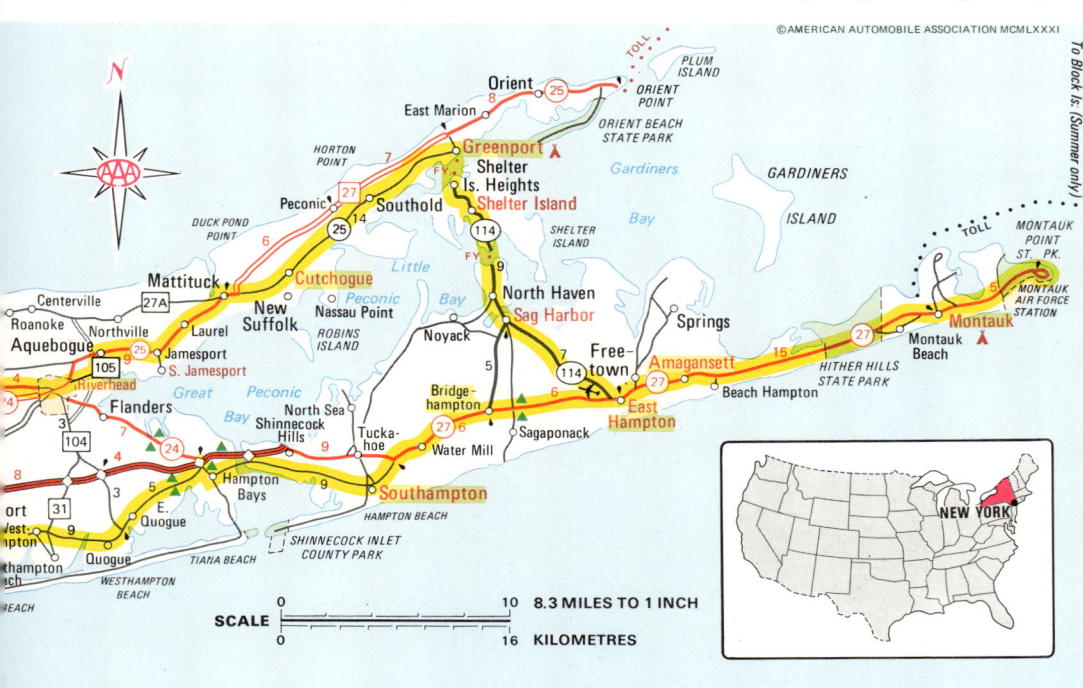

AROUND LONG ISLAND

The powdery white sands of Long Island's beaches, like this one at Amagansett, explain this coast's popularity

Amagansett
Nazi saboteurs came ashore from a submarine on the white sands of this attractive town during World War II. Fortunately they were captured without harm.
A 200-year-old Cape Cod house known as Miss Amelia's Cottage is maintained as a museum by the town's historical society. East Hampton Town Marine Museum, which depicts the history of whaling and commercial fishing, is also here. The garden is ideal for picknicking.
 Continue 4 miles west along State Route 27 to East Hampton.

East Hampton
Summer home of the rich and fashionable, East Hampton is surrounded by opulent estates and is itself a picturesque haven for writers and artists. At 14 James Lane is 'Home Sweet Home', the birthplace of John Howard Payne, who composed the famous song inspired by this very house. The 18th- and 19th-century china, glass, antiques and furniture collected in Payne's lifetime are now on view.
In beautiful tree-lined Main Street is the Guild Hall, a cultural centre where art exhibitions and theatre productions are held.
A rustic English scene is captured by the village green, which is complete with duck pond and a circle of stately homes. Close by is Mulford Farmhouse, built around 1660 and furnished in 18th-century style.
A Dutch windmill in working order, Old Hook Mill, is a charming feature. It was built in 1806 of oak and hickory wood brought from Gardiners Island, situated to the north.
 Drive for 5 miles westward on State Route 27 to Bridgehampton.

Bridgehampton
Working antique engines and farm machines are on display in the Hildreth-Simons Machine Shop which is a part of the Bridgehampton Historical Museum in Corwith House. The grounds also hold the George W Strong Wheelright Shop, which contains old tools once used to repair wagons. Local crafts and period furnishings from the late 18th century to the present day are on show in the Greek Revival-style Corwith House.
 Continue westwards along State Route 27 for 5 miles to Southampton.

Southampton
This largest and most famous of the chain of Hamptons stages a number of annual events including a colourful Fourth of July parade, an open air art sale in July and an Indian pow-wow at Shinnecock Indian Reservation in September. North-west of the town is the Long Island Automotive Museum, one of the largest motor museums in the world. South of the town is a restored two-storey house, the Old Halsey Homestead. Built in 1648, interesting features include 17th- and 18th-century furnishings and a colonial herb garden. There are a number of good museums in the town itself. Three miles north on North Sea Road, then 5 miles east on Noyack Road, is the Elizabeth Morton Wildlife Refuge, an Atlantic Flyway feeding and resting place for migrant birds.

Hotels
SHINNECOCK MOTEL: 240 Montauk Hwy, tel 283 2406. 24 rooms. Moderate.

Restaurant
BALZARINI'S: Northern Italian-American cuisine, pasta, seafood, and home-made desserts. Quiet family-owned restaurant. Moderate.

Drive west along the Montauk Highway (State Route 27) for about 30 miles, then take Lincoln Avenue and continue south-west to West Sayville.

West Sayville
Suffolk Marine Museum has a comprehensive collection of model ships, paintings and other mementos of early seafaring days. If you have the time and inclination, West Sayville Golf Course offers alternative entertainment.
 Return to State Route 27 and drive westwards for about 6 miles to join State Route 109. Continue westwards for 8 miles to Farmingdale, then take Main Street and drive north-west through Bethpage State Park to Old Bethpage.

Old Bethpage
Conditions of 150 years ago are recreated in this active farming community, where the visitor is taken back in time to the early 19th century. Twenty-five historic buildings from all over Long Island have been re-erected in the 200-acre village. Tours begin at the reception buildings, where an introductory film prepares you for a typical day in the life of a pre-Civil War community. Around the village you will see farmworkers, a cobbler, a tailor and a blacksmith at work.
 Leave Old Bethpage on Round Swamp Road north to the Long Island Expressway (Interstate 495) and drive westwards for about 20 miles to New York.

East Hampton's windmill. The tiller beam at the rear enabled the miller to turn the sails into the wind

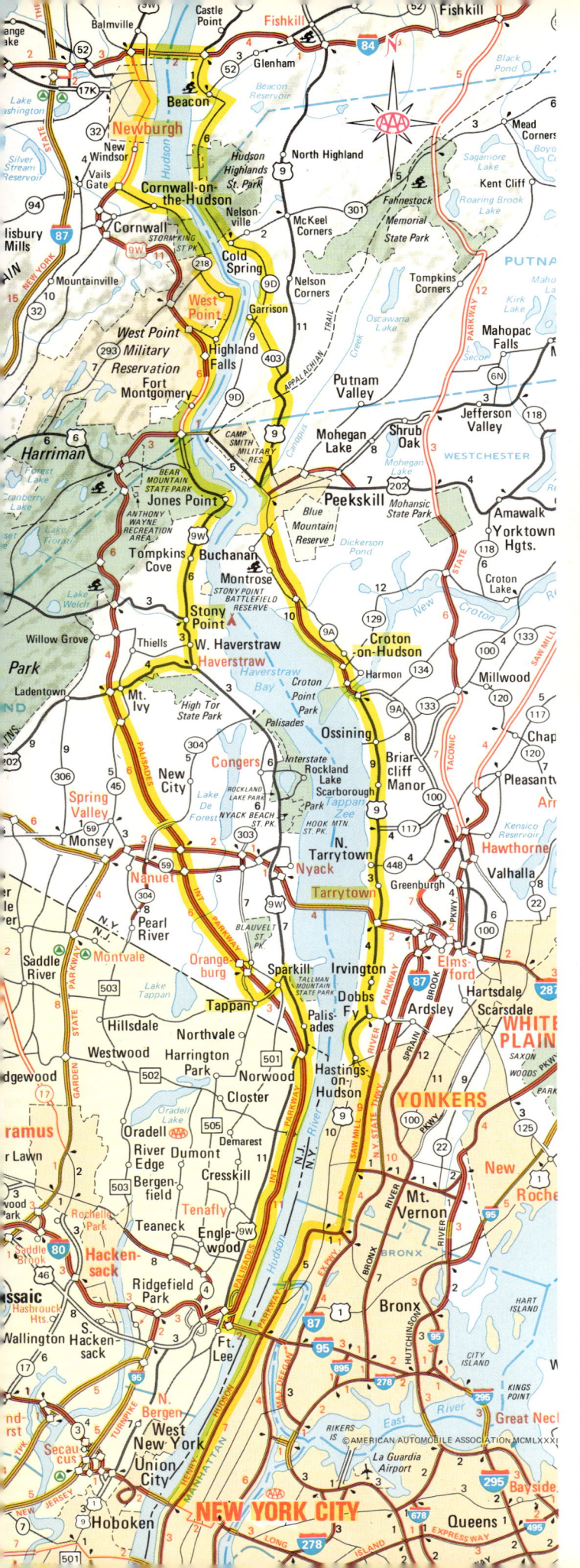

Along the Hudson River

2 days – 265 miles

Manhattan – Tappan – Stony Point – Bear Mountain State Park – West Point – Cornwall-on-the-Hudson – Newburgh – Beacon – Garrison – Croton-on-Hudson – Tarrytown – Yonkers – Manhattan.

The Hudson River and Bear Mountain Bridge in Bear Mountain State Park

Cross the Hudson River over the George Washington Bridge and turn right on to the scenic Palisades Interstate Parkway. Continue north for 11 miles then take the US 9W at the interchange and drive 3 miles north by Tallman State Park. Turn sharp left on to Washington Street and continue for about 2 miles to Tappan.

Tappan
Close to a picturesque lake, this town is the site of the George Washington Masonic Shrine, the DeWint House, on Livingstone Avenue and Oak Tree Road. The house was built in 1700 and was occasionally used as army headquarters during the Revolutionary War. Rooms are furnished in this period.

Drive north on State Route 303 to the first interchange and continue north on the Palisade Interstate Parkway for 12 miles. Turn right on to US 202 and drive east for 4 miles. Continue north for 3 miles on US 9W to Stony Point.

Stony Point
Stony Point Battlefield is a State Historic Site nearly a mile northeast of US 9W where a rocky promontory overlooks the Hudson River. Forty-five acres of land are preserved to commemorate the scene where General 'Mad Anthony' Wayne stormed a British post and captured 575 men in 1779.

Drive 6 miles north on US 9W, through Jones Point to Bear Mountain State Park.

Bear Mountain State Park
This magnificent 5066-acre park has dazzling views over the river to the east and across to stupendous Bear Mountain to the west. A visit to the 1305-foot summit along the George W Perkins Memorial Drive is unforgettable. If you want to stay overnight, Bear Mountain Inn is a beautiful old inn built in the style of a Swiss chalet, or there are small rustic lodges within the park. Phone 786 2731 for reservations.

Continue north on US 9W for about 3 miles to Highland Falls, then for 2 miles on the old Storm King Highway (State Route 218) to West Point.

West Point
Graduates of the United States Military Academy at West Point include Generals MacArthur, Patton and Eisenhower. The site was first occupied as a military post during the Revolution and the present academy was founded in

SCALE 5.25 MILES TO 1 INCH
KILOMETRES

65

HUDSON RIVER

1802. A huge chain was stretched across the river from West Point to Constitution Island in 1778 to block the British Fleet. Two years later Benedict Arnold, officer in charge of the post, attempted to betray it to the British.

Three chapels are on view to the public. Beautiful stained glass windows and one of the largest church organs in the world are features of Cadet Chapel, while Old Cadet Chapel has battle flags and marble shields on its walls commemorating the American generals of the Revolution, including one for Benedict Arnold. The Catholic Chapel of the Most Holy Trinity is built in Norman Gothic style and is modelled on St Ethelreda's Carthusian Church in England. Fort Clinton has a monument to the great Polish soldier, Thaddeus Kosciuszko, who built a series of defences around West Point in 1778 to foil the British. A stunning view of the Hudson River is seen from Trophy Point, where a collection of relics from the Revolution includes links of the enormous chain used to block the British Fleet. Battle Monument is dedicated to men of the regular army who were killed in the Civil War. One of the largest collections of military artefacts in the world is contained in Thayers Academic Hall.

Drive north on State Route 218 through the spectacular Storm King State Park for 6 miles to Cornwall-on-the-Hudson.

Cornwall-on-the-Hudson

Distant vistas of the Scunemunk Mountains to the west of this small town lend it an alpine atmosphere. The river narrows between the wooded hills of the Storm King State Park and the Hudson Highlands State Park. Seventy-five acres of woodlands three-quarters of a mile south-west of State Route 218, on Mountain Rd and the Boulevard, comprise a wildlife centre. Here native flora and fauna of the region may be seen from a number of nature trails.

Continue north-west along State Route 218 and rejoin US 9W. Drive 2 miles north to Newburgh.

Newburgh

This riverside city is noted for a host of reminders of George Washington's Revolutionary War successes. For over a year, from April 1782 to August 1783, Washington had headquarters at the Jonathan Hasbrouck House in Liberty Street. It was from here that the army disbanded after the successful conclusion of the war. Fascinating relics including paintings and period furnishings are on view and the landscaped grounds have a Tower of Victory and State Museum.

A mile north of Vails Gate on Temple Hill Road is a reconstruction of the Revolutionary Army's winter camp. The New Windsor Cantonment State Historic Site has guides wearing the uniforms of the Revolutionary Army who explain the history of the displays and exhibitions free of charge. Ironically, the camp is only open during the summer months! Nearly five miles south-west on State Route 94 is the Knox Headquarters, another State Historic Site. General Henry Knox, one of Washington's heavyweights, lived here. The John Ellison House was built in 1754 and there is also a 50-acre farm. Generals Green and Gates also occupied the house and Washington frequently visited them.

A full dress parade by cadets (inset) of the United Military Academy at West Point (above) on the Hudson River

> **Hotels**
>
> HOWARD JOHNSON'S MOTOR LODGE: on SR 17K, ¼ mile W of exit 17, tel 565 4100. 75 rooms. Expensive.
>
> RAMADA INN: 1055 Union Av, tel 564 4500. 115 rooms. Moderate.
>
> WINDSOR MOTEL: 2½ miles S on US 9W, tel 562 7661. 32 rooms. Moderate.
>
> **Restaurant**
>
> BEAU RIVAGE: 2½ miles N on US 9W, 2¾ miles E on River Rd, tel 561 9799. Views of the Hudson River, varied menu featuring continental cuisine. Strict dress code. Expensive.

Continue north and rejoin US 9W. After about 6 miles, turn right across the Hudson River on Interstate 84. At the first intersection east of the river, turn southwards on State Route 9D and drive for one mile to Beacon.

Beacon

Beacon is a small town with Dutch connections set amidst excellent skiing country. A notable early 18th-century building in Van Nydeck Avenue is the Madam Brett Homestead, dating from 1709. Authentic period furnishings and historic exhibits are on view. Handmade scalloped roof shingles and sloped dormers are interesting architectural features.

Continue southwards on State Route 9D for 10 miles, driving through beautiful Highlands State Park and Cold Spring to Garrison.

Garrison

Perched high above the Hudson Valley, Garrison offers spectacular views and two extraordinary mansions. North of the town, on State Route 9D is Boscobel, one of the finest New York Federal-style villas in the United States. It was scheduled for demolition in 1960,

HUDSON RIVER

Croton-on-Hudson
A Dutch-English mansion just off US 9 was the home of Pierre Van Cortlandt, a revolutionary patriot who became first lieutenant governor of New York State. Only 20 acres remain of the 18th-century estate of 86,000 acres. Of particular interest are the historic Ferry House and Ferry House kitchens which supplied food and lodgings to travellers on the Albany Post Road. Porcelain, silver, furniture and portraits of the Van Cortlandt family may be viewed in the manor house.
Two miles north of the town, on State Route 9A, is Chimney Corners Inn, an inexpensive and homely hostelry offering delicious pastries and Italian and American cooking.

Continue south on US 9 for 10 miles to Tarrytown.

Tarrytown
Deep in the *Sleepy Hollow* country immortalised by Washington Irving, Tarrytown and North Tarrytown sprawl along the banks of the 'Tappan Zee' – a shimmering three-mile-wide expanse of the Hudson River. In the 17th-century Old Dutch Churchyard at North Tarrytown lie the remains of Irving (1783–1859). Opulent estates and fantastic Gothic homes add glamour and gentility to the towns. Lyndhurst, 635 S Broadway, is perhaps the most flamboyant neo-Gothic mansion. Built in 1838 by Alexander Joeksan Davis, it later became the home of railway tycoon Jay Gould. The house is packed with interesting period pieces, and outdoor concerts and festivals are held on the 67-acre estate in warm weather. A magnificent rose garden is also open to the public.
The Sunnyside Estate, W Sunnyside Lane, off Broadway, was built to Washington Irving's designs in 1835. Relics of the 24 years he lived here are on view and the house is surrounded by beautiful grounds.
Through Patriot's Park on US 9 flows the André Brook, the dividing line between the Tarrytowns. A British spy, Major John André, was captured close to the brook during the War of Independence. He disclosed the treachery of Benedict Arnold, commander of West Point, who attempted to betray the military academy to the British in 1780. A Captors' Monument is topped by a bronze figure of one of André's captors, John Paulding.

Continue south on US 9 for 10 miles to Yonkers

Yonkers
In Westchester County's largest city, the tree-lined streets are the home of wealthy families and some of the state's biggest and best shopping centres.
Yonkers' Raceway has featured the 'Sport of Kings' since 1894 and trotting races are held nightly in season except on Sundays. Most fashionable is the August or September 'Yonkers Trot'.
In Trevor Park, the Hudson River Museum includes a mansion called Glenview which is a centre for festivals, concerts, films, lectures and children's entertainments and which has exhibits of art and local history.

Drive southwards for 9 miles on the Saw Hill River Parkway and for a further 10 miles south on the Henry Hudson Parkway to Manhattan.

Philipsburg Manor, a Dutch-American house on the shores of the Hudson at North Tarrington, was built in 1680

but was saved and moved 15 miles to its present site. Built in 1806 by S M Dyckman for his wife, the mansion houses a collection of remarkable antiques. Formal gardens are offset by magnificent glimpses of the River Hudson. Guided tours are available and 'son et lumiere' performances include an exciting and evocative historical narration. Close by is an amazing near-replica of the Spanish Alhambra, known as Dick's Hilltop Castle. Evans Dick, the eccentric builder, lost all his money on the stock exchange in 1911, so he failed to finish his fantasy.
On a mountain top just south of Garrison is the Graymoor Christian Unity Center, home of the Atonement Friars. It contains many chapels and shrines in grounds which give superb views of the Hudson Valley below.

Take State Route 403 south for 4 miles to join US 9 and continue south, passing the Camp Smith Military Reservation, for 15 miles to Croton-on-Hudson.

New York

'A beautiful and worthy catastrophe' is how the architect Le Corbusier described the New York of 1935, when the first flush of skyscrapers (the first were built in the early 1900s) dominated the Manhattan skyline.

These monsters, creating canyons of steel and glass, set the mood of New York. It is a city of extremes, light and shade, wealth and poverty, which lends itself to staggering statistics. Here, in the nation's largest city, is the world's busiest harbour, shipping 40 per cent of US foreign trade. Here 26,303 people live per square mile. Each of the five boroughs is inhabited by a kaleidoscope of nationalities. Libraries lend books in 30 languages, radio stations broadcast in 16. Nearly 50 per cent of the population is of foreign birth or parentage.

Yet among all the hard commercial dealing and the constant bustle, one sixth of the land in New York is devoted to parks and playgrounds; there are even two wildlife refuges and a bird sanctuary.

The financial, publishing and entertainment capital of the country,

New York is also the home of the United Nations, a fitting honour for the world's first truly cosmopolitan city.

Strolling along the streets of Manhattan, with cliffs of glass on either side of you so high as to appear to be leaning towards each other, it is interesting to consider that perhaps without one man, Elisha Graves Otis, a master mechanic at a bedstead factory who in 1854 invented the first passenger elevator, none of it may have happened.

▶*Downtown Manhattan as it appears from the Staten Island Ferry. The gleaming white twin towers of the World Trade Center which dominates the famous skyline are, at 1,350 feet high, the tallest in New York*
◀*Manhattan as evening falls, looking towards Staten Island past the Empire State Building, the World Trade Center, and in the distance, the Statue of Liberty*

New York makes the senses reel, the pulses quicken and the legs weary as no other city can. To spend a day in Manhattan is to invite a crick in the neck, as the eye follows the sheer cliffs of concrete stretching in some places more than 500 feet into the sky. To spend a week among these giants is not enough, but even a month would not be enough for a visitor to savour the scene fully. The New Yorker, fashioned and honed by years of overcrowded living in an environment he has chosen to create, admits barely knowing the place himself.

It all began in 1614, with the erection of four trading houses – Henry Hudson had claimed the territory three years earlier for the Dutch. The year 1626 saw one of the most bizarre commercial transactions of New York's history – Peter Minuit, made governor of the province in 1626, bought Manhattan Island from the Algonquin Indians for $24 worth of trinkets and baubles. By 1643 the population of New Amsterdam, as New York was called then, had a population of 500, who between them spoke 18 different languages.

Merchants and settlers from all over Europe, attracted by the opportunities in the New World, set up trading posts on the tip of Manhattan Island. They laid the foundations for New York City's prosperity and Manhattan's fashionable façade. Today, Manhattan has a population of 1.4 million people, although its 22 square miles constitute the smallest of the five boroughs that make up New York City. Manhattan is world-renowned for its skyscrapers, which make room for such an enormous population. They are not all imposing office buildings, although certainly many are the massive headquarters of giant corporations. There are also multi-storey apartment houses, and in the shadows of the giants are rows of Victorian-fronted villas built out of a soft, brown, porous sandstone that has given them the name of brownstones.

Very popular and cheap in the middle part of the 19th century, these houses have, since the 1950s, become fashionable residences for New York's 'in-crowd'. The sedate, select neighbourhoods like

NEW YORK CITY

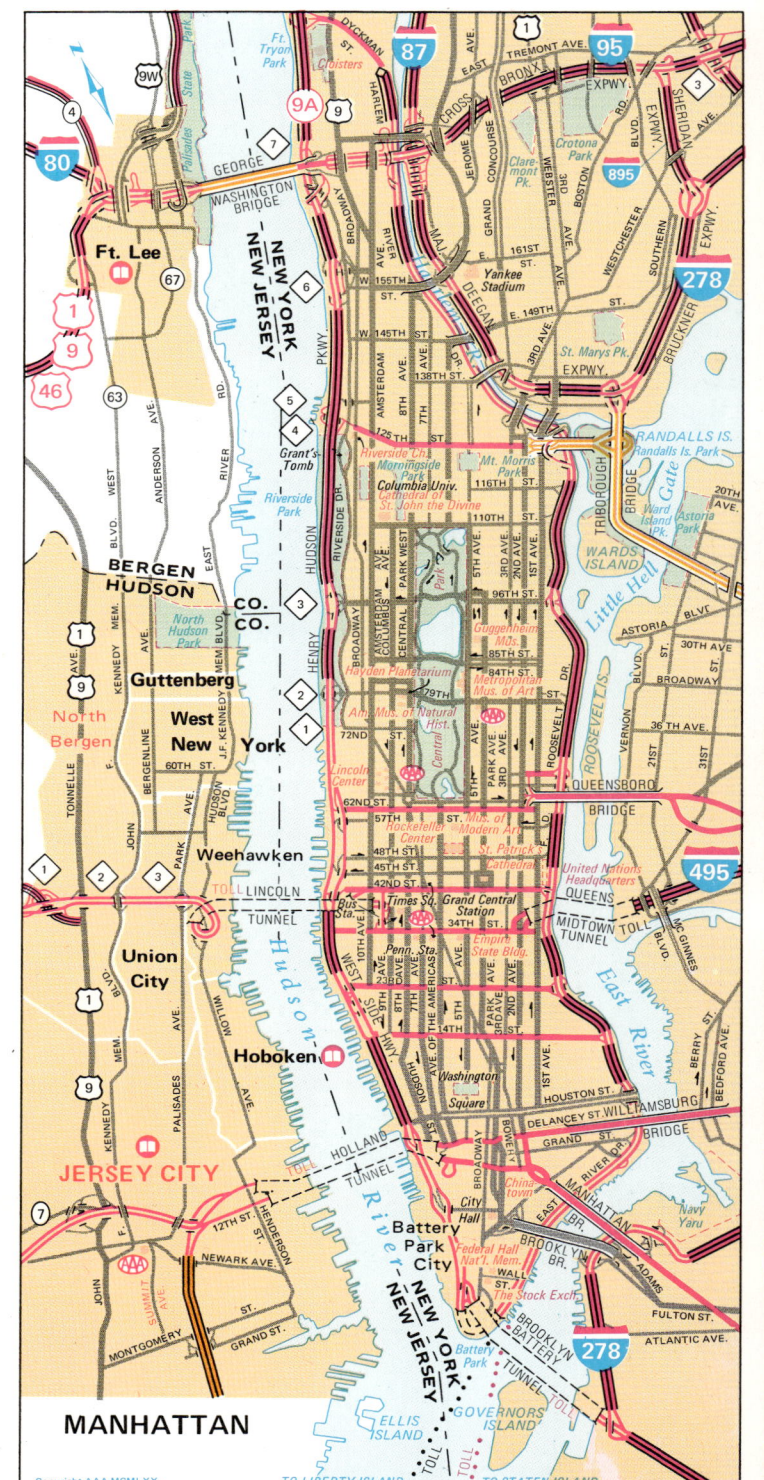

Murray Hill, with their brownstone terraces, have suddenly after many years of neglect taken on a new lease of life.

Like most cosmopolitan cities, New York also has its dark side and in Manhattan is the slumlike, derelict neighbourhood of the Bowery where the down-and-outs, surrounded by a surfeit of plenty, eke out a degrading existence. Harlem, where a white face is often too conspicuous for comfort, is also in the borough. Almost side by side with the shining glass and marble Leviathans, those monuments to wealth and plenty, are Manhattan's ethnic communities. Here the old European and Oriental customs are given free rein. Chinatown, Little Italy and that polyglot European 'principality' called SoHo (South of Houston Street) are townships in their own right as well as irresistible places for tourists to visit for their traditional food, shops and festivals.

No so much ethnic as bizarre, the best-known 'different' community in Manhattan is Greenwich

▲ *Garish and colourful, Times Square is the centre of New York's theatreland and the hub around which the city's street life revolves*

NEW YORK CITY

Village. Covering an area west of Broadway to Hudson Street and south from 14th Street to Spring Street, it reeks of Bohemia and is a certain draw for souvenir hunters and tourists in search of way-out lines in art jewellery, fabrics and food. And all this is still part of Manhattan.

To the New Yorker born and bred, New York is as much about the other four boroughs, Brooklyn, the Bronx, Queens and Staten Island, as it is about Manhattan.

Brooklyn, perhaps the best known, attracts visitors in search of candy floss, fairgrounds and toffee apples to its American-style Southend, Coney Island. This is where New Yorkers themselves can let their hair down. Some come from the adjoining residential borough of Queens which houses the two main airports serving the city – Kennedy International Airport and also the domestic airport of La Guardia.

From Manhattan the route to Brooklyn includes the famous Brooklyn Bridge which, since it opened nearly 100 years ago, has been the scene of numerous suicides and the object of outrageous attempts by confidence tricksters to sell it. Other ways across the East River are via the Brooklyn Battery Tunnel, the second longest underwater tunnel in America, the Manhatten Bridge or, from Staten Island, across the Narrows via the Verrazano Narrows Bridge which, until the opening of Britain's Humber Bridge, was the longest suspension bridge in the world. With only Bronx on the mainland, the 60 or so bridges that cross to the cluster of islands making up New York City are an important feature of the skyline. The Bayonne Bridge, at 1,652 feet long, linking Staten Island with New Jersey, is also the longest steel arch bridge in the world. More geared to tourists than the Bronx, which in its 43 square miles houses many of Manhattan's commuters and attracts principally baseball fans to its Yankee Stadium, Staten Island has many outdoor recreational amenities.

The five-mile trip across New York Harbour on the Staten Island Ferry allows you to escape the shadows of the skyscrapers and view downtown New York at a distance – the skyline is spectacular. One of the oldest ferries in America, it received its first charter in 1712. Nearly 270 years later it takes about twenty million passengers every year on the half-hour trip. Most are commuters, but a large number queue up at the pier to tour Liberty Island and climb the Statue of Liberty which, standing on its 156-foot pedestal, is itself 151 feet high. A gift from France to mark French support of the American Revolution, the statue was designed with the help of Gustave Eiffel (whose name is immortalised on another famous French landmark) and was dedicated by President Cleveland on 28 October 1886.

The statue, of course, is now dwarfed by the skyscrapers, which have a pedigree of their own. Among the first built was a 20-storey triangular highrise which earned the name of Flatiron because of its wedge shape. It was completed in 1902 and occupies the gap between Broadway and Fifth Avenue. It led the way to an architectural revolution.

The next towering milestone was the Woolworth Building which grew up on a site on Broadway in 1912. In 1930, just a year ahead of the most famous of them all, the Empire State Building, the 1,048-foot Chrysler Building was completed at 42nd Street and Lexington Avenue. But even the 1,472-foot Empire

▲ *America's most revered national monument, the Statue of Liberty, presented to America by France in 1884 to commemorate their alliance*

◀ *Two of New York's most familiar sights; the ubiquitous Yellow Cab and the magnificent Empire State Building, which towers 1,472 feet above the shadowy streets*

How to Find Your Way in Manhattan

Finding your way around New York is the easiest thing in the world, provided that you can do simple sums in your head and memorise a magic formula. Streets run east-west and avenues run north-south. Usually, when giving an address, Americans will not only state the number or the name of the building, and the street or avenue, but also specify the nearest intersection – for example: 357 5th Avenue at 72nd Street, so that you know precisely where the building is and do not have to travel the whole length of the avenue to find the number you want. Streets also have a west and east side, with 5th Avenue marking the dividing line between west and east.

There are two systems to help you pinpoint an address exactly, one for the street system and another for the avenues. House numbers on streets go in blocks of 100 between intersections with the avenues. It is assumed that there are 100 numbers in each block, regardless of whether there are in fact 100 buildings. If the address you want is, for example, the old Victorian Brownstone house at 41 E 72nd Street, a glance at the table below shows you that 41 must be in the block between 5th Avenue and Park Avenue. If, on the other hand, the address is 41 W. 72nd Street, the house will be between 5th and 6th Avenues.

East-West Numbered Streets
Addresses begin at the streets listed below.

East Side
1	5th Av
101	Park Av
201	3rd Av
301	2nd Av
401	1st Av
501	York or Av A
601	Av B

West Side
1	5th Av
101	6th Av (Av of the Americas)
201	7th Av
301	8th Av
401	9th Av
501	10th Av
601	11th Av

The formula for locating an address on the avenues running north-south is more complicated, but it does work. For example, the Downing Square Restaurant is at 500 Lexington Avenue. To find out which block that is, proceed as follows:
A. Cancel the last figure of the number.
B. Divide your answer by 2.
C. Find the key number of your avenue in the table below, and add or subtract that number to the result of step B.
Thus, for 500 Lexington Avenue, A = 50, B = 25, C = 25 + 22 = 47. The Downing Square Restaurant is therefore near 47th Street on Lexington Avenue. Exceptions to this formula are marked with an asterisk, but you can still pinpoint the address by leaving out step B. To find the apartment house at 11 Riverside Drive, for example: A = 1, C = 1 + 73 = 74. 11 Riverside Drive is near 74th Street.

North-South Avenues
*On streets or address numbers preceded by an asterisk, omit Step B from the computation.

Av A, B, C, D	3
1st Av	3
2nd Av	3
3rd Av	10
4th Av	8
5th Av:	
1-200	13
201-400	16
401-600	18
601-775	20
*776-1286	Deduct 18
Av of the Americas	Deduct 12
7th Av:	
1-1800	12
Above 1800	20
8th Av	9
9th Av	13
10th Av	13
11th Av	15
Amsterdam	59
Columbus	59
Lexington	22
Madison	27
Park	34
West End	59
*Central Park West	60
*Riverside Dr.:	
*1-567	73
*Above 567	78
Broadway:	
1-754 are below 8th St.	
754-858	Deduct 29
858-958	Deduct 25
Above 1000	Deduct 31

State Building can no longer offer the highest vantage point for visitors. In its upper observatory, 1,250 feet above the ground, has been superseded by as the most recent addition to the Goliaths of New York – the twin-towered World Trade Center, completed in 1975. From an open promenade on the 107th floor, 1,302 feet above the ground, the whole of New York is laid out before you.

The most diverse yet unified complex of skyscrapers is the Rockefeller Center, begun in 1936. Financed by millionaire John D Rockefeller, the original plan was for a cluster of 14 buildings, but after World War II another five were added. There are now 21 buildings on a 24-acre site. The tallest is the 850-foot-high RCA building on 49th Street, which is 70 storeys tall. A kind of city within a city, Rockefeller Center offers guided tours of its many facilities during weekdays. Among majestic pools and fountains is the Radio City Music Hall and the headquarters of NBC, one of the major radio and TV networks, together with several shopping plazas, an ice-skating rink, restaurants, film theatres and exhibition halls.

New York prides itself on a vigorous cultural life, with the Broadway area accommodating some of the world's most expensive and exclusive theatres. In truth, most of New York's theatres are off Broadway. Brooklyn alone has 29 theatres, many of them belonging to that coterie of drama known as the off-off-Broadway theatre. Some 230 experimental drama houses augment the 20 more legitimate off-Broadway theatres. On this outer fringe a faithful following pursue their heroes and heroines from makeshift stages in garages and derelict houses, sometimes climbing up to 'the gods' on a rickety skeleton of scaffolding hastily erected for the performance.

The hub of this extraordinary, extravagant, extrovert world which draws thousands every day, like moths, to the lights of Broadway, is Times Square. This is the place most people mean when they refer to

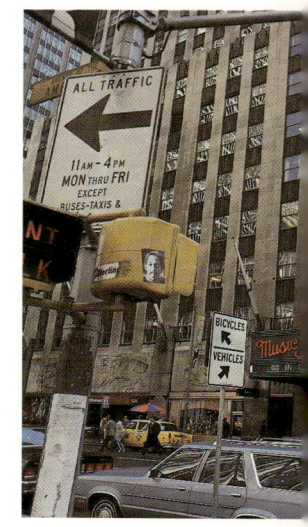

NEW YORK CITY

▲ *A world within a world – a visit to New York's Chinatown is a must, if only to sample the superb Chinese cuisine*

◄ *This plaza at the Rockefeller Center, overlooked by Paul Manslip's gilded Prometheus, serves as an ice rink in winter and as a sunken garden in summer. The Center, covering 17 acres, is one of New York's architectural marvels*

► *Several historic craft belonging to the South Street Seaport Museum are moored at South Street Pier, beneath the towering skyscrapers of Manhattan*

▼ *The art deco Radio City Music Hall Entertainment Center, built in 1932, is the world's biggest theatre, and the most spectacular feature of the vast Rockefeller Center complex*

Broadway – 'a centre of light, colour and decayed glamour'. Here, after dark, guitars strum, drunks and drug addicts cavort and shout, among the mass of people who provide an ever-changing scenario, day or night.

In contrast, the pavements almost everywhere else in New York are empty and only the roadways, packed with their distinctive yellow cabs adding a touch of mosaic colour to the grey pack of traffic jamming the streets, keep the city buzzing with life.

In daylight, it is always a pleasure to walk the streets in New York, but at night, even the New Yorker hesitates to pound the pavements alone in the dark sidestreets. Wherever possible, the wise tourist should take a taxi for safety's sake.

Everywhere in New York, shopping offers untold variety to the window gazer as much as to the actual buyer. Some of the shops and stores are an experience in themselves (see Directory). The restaurants, too, give New York a unique flavour. There is no end to the variety of ethnic food available in the national communities in New York. Most such restaurants are very reasonable, usually friendly and often only short on decor.

For international cuisine, some prices in restaurants are, of course, astronomical, but you don't need to rub shoulders with the fashionable at places like Sardi's or even in the in-places and trendy bars to face gargantuan portions, whatever the meal.

New York's prize speciality is the breakfast bar, which serves an enormous choice of food all day long, providing excellent value at very modest cost. At Reubens, where they claim that their sandwiches are a national institution, you can even have slices of turkey, bacon, lettuce and tomato with mayonnaise on white toast by simply asking for a Paul Newman. On the other hand, Virginia ham, turkey with Swiss cheese, coleslaw and Russian dressing, comes under the guise of Robert Redford.

The best way to make the most of New York is to

NEW YORK CITY

▲ *The green glass walls of the Secretariat Building of the United Nations is a familiar landmark on 42nd Street*

▶ *The extraordinary building of the Guggenheim Museum, designed by Frank Lloyd Wright, has been criticised in the past for upstaging the works of art it houses*

◀ *A visit to the landscaped and wooded acres of Central Park is the perfect antedote for the tourist weary of walking Manhattan's streets*

▼ *The calm Renaissance-style façade of the New York Stock Exchange on Wall Street hides the frenetic dealings of the city's stockbrokers*

walk. During the day, Central Park offers 840 acres of woods and landscaped grounds, including several lakes, two outdoor skating rinks, a swimming pool, a theatre, and a zoo which has a special children's spectator section. Some of the roads through the park are closed to motor traffic in summer, when certain stretches become cycle tracks.

Park Avenue has major office buildings and select apartment houses. Madison Avenue is the home of America's advertising industry. Fifth Avenue houses the most luxurious and expensive hotels and shops and apartment stores with world-famous reputations and sumptuous premises. Above 50th Street, Fifth Avenue becomes an exclusive residential area. Although it is now grandly called Avenue of the Americas, 6th Avenue begins to show signs of the west side. And the further west one goes in New York, the rougher and tougher the neighbourhood becomes. Some of the names of the streets also have a familiar ring to them. 42nd Street, for instance, is synonymous with jazz and the 1930s when with Prohibition came the speakeasys. Behind 42nd Street, the bustle of New York is left behind in a neat square called Tudor City.

This is a delightful backwater which retains the atmosphere of New York as it was in 1920. Flanking one side of the square is the elegant 21-storey Tudor Hotel whose 500 rooms are often as much occupied by visiting diplomats and delegates to the United Nations as by the coachloads of tourists, for whom they seem always to find room. The hotel is something of an anachronism. Built around the time the Empire State Building was completed, its 1930s appearance is in sharp contrast to the daunting black facade of the United Nations Plaza Hotel just across the street. There many of the 7,000 diplomats and bureaucrats from 140 nations working at the UN building come and go.

The United Nations' massive slab of concrete and glass on the riverside occupies 18 acres at the end of 42nd Street. More than one million visitors pass through its doors every year, many of them making for the basement where the United Nations Post Office mails messages franked with United Nations' stamps only – a unique souvenir – and where souvenir shops sell goods from many of the countries represented at the United Nations. A model of Sputnik 1, the first Russian space shot, a chunk of moon rock, and the Foucault Pendulum indicating the earth's rotation, are some of the main attractions for visitors. Even for those who merely stop and stare at the buildings, the passing scene is riveting. Instead of the famous New York cops, the United Nations police force in their Ruritanian-style uniforms stand guard and, like the sentries at Buckingham Palace, attract the crowds to themselves as much as to the parade of imposing cars to-ing and fro-ing through the gates.

Quietly, in this way, the world's most enduring debating society has found a secure home in the world's most cosmopolitan city – a part of New York City's life and yet, at all times, aloof and independent from what has been called the only truly 20th-century city.

New York Directory

HOTELS

Hotels and restaurants shown here are either recommended by the American Automobile Association (AAA) or chosen because they are particularly appealing to tourists. As an approximate guide to cost, they have been rated as either expensive, moderate or inexpensive. Unless otherwise stated, the hotels all have private bathrooms and colour television in rooms, and are in the Manhattan area of the city.

ABBEY VICTORIA HOTEL: 7th Av and 51st St, tel 246 9400. Cosy, attractive rooms in plush surroundings. Many facilities including two restaurants and a coffee shop, barbershop, beauty salon, health club for men, theatre and sightseeing ticket desk. Moderate.

BEST WESTERN BARBIZON PLAZA: 106 Central Park South and 6th Av, tel 247 7000. 800 rooms, special-stay 'packages' available at this pleasant hotel which has restaurants and a bar. Moderate.

BILTMORE HOTEL: Madison Av at E 43rd St, tel 687 7000. 840 rooms. One of the Big Apple's most distinguished old hotels. Restaurant and bar plus pay valet garage.

CARTER HOTEL: 250 W 43rd St, tel 947 6000. 700 rooms. Generous amenities and friendly service make this a good budget-price hotel. Some TV black and white. Inexpensive.

CENTURY PARAMOUNT: 235 W 46th St, tel 246 5500. 700 rooms. Plenty of amenities at a reasonable price. Adequate rooms (some TV black and white). Moderate.

HOTEL DIPLOMAT: 108 W 43rd St, tel 279 3707. A family-run hotel. The rooms (25% of them without a bath) reasonably sized and adequate considering the low rates. Bar/cocktail lounge plus a theatre and two discos. Inexpensive.

DORAL INN: 541 Lexington Av at E 49th St, tel 755 1200. 650 rooms. Restaurant, coffee shop and bar. Moderate.

EDISON: 228 W 47th St just off Times Square. 1,000 rooms. A big and bustling hotel with modern facilities. Clean, pleasant accommodation. Garage facilities. Inexpensive.

HILTON INN AT JFK: 138-10 135th Av, tel 322 8700. 350 rooms. Opposite the entrance to the John F Kennedy International Airport. Restaurant, bar and coffee shop. Moderate.

IROQUOIS: 12 W 44th St. A particular favourite with many families. Bargain rates are enhanced by the availability of weekly rates. Inexpensive.

PICCADILLY: 227 W 45th St, tel CI 6-6600. 600 rooms. A hospitable and cheerful hotel. Rooms with two double beds can comfortably accommodate a family of four. Coffee shop for quick meals and attractive cafe serving American food and drinks. Moderate.

PICKWICK ARMS: 230 E 51st St. 400 rooms. There's a warm and friendly atmosphere here. On the east side of the city, it is still quite conveniently located. Close to the UN building. Moderate.

RAMADA INN – MIDTOWN: 790 8th Av, between 48th and 49th Sts, tel 581 7000. 366 rooms. Rooftop swimming pool, restaurant and coffee shop. Moderate.

RESTAURANTS

The cuisine of virtually every country in the world is represented in New York, and there are restaurants to suit every taste. Only a few can be included in this list, and they are restricted to the tourist areas of the city, Manhattan and Greenwich village.

AMY'S: 108 University Pl, between 12th and 13th Sts, tel 741 2170; 151 Bank St, corner of West St, tel 929 7410, and many other branches in Manhattan. Provides 'fast food' with an Israeli and Middle-Eastern flavour. Inexpensive.

WALDORF ASTORIA: Lexington Av, between E 49th and 50th Sts, tel 355 3000. 1855 rooms. Lush, plush and long-established, this is *the* New York hotel where you rub shoulders with the stars. Five restaurants, bars, pay valet, garage. Expensive.

WINDSOR: 100 W 58th St, tel 265 2100. A small, gracious hotel with an old world theme. Close to Central Park, it has peaceful, generously-sized rooms with French Provincial furniture, and computerised no-key door locks for maximum security. Expensive.

BOSS: 253 Broadway, opposite City Hall, tel 563 7440, and other branches along Broadway; 380 Lexington Av; 3rd Av at 52nd St; 260 Madison Av; 4 Park Av. Unlimited helpings of salad, wine, and beer, with American-style food. Inexpensive.

DUMPLING HOUSE: 207 2nd Av at 13th St, tel 777 5290. Mandarin and Szechuan dishes are a speciality of this Chinese restaurant. Inexpensive.

FONDA LA PALOMA: 256 E 49th St, between 2nd and 3rd Avs, tel 421 5495. Strolling guitarists play to diners in the evenings. Delicious Mexican cuisine.

FRAUNCES TAVERN: 54 Pearl St, corner of Broad St, tel 269 0144. Traditional American food is served here in the 'oldest restaurant in New York'. The restaurant has associations with George Washington, and there is a museum to visit after your meal. Moderate.

HARVEY'S CHELSEA RESTAURANT: 108 W 18th St between 6th and 7th Avs, tel 243 5644. Elegant 19th-century restaurant serving fine American cuisine. Moderate.

JACK'S NEST: 310 3rd Av at 23rd St, tel 260 7110. Specialises in recipes from America's 'Deep South'. Moderate.

LINDY'S: 50th St and Av of the Americas, tel 586 8986; Broadway, between 44th and 45th Sts, tel 840 1054. Delicatessen food, steaks and salads. Lindy's cheesecakes are world-famous. Moderate.

LUTECE: 249 E 50th St, between 2nd and 3rd Avs, tel 752 2225. One of New York's most popular French restaurants. Closed Sundays and during August. Expensive.

MARCHI'S: 251 E 31st St, between 2nd and 3rd Avs, tel 679 2494. Northern Italian dishes, home-made pasta, pastries and delicious coffee. Moderate–expensive.

MARINER 15: 15 State St, 2nd Floor, tel 344 6055. Well-known for the fresh seafood served here in nautical surroundings. Closed weekends. Moderate.

NATHAN'S: 3rd Av and 53rd St, tel 752 6881; 5th Av at 58th St, tel 751 9060. Anything from a sandwich to

NEW YORK DIRECTORY

a banquet can be had at either branch of this famous restaurant. Moderate.

RIVER CAFE: 1 Water St, tel 522 5200. On the waterfront, this romantic restaurant serves an international selection of dishes. Moderate.

ROCK GARDEN OF TOKYO: 34 W 56th St, tel 245-7936. Delicious, genuine Japanese food. Expensive.

SARDI'S: 234 W 44th St, between Broadway and 8th Av, tel 221 8440. A well-known restaurant in the heart of theatreland. Expensive.

WINDOWS ON THE WORLD: 107th Floor, World Trade Center, tel 938 1111. A restaurant complex taking advantage of its lofty position. Expensive.

TRANSPORT

JOHN F KENNEDY INTERNATIONAL AIRPORT: Covering an area of 5,000 acres, this airport is one of the largest and most modern in the world. It is situated in the district of Queens, at the junction of Van Wyck Expressway (Interstate 678) and Belt Pkwy and boasts ten terminals serving travellers from all over the world.

LA GUARDIA AIRPORT: Also in Queens, La Guardia is situated at Grand Central Pkwy and Flushing Bay. There is a bus service to and from East Side Airlines Terminal.

TRAINS: New York's two railway stations are to be found in Manhattan. Grand Central Station is at Park Av and E 42nd–44th Sts (terminal building is between Lexington and Vanderbilt Avs); Pennsylvania Station is at 7th Av and W 33rd St. For information ring AMTRAK at 736 4545.

BUSES: A total of 210 bus lines criss-cross the city. Whenever possible check fares in advance, tel 330 1234, as the exact fare is required.

SUBWAY: The 237-mile underground network provides the tourist with a cheap and efficient means of transport. Morning and evening rush hours are best avoided, as is late night travel. It is relatively easy to get from A to B, as all stations are clearly signposted and good maps are available at change booths. There are two types of train, express and local, and if you are unsure of where you are going, it is best to take the local train which stops at each station, rather than the express limited-stop train.

TAXIS: If speed is the important factor in your journey, rather than cost, then the taxi is your best mode of travel. The two airports are served by a plentiful supply of taxis, waiting to whisk you into Manhattan for a tidy sum.

CAR HIRE: Driving through Manhattan's overcrowded streets is not advisable. The dense traffic conditions and the lack of parking places can turn the tourist's pleasure ride into a nightmare. But if you must drive yourself there are plenty of car hire agencies, the main ones are: Airways, tel 244 0440; Avis Rent-a-Car, 217 E 43rd St, tel 331 1212; Dollar Rent-a-Car, tel 569 8290; and Hertz Rent-a-Car, tel 654 3131. Many more are listed in the Yellow Pages of the telephone directory.

TOURING INFORMATION

AAA: The Automobile Club of New York is an invaluable source of information for the newcomer to the city, in the form of brochures, maps and helpful advice. Should you lose your way in the city just ring 594 0070 and explain where you are and where you want to get to; friendly AAA staff will then give you directions, irrespective of whether you are travelling in a car or by public transport. Head office is at 28 E 78th St at Madison Av, tel 586 1166. Branches can be found at the Hilton Hotel, 7th Av at 33rd St; the Lincoln Center, 1881 Broadway at W 62nd St; 1781 Flatbush Av, Brooklyn; 186–06 Hillside Av, Jamaica; and at 729 Smithtown Bypass, Long Island.

NEW YORK CONVENTION AND VISITORS' BUREAU: Maps, guides and a number of helpful lists of shops, restaurants, events etc are produced by the Visitors' Bureau at 2 Colombus Circle, tel 397 8200. Telephone 397 8222 for information on events.

PLACES TO SEE

CITY HALL: At the end of Brooklyn Bridge between Park Row and 250 Broadway, tel 566 8681. This fine 19th-century building stands in gracious contrast to the skyscrapers that crowd the city streets. Here, in 1865, 120,000 grief-stricken New Yorkers viewed the body of their assassinated President Abraham Lincoln as it lay in state.

EMPIRE STATE BUILDING: 34th St and 5th Av, tel 736 3100. At 1,472-feet high, the Empire State Building is the tallest office block in the world, and the third tallest structure. Some 1½ million visitors are attracted each year to its lofty observatories, on the 86th and 102nd floors, to see the spectacular views.

FEDERAL HALL: At the corner of Wall and Nassau Sts, tel 264 4367. This striking marble building stands on the site of the first United States Capitol where, in 1789, George Washington was sworn in as president.

LINCOLN CENTER: Broadway and W 66th St, tel 877 1800. The Lincoln Center is a 14-acre site comprising six buildings devoted to educational and artistic pursuits. More than 13,700 spectators can be accommodated at any one time within its magnificent marble walls. The six principal buildings are: the Metropolitan Opera House, lavishly decorated with huge murals by painter Marc Chagall; the Avery Fisher Hall, home of the New York Philharmonic Orchestra; the Juilliard School, a training ground for musicians, actors and dancers; New York Public Library, a library and museum of the performing arts; the New York State Theater and the Vivian Beaumont Theater.

MADISON SQUARE GARDEN: 4 Pennsylvania Plaza, W 33rd St, between 7th and 8th Avs, tel 564 4400. A modern complex, this, the fourth Madison Square Garden, stands in striking contrast to the canvas-covered railroad shed that was the first structure erected in 1874. The present Garden boasts a theatre, bowling centre, convention area and facilities for handling seven major events at one time. World class boxing, the National Horse Show, circuses and rock concerts all take place here. It is also home for the New York Knicker-bockers basketball team and the Rangers ice hockey team.

NEW YORK STOCK EXCHANGE: 20 Broad St, tel 623 5167. At the entrance to the stock exchange there stands a single tree which symbolises the buttonwood tree under which, in 1792, the first transaction took place. Today, the striking building with its Corinthian columns and sculpted figures houses a much more sophisticated system of finance. Free tours are available and visitors can view the complicated goings-on from a glass-enclosed gallery.

An organised sightseeing trip is often the most convenient way to take in all major points of interest at an unfamiliar holiday destination, and New York is no exception. However, in this city you may choose to take a tour by bus, boat or helicopter. The Gray Line, tel 765 1600, is one of the best known bus companies, and boat trips are organised by Circle Line, tel 563 3200. If you really want something to tell the folks back home, why not settle for the helicopter tour by Island Helicopters, tel 895 5372?

SHOPPING

New York attracts world acclaim as a shoppers' paradise, and nowhere more so than the celebrated Fifth Avenue with its magnificent department stores and exclusive speciality shops. All the famous names are here: Saks Fifth Avenue is near the Rockefeller Center at 50th St, and Tiffany's with its fabulous display of jewellery, and often less expensive gifts, is at 57th St. Among the city's leading department stores are B Altman & Co at 34th St; Bloomingdales, Lexington Av at 59th St; Gimbels at 33rd St and 6th Av; and Macy's ('the largest department store in the world') at 34th St and Broadway. Antiques can be bought from the Manhattan Art and Antique Center, an attractive, three-storey arcade containing the shops of over 72 antique dealers, jewellers and craftsmen; address: 1050 2nd Av at 56th St. On Sundays you can browse through a wide assortment of bric-a-brac at the outdoor 'flea' markets at 6th Av and 25th St, and at 335 Canal St corner of Greene St (also open Saturdays).

MUSEUMS

THE BROOKLYN MUSEUM: Eastern Pkwy and Washington Av, tel 638 5000. One of the finest Egyptian collections in America is housed in this huge museum, which also holds a superb collection of primitive and prehistoric art.

CHINESE MUSEUM: 8 Mott St, Chinatown, tel WO 4-1542 Brightly coloured costumes, ancient coins and beautiful antique chopsticks are among the fascinating exhibits here. Educational quizzes and push-button displays provide additional delight for youngsters.

THE CLOISTERS: Fort Tyron Park, Fort Washington Av and W 190th St, tel 923 3700. Occupying a dramatic clifftop setting, with views across the Hudson River, is this most unusual museum which has been painstakingly constructed from a number of medieval monasteries transported from the south of France. Stained glass windows, the 15th-century tapestry *Hunt of the Unicorn*, paintings and precious stones are among the many treasures held here.

THE GUGGENHEIM MUSEUM: 5th Av, between E 88th and E 89th Sts, tel 860 1300. In its time this controversial building, designed by architect Frank Lloyd Wright (1867–1959) for copper magnate Solomon R Guggenheim, has been described by critics as 'a monstrous concrete mushroom' and 'a corkscrew' However, this does not alter

NEW YORK DIRECTORY

the fact that many visitors are as interested to see this striking cream-coloured building with its spiralled cone as they are in its contents. The museum's exhibits includes works by Kandinsky, Klee, Chagall, Delauney and Leger. Other artists represented here include Renoir, Van Gogh, Picasso, Cezanne, Degas and Toulouse-Lautrec.

HAYDEN PLANETARIUM: Central Park West and W 81st St, tel 873 8828.
Part of the American Museum of Natural History, the Planetarium has a lot to offer those interested in the many faces of the sky, be it space travel, meteorites, UFOs, comets or the stars.

METROPOLITAN MUSEUM OF ART: 5th Av at 82nd St, tel 535 7710. Numbered among the great museums of the world, the Metropolitan occupies a fine neo-Renaissance building of grey Indiana limestone. Its 26 galleries are filled with exhibits of European sculpture, ceramics, glass, metalwork, decorative art, arms and armour, medieval art, musical instruments, Far-Eastern art, costume and primitive art. There is also an impressive collection of American paintings, sculpture and design.

MUSEUM OF MODERN ART: 11 53rd St, tel 956 6100.
The light, airy, geometric building in which this museum is housed is a popular meeting place with New Yorkers. Among its greatest treasures are Van Gogh's masterpiece *Starry Nights* and Claude Monet's *Water Lilies*. Another attractive feature is the sculpture garden where works by Rodin, Renoir and Henry Moore are displayed. Classic, documentary, artistic and foreign films are shown here daily.

THE MUSEUM OF NATURAL HISTORY: Central Park West and W 79th St, tel 873 1300.
One of the largest of its kind in the world, the museum houses over 24,000 items including prehistoric monsters, oceanic birds and life-size dioramas of animals in their natural habitats. Also featured are exhibits on the origin of man and the wonders of the plant world. Free film shows, slide lectures and gallery talks take place throughout the week at certain times of the year.

COOPER HEWITT MUSEUM: 5th Av at 91st St, tel 860 6868. Part of Washington's Smithsonian Institution complex, this museum of design is housed in a beautifully-renovated Carnegie mansion. Primarily a centre of reference for the study of design, its exhibits include many decorative objects from all parts of the world, some over 3,000 years old, including jewellery, metals, sculpture, drawings and prints, ceramics, fabrics, wallpaper and furniture.

THE FRICK COLLECTION: 1 E 70th St, tel 288 0700. Designed in 1913 for Pittsburgh industrialist Henry Clay Frick (1849–1919), this luxurious mansion abounds with his beautiful collection of works of art gathered from all parts of the globe. French bronzes from the 16th and 17th centuries, portraits and landscapes of the Dutch, French, Spanish and British schools, Chinese porcelain and Swedish miniatures are just some of the treasures that are shown to great advantage against a background of exquisitely furnished rooms.

PARKS AND GARDENS

BATTERY PARK: Situated on the southern tip of Manhattan Island is this attractive park, which takes its name from a fort which used to stand here, built by the first Dutch settlers in 1624. The park affords fine views of New York Harbour and the Statue of Liberty.

BROOKLYN BOTANIC GARDEN: Entrances to this 50-acre garden are to be found on Flatbush Av, Empire Blvd, Washington Av and Eastern Pkwy. There are many types of garden here, including a garden of fragrance for blind visitors and a rose garden which boasts no fewer than 700 varieties. The Ryoanji Temple Stone Gardens feature interesting examples of a traditional Japanese garden and an abstract temple garden.

CENTRAL PARK: These 840 acres of parkland, bordered by 59th and 110th Sts, 5th Av and Central Park West and South, offer the city-weary tourist a welcome touch of the countryside. Hire a horse-drawn carriage and be transported through the landscaped, wooded grounds at a leisurely pace; meditate by a lakeside or take in the more man-made attractions, like the zoo, swimming pool, skating rinks or open-air Delacorte Theater, where performances of Shakespeare are given in summer. At E 81st St is 'Cleopatra's Needle', an Egyptian obelisk which was presented to the United States by the Khedive of Egypt a century ago. You must enjoy this park in the hours of daylight only and, even then, it is advisable to stay on the more frequented paths.

FLUSHING MEADOWS – CORONA PARK: The largest park in Queens, it is bounded by Roosevelt Av, Van Wyck St, Union Turnpike and 111th St. As well as miles of cycle paths, a zoo, boating lake, swimming pool, ice rink, putting green, children's farm and restaurant, Flushing Meadows – Corona Park also accommodates a Hall of Science, the Arena Aquacade Amphitheater and the Pavilion – Sugar Bowl. In 1939–40 and again in 1964–5, the park was the site of New York's World Fairs.

NEW YORK BOTANICAL GARDEN: Covering a magnificent 230 acres in north-west Bronx Park, the New York Botanical Garden has one of the largest botanical collections in the world, as well as some fine buildings, one of which is the Museum Building. It houses a herbarium with 4 million plant specimens, a research library, and various botanical and horticultural exhibits. The garden's natural features include the Bronx River Gorge and Falls, the Hemlock Forest and 40 acres of natural forest.

NEW YORK ZOOLOGICAL PARK: Fordham Rd and Southern Blvd. Known as the Bronx Zoo, it boasts a large collection of animals, birds and reptiles. The safari park can be seen to advantage by monorail and, for children, there are animal rides and a children's zoo.

WASHINGTON SQUARE PARK: Situated in a residential section of Greenwich Village, at the foot of 5th Av, the park is a gathering place for artists who display their work at open-air shows here during spring and summer. Other events, which attract residents and tourists alike, are the folk singing concerts and poetry readings. During the summer months, chess and draughts players have their own special corner of the park.

SPORT

All sports enthusiasts should head for Central Park in the heart of Manhattan; that is where all the popular sports can be enjoyed, be it horse riding, jogging, cycling, rowing or tennis. Cycles can be hired from the Bicycle Club of America, corner of 61st St and Broadway, tel 757 7957; and horses are available from the Claremont Riding Academy at 175 W 89th St. Both lakes in Central Park have rowing boats for hire. New York also has its share of spectator sports. You can watch the New York Knicks play basketball and the New York Rangers ice hockey at Madison Square Garden, and baseball fans have a choice of Yankee Stadium in the Bronx or Shea Stadium in Queens.

NIGHTLIFE

All conceivable forms of evening entertainment are available in abundance in New York. Whether your choice is the intimate jazz club, the classical concert, contemporary ballet or a Broadway show, you will find information concerning those, and all of the latest events, in *New York*, *The New Yorker*, *Village Voice* and *Cue* magazines. The Visitors' Bureau also publish a calendar of events.

THEATRES

The number of theatres in New York is so great that to attempt to list them here is pointless. To find out what's on and where, look in the *New York Times*, *Village Voice*, and *New York* magazine. Tickets are expensive, so if on a budget, go to a low-priced preview or buy 'twofers' – tickets sold to fill seats. You may obtain these from 'Hit Shows', 303 W 42nd St, Room 700, tel 581 4211. Alternatively 'Tkts', Times Square Theater Center at Broadway and 47th St, tel 354 5800, sell half-price tickets on the day of the performance. Listed below are theatres specially selected for their particularly interesting programmes.

THE DRAMATIC WORKSHOP: 55 W 21st Street, tel 243 9225. Performs free at weekends. One-act plays by authors such as Shaw, Kafka, Thornton Wilder, and unknowns of promise.

CHELSEA THEATER CENTER: 30 Lafayette Av, tel 783 5110, in Brooklyn Academy of Music; and at the Chelsea West Side Theater, 407 W 43rd St, tel 541 8394. Both show same productions – avant garde and experimental plays.

LIBRARY & MUSEUM OF PERFORMING ARTS: 111 Amsterdam Av, tel 799 2200. In the Lincoln Center. Gives daily performances of plays, concerts, dance and films.

MANHATTAN THEATER CLUB: 321 E 73rd St, tel 472 0600. Three theatres offering plays, opera, poetry and cabaret. Workshop productions and well-known plays with Broadway casts.

PLAYWRIGHT HORIZONS: 416 W 42nd St, tel 564 1235. An off-off-Broadway theatre where only new works are produced.

PUBLIC THEATER: 425 Lafayette St. Seven playhouses under one roof offering high-quality theatre. Home of the New York Shakespeare Festival, which performs in Central Park in the summer for free.

CLIMATE

Summer can be extremely hot and humid and winter very cold in New York, but spring and autumn can be extremely pleasant. However, weather is not really a problem because central heating and air-conditioning are almost universal.

Southern New England

Massachusetts is a land of delightful old towns, ocean resorts and green mountains. To visit the Revolutionary War battle sites, or the Witches Court at Salem, or the whaling ports along the coast, is to gain a fascinating insight into the early history of the United States. It is a history proudly displayed, which began with the arrival of the Pilgrim Fathers at Plymouth in Cape Cod Bay.

Their uncompromising regime and the intolerance of the Puritans who dominated those first colonies caused many of the early settlers to migrate south to Connecticut and Rhode Island. In Connecticut the excellent farming lands, the availability of water-power and the fine natural harbours along its coastline gave the state a head start when the race towards industrialisation began.

Rhode Island, despite being America's smallest state, has 400 miles of glorious seaside, and although some parts are heavily industrialised, two-thirds of the land remains uncultivated woodland.

Connecticut, Massachusetts, Rhode Island

Gloucester harbour is typical of many New England ports found along the rocky and often inhospitable coast of Massachusetts Bay

These three states are inextricably entwined with the early history of the United States. Here the American Revolution was sparked off, the Industrial Revolution flowered, and the great universities of Harvard and Yale were founded. The countryside is green and the climate temperate, the towns and villages, the streets of Boston, not so different from those found in England – nowhere else in the United States comes so close to emulating the England which the Pilgrim Fathers scorned.

The great states which between them make up southern New England not only share the distinction of having borne the military and political battles of the Revolutionary War, but also can claim to have laid the foundations of America's prolonged prosperity. The pilgrims who first set foot on these shores with the resolve to build a future out of the soil of the New World brought with them new ideas and philosophies of government, religion and education which had a profound effect on the development of the new nation.

When the 102 pilgrims aboard the *Mayflower* (two had died at sea) landed at the tip of Cape Cod on 21 November 1620, after more than two gruelling months at sea, they rested for a month before setting sail across Cape Cod Bay to found the first permanent European settlement in New England, on a site they were to call after their point of departure – Plymouth. The Pilgrims were determined to found a community free of bigotry and prejudice. They sought their own religious freedom, but persecuted all others. During the hard months of that first winter, 58 of the 102 survivors died. By 1640, with the arrival of new settlers, about 2,500 immigrants were living in the eight settlements along the Massachusetts coast. The differing ideas and convictions found among the increasing numbers of immigrants soon created conflicts. Many moved away, migrating west and south into Connecticut and Rhode Island.

As well as tilling the soil for crops, the

'Mayflower II', moored at State Pier in Plymouth, is a replica of the ship which brought the Pilgrims to the New World

early settlers also sifted crude iron as they cleared the land and drained the swampy areas. They built simple smelters with which they were able to separate the metal from the ore and fashion their own nails and tools. Even children learnt how to make nails, and these skills were passed down the generations. In 1819 Isaac Jarred Pratt established the first nail manufacturing plant on the site of what is now the Tremont Nail Company at Elm Street in Wareham on Massachusetts' south-east coast. The present mill has been in operation there since 1848, and tourists can look around the building and see a film which explains the history and process of nail-making.

New England became heavily industrialised from the late 1700s onwards, supported by sheep and dairy farming. Weaving was among the first industries to gain a foothold, and today many of the mills remain to mark the 'spindle cities' which prospered in New England in the 19th century. The secret of machine spinning was first introduced to America by Samuel Slater, a Derbyshire engineer, who could be said to have been one of the earliest 'industrial spies'. Born at Belper in 1768, he went to the States in 1789, committing the design of a patented machine to memory. By re-building the machine, he founded North America's first successful cotton manufacturing plant in Pawtucket, Rhode Island, in 1790. The water-powered mill, at the Slater Mill Historic Site on Roosevelt Avenue, has been restored, and several of the historic machines are shown in action.

One of the busiest 'spindle cities' was Fall River, Massachusetts, about 30 miles from Pawtucket. More than 120 mills were in operation by 1875, and the money made during this boom period built many of the stately mansions which today command the heights overlooking the city. The history of the textile industry is not, however, the only

FALL RIVER

Hotels

4-D MOTEL: 3½ miles W on US 6, tel 678 9071. 24 rooms. Inexpensive.

HOWARD JOHNSON'S MOTOR LODGE: 1878 Wilbur Av, tel 678 4545. 62 rooms. Expensive.

MOTEL SOMERSET: 537 Riverside Av, tel 678 7665. 24 rooms. Inexpensive.

Restaurant

VALLE'S STEAK HOUSE: junc SR 24 and SR 81, tel 679 0155. Extensive menu, also children's menu. Inexpensive-moderate.

Places of Interest

FALL RIVER HISTORIC SOCIETY: 45 Rock St. Rooms furnished in Victorian era, with exhibits about Lizzie Borden, and Fall River mills and steamships.

ST ANNE'S CHURCH AND SHRINE: 818 Middle St. Contains shrine of St Anne.

SOUTHERN NEW ENGLAND

reason for a visit to Fall River. It has, for instance, the dubious distinction of being the home town of Lizzie Borden who, on 4 August 1892, 'took an axe and gave her mother 40 whacks, and when the job was nicely done, she gave her father 41'. The house where she did the bloody deeds is on Second Street, but has been closed for several years. Fall River's greatest attraction is Battleship Cove where the United States Navy harbours several famous ships that saw service in World War II. All have now been pensioned off. They include the USS *Massachusetts*, affectionately called Big Mamie – a 680-foot battleship which survived 35 battles in the Atlantic and Pacific. The vessel, together with others on show, can be boarded. There is also a Marine Museum which houses more than 1,000 items in a maritime collection (including 19th- and 20th-century ship models), dedicated to the history of steam shipping.

The undisputed leader of America's textile cities is Lowell, near the New Hampshire boundary. Its namesake, Francis Cabot Lowell, set up his first successful power loom about 15 miles south at Waltham. Lowell, a thriving city of 90,000 people, has a National Historical Park which traces the history of the Industrial Revolution. At the Lowell Museum in Suffolk Street, recreated rooms of a typical boarding house for mill girls reflect the awful conditions endured during the 19th century by farm girls enticed from the country by the prospect of earning a higher wage.

Another important New England industry is papermaking. At Dalton, 150 miles west of Boston, and near the New York State boundary, they make the paper for American dollar bills. The Crane Museum of Papermaking, sited in an old stone mill, traces the history of the industry. A few miles south, at Lee, they also make paper, but the more prestigious output is marble – Lee marble was used in the building of the Capitol in Washington 200 years ago, and more recently, for St Patrick's Cathedral in New York. New England's robust industrial past is preserved at Old Sturbridge Village on the Quinebaug River about 60 miles south-west of Boston. Here, on a 200-acre site, 38 buildings have been erected to represent a complete New England country town of the early 19th century, including a grist mill, herb farm, a blacksmith's shop and village stalls filled with contemporary goods of the period. Among the crafts on display are spinning, weaving, horse shoeing, cabinet making, and candle dipping.

The craft the village does not demonstrate is witchcraft. This ancient black art is more at home in Salem, a proud and prosperous seaport which in 1692 earned its place in the history books by hanging 19 people suspected of being witches. Salem deserves to be taken more seriously than this kind of reputation suggests. For the first four years after it was founded in 1626, it was the capital city of the Massachusetts Bay Colony. Today, it has docks and wharfs bristling with cranes and all the trappings of a great commercial and industrial centre. In the 18th century Salem exploited its seafaring role by encouraging ships laden with rare and costly cargoes from all corners of the earth. The captains of these vessels settled there and built fine houses which form part of the character of modern-day Salem. For its size, the city is unusually well-endowed with things worth seeing. The Peabody Museum, for instance, recounts the maritime history of the port, and the Salem Maritime National Historic Site depicts the wharfs and houses of Salem Harbour as they were during the Revolutionary and 1812 wars. The Custom House, the Bonded Warehouse (both dating back to 1819), are preserved with a motley collection of their contents – tea chests and rum barrels among them. The Essex Institute in Essex Street comprises a collection of several 18th-century houses reflecting Salem's era of prosperity. Nearby is the Bebe Summer House and a flower garden specializing in plants of the type grown in New England before 1700. In the grounds of 54 Turner Street, the original House of Seven Gables, which was the inspiration for Nathaniel Hawthorne's famous novel, is the house where Hawthorne was born in 1804. Both are open to the public. Salem, too, is where Alexander Bell laid the groundwork for the invention of the telephone; Nathaniel Bowditch earned the undying gratitude of seamen all over the world for compiling, in 1802, the *New American Practical Navigator*, which is still considered to be the standard text for seamen all over the world; and from where Elias Haskett Derby set out to become America's first millionaire. Born in Salem

SALEM

Hotel

THE HAWTHORNE INN: 18 Washington Sq, tel 744 4080. 85 rooms. Moderate.

Places of Interest

COURTHOUSE: Washington and Federal Sts. Scene of the sensational witchcraft trials of 1692. Original case files and artefacts.

ESSEX INSTITUTE: 132–134 Essex St. Extensive collection including portraits, toys, china, silver, clocks and a large library.

PEABODY MUSEUM: 161 Essex St. Huge collection, with the three main themes being maritime history, ethnology and natural history.

Salem Pioneer Village reconstructs the houses of a typical 1630s settlement

SOUTHERN NEW ENGLAND

in 1739, he made a fortune out of ships plying the trade routes.

Most of all, however, Salem has fired the public imagination for its dealings with witches. In recent years, Salem's population of 38,000 is said to have produced about 350 witches. One of them has been officially designated by the State as the official Witch of Salem. The Witch House, 310½ Essex Street, home of Judge Jonathan Corwin, one of the judges of the witchcraft trial of 1692, is open to tourists. Some of the preliminary interrogations of witches took place here. There is also a Witch Museum in Washington Square North which depicts the witch trials in great and often gruesome detail. Not surprisingly, the city's witch watch is most profitable at Halloween. At a 'witches weekend' the Town Hall is turned into a haunted house and there are such spine-chilling attractions as the Witches' Ball and the 'Grand Ghoul Parade'.

Strong black-magic overtones are also apparent about 20 miles north along the coast. A heath on the outskirts of Gloucester is the site of a small village. It was named Dogtown in 1830, because after many of the men had died at sea or in war, the women took charge of running the community, and acquired dogs for protection. Inevitably the word soon spread that the wives were witches.

Though he is popularly associated with Salem, Nathaniel Hawthorne lived for much of his life at Concord. There he acquired The Wayside, home of the Alcott family (of *Little Women* fame). He was a friend of Bronson Alcott, father of the five girls, of which author Louisa (Jo in the book), Anna (Meg) and Elizabeth (Beth) are best known. Although Hawthorne died at The Wayside in 1864, the cottage bearing his name stands at Lenox, near the New York State boundary, over 120 miles west. This building is now part of a 200-acre music-center complex called Tanglewood. It is the summer home of the Boston Symphony Orchestra and is where a celebrated music festival is held every year in July and August.

Though more famous for its part in the events leading up to the American War of Independence, Concord enjoyed a strong literary tradition – thanks not only to Hawthorne and Louisa May Alcott, but also because Concord was where poet and essayist Ralph Waldo Emerson and the naturalist and writer Henry David Thoreau lived. Louisa wrote *Little Women* in Orchard House, one mile south-east of the town centre on State Route 2A. Emerson lived in a house at Cambridge Turnpike and State Route 2A from 1835 until his death in 1882, and Thoreau's legacy is the Lyceum in Belknap Street, a 19th-century shingled house displaying some of his belongings. Concord's most visited shrine is the Minuteman Statue and the bridge – 'the

The Old North Bridge, near Concord, where patriots defeated the British in 1775

rude bridge that arched the flood' – where the Battle of Concord was fought. Here 800 British soldiers under the command of 56-year-old General Thomas Gage were ordered to seize supplies and arms stock-piled about 20 miles west of Boston by the recalcitrant colonists. The action was to set off further conflict between the British and the colonists. On 19 April 1775, both sides clashed across the Concord River at the North Bridge. The Americans had been warned of the British troops' movements by Paul Revere, a 40-year-old silversmith and engraver who rode out of Boston under cover of darkness. When he reached Lexington, about six miles east of Concord, he was captured, but two of his compatriots reached Concord in time to give the alarm. The 100-strong local militia came to be known as the Minutemen because they pledged to be ready at a minute's notice to fight the advancing Redcoats. Eight Americans died and ten were wounded in the battle, and there is a monument commemorating the battle with the words: 'On the opposite bank stood the American Militia. Here stood the invading army, and on this spot the first of the enemy fell in the war of that revolution which gave independence to these United States.' When the British column withdrew they were soon caught in crossfire as more and more militia men gathered to harass their retreat along the road back to Boston. More than 230 Redcoats died that day. So did 95 Americans. The victory was to give the colonists the heart and spirit to unify in their struggle against the British. At Lexington, too, the clash is commemorated by an inscription on a boulder. It reads: 'Stand your ground. Don't fire unless fired upon, but if they mean to have a war, let it begin here.'

In another war with the British, between 1812 and 1815, a seaborne contingent of British soldiers was repelled before they landed by the most implausible force ever fielded in a military campaign – two sisters, aged 15 and 16. The incident took place at Scituate Lighthouse, about 20 miles down the coast from Boston, where today the beaches of Minot, Humarock and North Scituate are popular with tourists. The sisters, Abigail and Rebecca Bates, daughters of the lighthouse keeper, were the first to notice the approach of two barges filled with Redcoats. Hiding behind the trees, they found a fife and drum, and with these made such a noise that the British soldiers,

---

NEW HAVEN

Hotels

HOLIDAY INN – PARKWAY: 1605 Whalley Av, tel 389 9504. 86 rooms. Moderate.

HOWARD JOHNSON'S MOTOR LODGE: 400 Sargent Dr, tel 562 1111. 154 rooms. Moderate.

SHERATON PARK PLAZA: On Temple St, between Chapel and Crown Sts, tel 772 1700. 300 rooms. Expensive.

Restaurants

RED COACH GRILL: at I-95 exit 42, tel 932 2235. Children's menu. Inexpensive.

TIVOLI RESTAURANT: 311 Orchard St, tel 787 5725. Very good Continental cooking, specialising in Italian dishes. Moderate.

Places of Interest

THE GREEN: 16 acres in centre of city on which three churches of the 19th century stand.

PARDEE HOUSE: 325 Lighthouse Rd. Built about 1750 and restored in 1780 after fire damage. Herb and formal gardens.

thinking that an entire regiment was gathered in the woods, turned around and beat a hasty retreat.

A few miles north of Springfield, which like Worcester has a population of around 168,000 – both cities sharing the second largest population in Massachusetts – is South Hadley. Here, at the 390-acre Joseph Allen Skinner State Park, the Devil's Football, a 300-ton magnetic boulder, is one of the main attractions on the 950-foot climb to Mount Holyoke. Yet South Hadley's most bizarre promotion must be the trade in dinosaur footprints. Estimated to be 180 million years old, these footprints were discovered by a young geologist in 1933 on a two-acre stony ledge. Volcanic action and the erosion of the earth's crust has only recently brought these prints to light. Now they are being lifted, packed, insured and sold from between £7 to £1,500 a time, depending on how long, unusual, and distinct each is. Customers put them in their garden as the ultimate line in one-upmanship. South Hadley nowadays has its Dino Museums, but the remains of these pre-historic creatures get much fuller and more serious exposure in the Dinosaur State Park at Rocky Hill, Connecticut. Here, too, dinosaur tracks have been found in profusion. Most of the specimens are three-toed tracks, the largest only 16 inches across. On a sandstone terrace, over 500 of these fossilised footprints have been preserved, and visitors can make casts of them. Come equipped with 10lbs of plaster of Paris, a quarter cup of cooking oil and lots of rags for cleaning up.

A more valuable export from Connecticut are the brilliant graduates turned out by Yale University at New Haven. Founded in 1701 by ten ministers who gave their books to a college in nearby Branford, it was named Yale in 1718 after an East Indian trader who became its early benefactor. The campus at Phelps Archway in College Street is open for guided tours and includes Connecticut Hall, the oldest of Yale's ivy-covered buildings, the Memorial Quadrangle and Wrexham Tower, a duplicate of the Cathedral Tower in Wrexham, Wales. Apart from its academic work the University also has a school of forestry which was established at the turn of the century. Other places worth visiting at Yale are the College of Musical Instruments and the Beinecke Rare Book and Manuscript Library.

Arguably, Yale's most far-reaching influence was generated by Noah Webster. He had a unique vision when he left Yale: to provide America with its first indigenous dictionary – one that did not rely on the

HARTFORD

Hotel

RAMADA INN: 1330 Silas Deane Hwy, tel 563 2311. 119 rooms. Moderate.

Restaurants

THE CLAM BOX: 1291 Silas Deane Hwy, tel 529 7761. Excellent sea-food menu. Reservations advised. Moderate.

THE SIGNATURE RESTAURANT: 1 Civic Center Plaza, tel 249 1629. Superb dining. Strict dress code. Expensive.

Places of Interest

HARRIET BEECHER STOWE HOUSE: on Nook Farm. Restored home of the authoress of *Uncle Tom's Cabin*. Many original exhibits.

MARK TWAIN MEMORIAL: 351 Farmington Av. Large late 19th-century home of the famous author for many years. Interesting interior decor.

WADSWORTH ATHENAEUM: between Main and Prospect Sts. Hartford's culture centre, an extensive collection of art and antiques from ancient times to the present day.

British vocabulary. His first volume appeared in 1806, when he was 48, and the definitive work, the one on which all Webster's modern American dictionaries are based, in 1828. Webster spent the first 40 of his 85 years at West Hartford which, though connected to Hartford, is a city in its own right. His home, a restored farmhouse at Main Street, has a museum and other reminders of the great lexicographer. Lake Webster, a small lake in Massachusetts, is distinguished only by its original name – the longest sounding lake in the world: *Chargoggagoggmanchaugagoggchaubunagungamaugg*. It is Indian for 'You fish on your side. I fish on mine. Nobody fish in the middle.'

Hartford, with a population of 135,000, boasts of having published the oldest newspaper in the States, the Hartford Courant, (it was founded in 1764), and of having given houseroom to one of the greatest 19th-century exponents of journalism, Mark Twain. The Mark Twain Memorial in Farmington Avenue is an 18-roomed house where the author lived for many years. Adjacent is the Harriet Beecher Stowe House on Nook Farm, named after the authoress of *Uncle Tom's Cabin*. Many of her possessions are preserved within.

It is only natural that Connecticut's long, south facing coastline should give rise to a thriving shipbuilding industry. In 1954, the first atomic-powered submarine, the *Nautilus*, was launched at Groton. It was to help make this town of 40,000 people the largest submarine base in the western hemisphere. Visitors can enjoy a close look at some of the latest designs in the United States Navy's submarine fleet, including those carrying Polaris and Poseidon missiles. The technology of these weapons is a long way from that used in the world's first experimental submarine, the *Turtle*. She was built by David Bushnell, a courageous maritime adventurer, a few miles west at Old Saybrook, during the American Revolutionary War. Bushnell dived with the craft off Saybrook Point and infiltrated New York harbour in an attempt to sink a British man-'o-war, the *Eagle*, but failed to attach a charge to the hull.

As in Connecticut and Massachusetts, fishing is one of Rhode Island's traditional industries. Although it is one of America's smallest states, with a total land area of just over 1,000 square miles (about the size of Shropshire), it has 400 miles of shoreline which was once the home of a great whaling fleet. Today's catches of lobster, scallop and clam are rather smaller, but a good deal tastier. Rhode Island's best-known food product, however, is its famous Red Chicken. First successfully bred in 1854 at Adamsville, in the heart of Rhode Island's farming belt, the breed has been immortalised in songs, and by a monument in the centre of the village.

Author Mark Twain's extravagant Victorian mansion outside Hartford

SOUTHERN NEW ENGLAND

The State Capitol in Providence – the unsupported dome is the second largest in the world

Rhode Island was the first colony to declare itself independent of Britain – two months before the Declaration of Independence was signed in Philadelphia on 4th July 1776. It even wanted to remain independent of the Union, opposing the Federal Constitution until in 1790 it was forced to join.

Roger Williams is credited with being the founder of the state. Rebelling against the strict Puritan hold on Massachusetts, this passionate reformer was banished from the state and built the first settlement at Providence in Rhode Island in 1636. He was followed two years later by Anne Hutchinson, who having formed a non-conformist group in Boston, was reviled by the Puritans for speaking out against them. So with her husband and a small group of her followers, she bought Aquidneck Island from the Indians and founded Portsmouth. Once the town with the largest population in the state, Portsmouth is now a modest village of 14,000 people.

Under Roger Williams's leadership, Rhode Island became a haven of peace surrounded by the turmoil of ideological and political conflicts. The grievances of the Indians eventually led to a war in 1676; Providence was besieged and successfully defended by only 21 men. Today Providence is the State Capital as well as its largest city. Though a busy port with a 600-foot pier and a 3,000-foot municipal quay, it is 27 miles from the open sea in the Narrangansett Bay. At the Providence Civic Center on Sabin Street are portraits and photographs of famous Rhode Islanders. Only 22 years after Williams settled in Providence, 15 Jewish families, attracted by the new freedoms in Rhode Island, landed from Spain and Portugal. One hundred years later they built their first synagogue. It was completed in 1763, and is the oldest in America, a colonial structure of austere classic beauty, and the first Jewish temple to become a National Historic Site. Thanks to Williams's encouragement, Providence also became home to the first Baptist Church in America. The building was erected in Main Street in 1638, and the present church on the same site was built in 1775, and is open to the public. It has a magnificent Waterford chandelier made in 1792. The other large tourist draw in Rhode Island is Newport. The town is noted for its 19th-century architecture, some of which has been modelled on 18th-century European mansions. In particular, the Elms was fashioned after the 18th-century Château d'Asnières near Paris. It is now a museum of antique furniture and objets d'art. Also worth seeing is The Breakers on Ochre Point Avenue, an over-sized summerhouse once owned by Cornelius Vanderbilt, founder of one of America's wealthiest families. Sea, surf and rocks form a dramatic setting for Millionaires' Row, the nickname of Bellevue Avenue, where another branch of the family lived in the Marble House, a columned mansion, which like many other opulent homes in the area, dominates the three-and-a-half-mile stretch of clifftop road. The Marble House is one of several now owned and kept up by the Newport Preservation Society. Full of gold and marble, the ballroom, with its carved and gilded woodwork, chandeliers and large ceiling mural, was the scene of an extraordinary, lavish party thrown by the Vanderbilts in 1895 – just a year before they divorced and closed the place down. The party was in honour of a daughter, Consuelo, who was shortly to become the Duchess of Marlborough. Thirteen years after she remarried, the mother returned to Marble House and though she only lived in it for a few more years, preferring to spend the last years of her life in France, she kept the place until shortly before her death in 1933. Her marvellous mansion remains symptomatic of the wealth and variety of attractions in southern New England.

PROVIDENCE

Hotels

CRANSTON HILTON INN: 1150 Narragansett Blvd, tel 467 8800. 123 rooms. Moderate.

MARRIOTT INN: Charles and Orms Sts, tel 272 2400. 345 rooms. Expensive.

Restaurants

EILEEN DARLING'S RESTAURANT: 5 miles E on U6, tel 336 9222. Family atmosphere. Home-made pastries. Inexpensive.

Places of Interest

BENEFICENT CONGREGATIONAL CHURCH: 300 Weybosset St. Early 19th-century example of Revival architecture.

FIRST BAPTIST CHURCH: 75 N Main St at Waterman St. Believed to be the oldest American Baptist church. Superb Waterford chandelier.

NEWPORT

Hotels

HARBOR-BASE MOTEL: 2½ miles NW on Coddington Hwy, tel 847 2600. 47 rooms. Inexpensive.

NEWPORT HARBOR TREADWAY INN: on harbour off America's Cup Av, tel 847 9000. 134 rooms.

Restaurant

THE PIER: W Howard St at Williams & Manchester Shipyard, tel 847 3645. Pleasant dining with views of pier and harbour. Children's menu. Moderate.

Places of Interest

ARTILLERY COMPANY OF NEWPORT – MILITARY MUSEUM: 23 Clarke St. Displays from over one hundred foreign countries, especially uniforms.

FRIGATE ROSE: King's Dock. Replica of an 18th-century British frigate. Interesting cannons and cabins.

INTERNATIONAL TENNIS HALL OF FAME AND MUSEUM: 194 Bellevue Av. Memorabilia of the great players, record library and courts open to the public.

TOURO SYNAGOGUE NATIONAL HISTORIC SITE: 72 Touro St. The oldest synagogue in America (1763), prized for its interior architecture.

Cape Cod and Rhode Island

Four days – 350 miles

Boston – Pawtucket – Providence – Mystic – Saunderstown – Jamestown – Newport – Fall River – New Bedford – Fairhaven – Bourne – Falmouth – Woods Hole – Hyannis – Harwich – Chatham – Eastham – South Wellfleet – Wellfleet – Provincetown – Plymouth – Duxbury – Braintree – Quincy – Boston

From downtown Boston, take Insterstate 93 for 10 miles south. Drive 5 miles west, still on Insterstate 93 to the junction with Insterstate 95. Take Interstate 95 south for 30 miles to Pawtucket.

Pawtucket

The birthplace of America's Industrial Revolution, it was here in 1790 that Samuel Slater started the continent's first successful cotton-manufacturing plant, operated by waterpower. The Slater Mill Historic Site on Roosevelt Avenue has been restored to its early appearance and recreates life in a 19th-century industrial village, and there are demonstrations of old textile machine tools and of allied handicrafts in three of the original buildings.

Continue south for 6 miles on Interstate 95 to Providence.

Providence

State capital of Rhode Island and second largest city in New England, Providence is also an important port at the head of navigation on Narragansett Bay. The city was founded in 1636 by the liberal Roger Williams, who, banished from Massachusetts, set about establishing America's first free-religion settlement. Evidence of this freedom is still to be seen in the numerous churches representing every conceivable denomination. However, the same city prospered from running the old Triangular Trade of slaves, rum and molasses between Africa, the West Indies and the Colonies.

The Arcade, which runs from Westminster to Weybossett Streets, was opened in 1828 and is an exquisite 'temple of trade' once commonly found in eastern seaboard towns.

Rhode Island School of Design, at 224 Benefit Street, has a Museum of Art which houses a collection of classical art, 18th-century European porcelains and Oriental textiles as well as work by 19th-century Latin-American and French artists. A replica of an early Providence house, Pendleton House, features a collection of American furniture and decorative arts.

Other attractions include the imposing State House on Smith Street. Here is a Gilbert Stuart portrait of George Washington and the original 1663 charter granted by Charles II. John Brown House (1786) on Power Street was described by John Adams as the most magnificent in the country. On display are Rhode Island antiques.

As well as meriting a National Memorial above his grave on Prospect Terrace, Roger Williams is commemorated by a beautiful 430-acre park with a chain of 10 lakes, extensive flower gardens and nine miles of drives. There is also a natural history museum, a zoo, and an amphitheatre. (For recommended hotels see page 84.)

Drive south-west for 55 miles on Interstate 95, then drive south at the interchange for State Route 27. Mystic lies at the end of State Route 27, 2 miles south.

Mystic

The fastest clipper ships in the New World were being built at this historic seaport by the middle of the 19th century. Along the Mystic River, half a mile north of the town, Mystic Seaport Museum recreates the past on the waterfront. Homes, shops, lofts and historic sailing ships are all exhibited, including the square-rigged *Joseph Conrad* and the great three-masted *Charles W Morgan*, last of the wooden whalers. Museum buildings lining the cobbled streets display figureheads and ship models and demonstrations of shipbuilding, sail-setting and whale-rowing are given. Adventure boat trips depart from Steamboat Wharf, by the drawbridge, for cruises along Mystic River, Fisher's Island Sound and Long Island Sound.

Half a mile north of the town is Olde Mistick Village, a shopping and recreational complex with 25 colonial-style buildings, a handmade water wheel and community meeting houses.

Hotels

HOWARD JOHNSON'S MOTOR LODGE: at junc I–95 exit 90 and SR 27, tel 536 2654. 72 rooms. Expensive.

SEAPORT MOTOR INN: at junc I–95 exit 90 and SR 27, tel 536 2621. 118 rooms. Moderate.

Drive east along US 1 for 9 miles to Pawcatuck. Cross into Rhode Island, continuing along US 1 for 22 miles to its junction with State Route 108 and State Route 1A. Take State Route 1A north for 8 miles to Sanderstown.

The Mystic Seaport Museum recreates life in a mid-19th-century seaport

BOSTON
Cambridge
Brookline
Newton
Waltham
Quincy
Milton
Dedham
Braintree
Weymouth
Norwood
Walpole
Canton
Sharon
Stoughton
Foxboro
Mansfield
Brockton
Franklin
Attleboro
Taunton
Norton
Raynham
PROVIDENCE
Pawtucket
E. Providence
Seekonk
Cranston
Warwick
E. Greenwich
Fall River
NEW BEDFORD
Tiverton
Portsmouth
Middletown
Newport
Jamestown
Wickford (N. Kingstown)
Wakefield (S. Kingstown)
Narragansett Pier
Point Judith
Charlestown
Westerly
Watch Hill
Pawcatuck
Mystic
Stonington
Groton
Noank
Ledyard
Norwich
Plainfield
Moosup
Hope Valley
Coventry
Westport
North Dartmouth
Little Compton
Rhode Island Sound
Fishers Island Sound
Narragansett Bay
WINDHAM
NEW LONDON
KENT
WASHINGTON
BRISTOL
NORFOLK
SUFFOLK
CONN.
R.I.
MASS.
©AMERICAN AUTOMOBILE ASSOCIATION MCMLXXXI

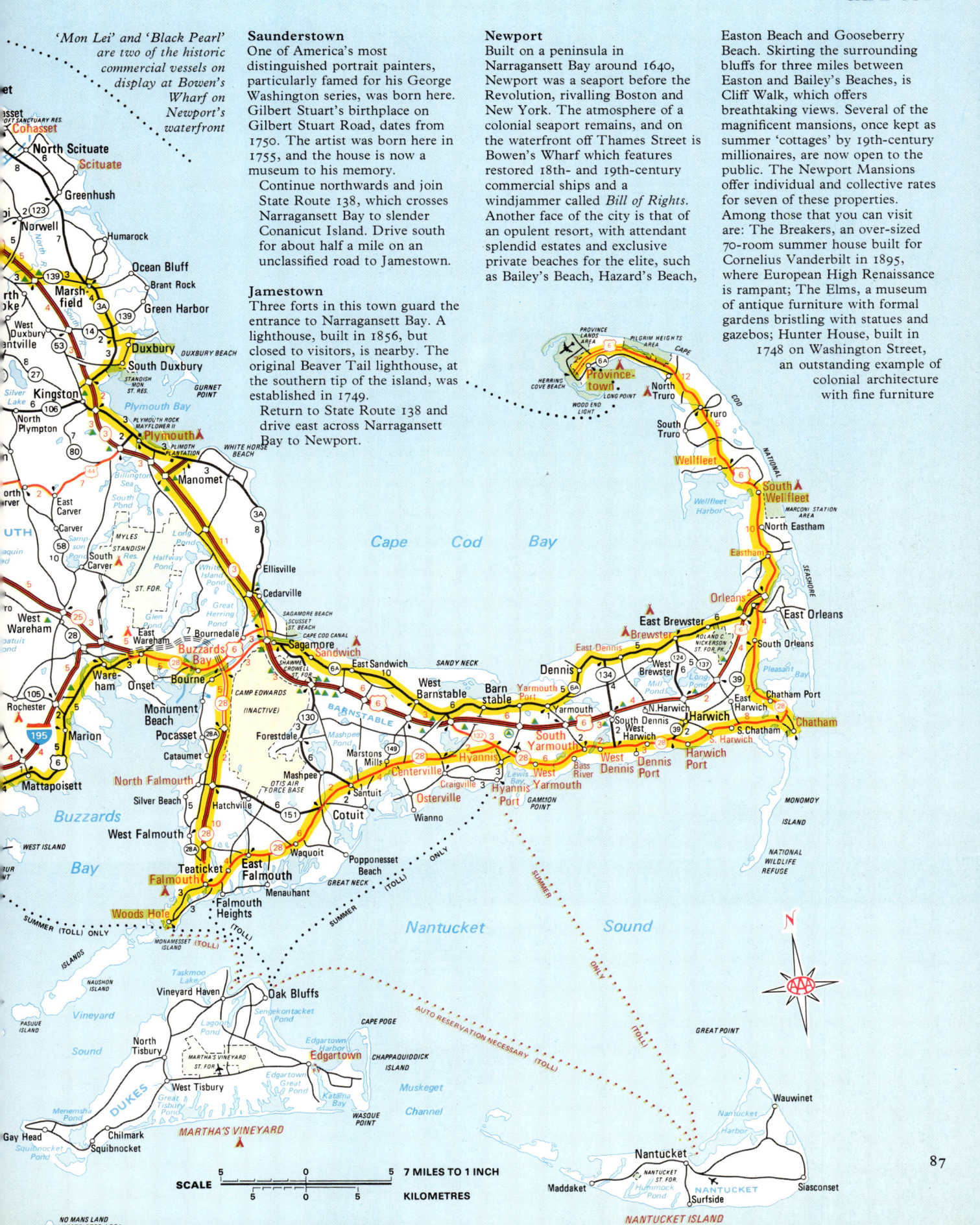

CAPE COD

'Mon Lei' and 'Black Pearl' are two of the historic commercial vessels on display at Bowen's Wharf on Newport's waterfront

Saunderstown
One of America's most distinguished portrait painters, particularly famed for his George Washington series, was born here. Gilbert Stuart's birthplace on Gilbert Stuart Road, dates from 1750. The artist was born here in 1755, and the house is now a museum to his memory.

Continue northwards and join State Route 138, which crosses Narragansett Bay to slender Conanicut Island. Drive south for about half a mile on an unclassified road to Jamestown.

Jamestown
Three forts in this town guard the entrance to Narragansett Bay. A lighthouse, built in 1856, but closed to visitors, is nearby. The original Beaver Tail lighthouse, at the southern tip of the island, was established in 1749.

Return to State Route 138 and drive east across Narragansett Bay to Newport.

Newport
Built on a peninsula in Narragansett Bay around 1640, Newport was a seaport before the Revolution, rivalling Boston and New York. The atmosphere of a colonial seaport remains, and on the waterfront off Thames Street is Bowen's Wharf which features restored 18th- and 19th-century commercial ships and a windjammer called *Bill of Rights*. Another face of the city is that of an opulent resort, with attendant splendid estates and exclusive private beaches for the elite, such as Bailey's Beach, Hazard's Beach, Easton Beach and Gooseberry Beach. Skirting the surrounding bluffs for three miles between Easton and Bailey's Beaches, is Cliff Walk, which offers breathtaking views. Several of the magnificent mansions, once kept as summer 'cottages' by 19th-century millionaires, are now open to the public. The Newport Mansions offer individual and collective rates for seven of these properties. Among those that you can visit are: The Breakers, an over-sized 70-room summer house built for Cornelius Vanderbilt in 1895, where European High Renaissance is rampant; The Elms, a museum of antique furniture with formal gardens bristling with statues and gazebos; Hunter House, built in 1748 on Washington Street, an outstanding example of colonial architecture with fine furniture

CAPE COD

and panelling, and Rosecliff, built in 1902 to outdo all the other Bellevue Avenue mansions. Fashioned after Marie Antoinette's Grand Trianon at Versailles, it boasts a vast ballroom, a heart-shaped staircase and innumerable sculptures. Also in Bellevue Avenue is the Newport Automobile Museum, where you can see antique and classic cars, historic flags, and murals by Louis Burnstein.

Before leaving Newport, cruise along Ocean Drive, a 10-mile circuit with panoramic views of the rugged Atlantic coastline. (For recommended hotels see page 84.)

Take State Route 114 north of Newport and drive for 7 miles to join State Route 24. Continue along State Route 24 for 12 miles to Fall River, joining Interstate 195.

Fall River

This large town, bordered by water to the east and west, is the home of Battleship Cove, where you may board a battleship, submarine or destroyer. Among the several Navy craft preserved here is the 680-foot battleship *USS Massachusetts* (Big Mamie) survivor of 35 battles in both the Atlantic and Pacific.

An infamous 19th-century trial in which Lizzie Borden was accused of axing her mother and father to death, is recalled at the Fall River Historical Society, 451 Rock Street, which also displays relics of the Fall River Mills and Steamships. The house where the dirty deed (for which Lizzie was aquitted) allegedly took place is in Second Street, but you can't see inside. (For recommended hotels see page 80.)

Take Interstate 195 east for 10 miles to New Bedford.

New Bedford

A large city on Buzzard's Bay, New Bedford was once a great whaling port, and is still an important fishing centre.

A whaling museum, which is sponsored by the Old Dartmouth Historical Society, is open at 18 Johnny Cake Hill. Here you can see a half-size model of the whaling bark *Lagoda*, full-rigged. Replicas of cooperage, sail loft and rigging loft shops are also on view. Close by is the Seamen's Bethel at 15 Johnny Cake Hill. Opened in 1832, it contains cenotaphs described by Herman Melville in *Moby Dick*. Next door is Mariner's Home, once a refuge for shipwrecked sailors.

Fort Taber, on East Rodney French Boulevard, is a restored mid-19th-century seacoast fortification designed by Robert E Lee and Richard Dalafield.

Drive east on Interstate 195 and turn right at the first interchange for Fairhaven.

Fairhaven

This small town is remarkable for the Unitarian Memorial Church on Green and Center Streets. A Gothic church, with sculptured bronze doors and mosaic and marble floors, it contains carvings and symbols which depict the history of Christianity.

Take US 6 from Fairhaven and drive east along Buzzard's Bay for 15 miles to Wareham. Drive east on US 6 for 2½ miles before joining State Route 28 for 5½ miles to Cape Cod Canal. Turn right past the canal on State Route 28A for 1 mile to Bourne.

Bourne

Called the Gateway to Cape Cod, Bourne was established as a town in 1884 when it became separated from Sandwich. Highway and rail bridges across Cape Cod Canal are close to the town. Winding and beautiful, the canal provides transit for some 30,000 vessels of all sizes every year, and effectively makes Cape Cod an island.

The Aptucxet Trading Post was established here in 1627 under the Charter of the Governor of Plymouth. A replica may be viewed on the actual site, one mile west of State Route 28 and US 6 junction. Dutch, Indian and Pilgrim relics are exhibited and there is a saltworks, an old windmill and a herb garden. You may picnic in the grounds.

Drive south on State Route 28 for 17 miles to Falmouth.

Falmouth

This charming village, built around an enchanting green, was originally named Succanesset when it was settled in 1660 by a group of Quaker sympathisers. A bronze tablet on the beach marks the spot where the settlers landed. Named Falmouth since 1694, smooth, sandy beaches and an average water temperature of over 70°F are now a main attraction.

Ashumet Holly Reservation and Wildlife Sanctuary north of Falmouth is a haven of flora and fauna, offering self-guided tours along well-marked trails. On Woods Road, near the town square, is Falmouth Historical Museum and Garden. The museum, housed in what was once a sea captain's house, exhibits whaling tools and ship models.

The Saconsset Homestead is 3¼

Among the many exhibits at New Bedford's whaling museum, this impressive skeleton testifies to the importance of the industry in years gone by

In winter the Woods Hole ferries, plying from Cape Cod to Martha's Vineyard, have to contend with ice

---

FALMOUTH

Hotels

THE CAPEWIND: 34 Maravista Av, tel 548 3400. 31 rooms. Moderate.

OX-BOW MOTEL: 179 Main St, tel 548 6677. 25 rooms. Moderate.

SHERATON INN: 291 Jones Rd, tel 540 2000. 96 rooms. Expensive.

Restaurant

THE FLYING BRIDGE RESTAURANT: ¾ mile SE on Scranton Av, tel 548 2700. Good food. Dining rooms have nautical theme. Moderate.

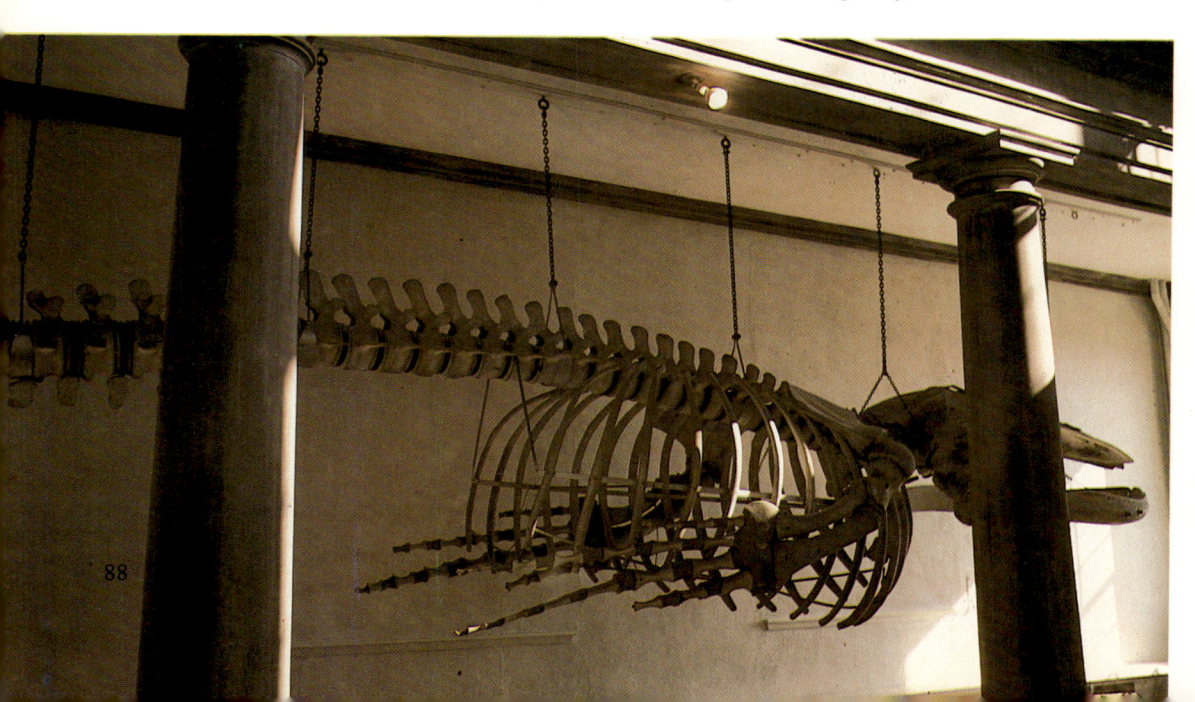

CAPE COD

resort satellites have made Hyannis the playground of the very wealthy – in particular the Kennedy family. The late President John F Kennedy's family compound is concealed behind a high fence in Hyannis Port. A circular fieldstone wall on Ocean Street bearing the Presidential seal serves as a memorial to the murdered leader.

Melody Tent on West Main Street is the entertainment centre where the big names in the showbusiness world appear throughout the summer.

Ferry services operate from the harbour, plying between expensive ocean-going yachts to Falmouth, Martha's Vineyard and Nantucket Island.

Continue east along State Route 28 for 11 miles, then take State Route 39 for 2 miles north to Harwich.

Harwich
This town is famed for Brooks Library, in the centre on State Route 39, which contains figurines by John Rogers.

Harwich Port has a fine harbour, ocean bathing, and excellent sea and freshwater fishing.

Drive south-east to State Route 28 and continue east for 6 miles. Turn right on to an unclassified road and drive one mile south to Chatham.

Chatham
Chatham sits on the most south-easterly tip of Cape Cod. Facing the Atlantic to the east and Nantucket Sound to the south, this fashionable shopping centre and long-established fishing town offers superb views of the ocean from Chatham Light. Free of the commercialism that mars so many other Cape towns, Chatham has changed little since the turn of the century. You can still watch the boats unloading their catch of haddock, cod, flounder and pollock at the Fish Pier on the corner of Shore Road in the afternoons. Within the bounds of Chatham township is needle-like Monomoy Island, home of the Monomoy National Wildlife Refuge which is vital to migratory wildfowl on their journey from Canada to Florida. Boats are available for visiting ornithologists.

Rejoin State Route 28 and drive north past Pleasant Bay for 11 miles to Orleans. Here join US 6 for 4 miles to Eastham and the Cape Cod National Seashore.

Eastham
Surrounded by great rolling, lonely beach dunes, ocean surf, picturesque inlets and marshes and tranquil freshwater ponds,

Winter in Falmouth: the scene reminds one of an English village green

Eastham is close to the headquarters of the Cape Cod National Seashore Project. Greater contrast to the Cape's bustling southern shore is impossible to imagine. Here 28,000 acres of primitive beauty are conserved for posterity. Five areas in the project include Nauset Beach – miles of broad sands ideal for swimming, surfing, surf-casting or simply sunbathing. Five more splendid beaches stretch to the north, with Great Island, Marconi Station, Pilgrim Heights and Province Lands offering heaths, pine forests, glowing red cranberry bogs and shining white lighthouses which you can admire as you venture along nature trails or on guided walks. The Visitor Centre at Salt Pond, off US 6, will give further information.

Also on US 6, near Eastham town hall is Old Windmill. Dating from 1793, this is the oldest windmill on Cape Cod.

Continue north on US 6 for about 6 miles to South Wellfleet.

South Wellfleet
Spectacular views of the beach and ocean from high cliffs and a nature trail through an eerie white cedar swamp are two attractions. The site of the first Marconi wireless station is in a desolate spot nearby.

South of the area is the Wellfleet Bay Wildlife Sanctuary, a 750-acre nature reserve with hiking trails and wildlife tours.

Continue north on US 6 for about 4 miles, then turn west on a small road to Wellfleet.

miles north on State Route 28A. Home of the settlers for nine generations, the site includes the original house, furniture, wagons and farm implements.

Take State Route 28A and drive south-west for 3 miles to the heel of Cape Cod and Woods Hole.

Woods Hole
The chief port of the cape, Woods Hole, is connected by ferry to a pair of delightful islands. Martha's Vineyard is only seven miles away and a car ferry operates daily between Woods Hole and Vineyard Haven, the shopping centre of the island. In summer, ferries sail to Oak Bluffs, with its 19th-century flower-decked gingerbread houses. Nantucket Island is 30 miles from the shore. Once a lively whaling centre, the cobblestone streets of this island are still lined with the mansions of whaling captains.

Woods Hole is the home of the nationally-famed Oceanographic Institute, and also boasts a Marine Aquarium. Maintained by the National Marine Fisheries on Albatros Street, the aquarium contains exhibits of local and commercial species and a seal pool.

Return to Falmouth on State Route 28A and join State Route 28, driving east for 18 miles to Hyannis.

Hyannis
Bordered on both sides by neon signs, drive-ins, stores and restaurants, your drive along State Route 28 will have prepared you for this commercial hub of tourism on the southern shore of Cape Cod. Superb beaches such as Craigville Beach and fashionable

89

CAPE COD

Wellfleet
The centre of Wellfleet is bypassed by the main highway, so the old buildings and charm of the village are intact. The church clock still strikes nautical time, reflecting the maritime past, when Wellfleet was a thriving whaling port and the centre of the oyster industry.

Visit Wellfleet Historical Museum in Main Street which captures the flavour of this whaling heritage.

Rejoin US 6 and drive north for 17 miles to Provincetown.

Provincetown
At the very tip of Cape Cod is this bustling artists' colony, famous as the first landfall of the Pilgrim Fathers. Though Plymouth has long taken the credit for this, in fact the *Mayflower* was at anchor in Cape Cod Bay for four weeks while the Pilgrims suffered on the windswept marshes around Provincetown. A 252-foot stone tower now marks the place where the Pilgrims landed and a Heritage Museum on Commercial Street houses an excellent collection of relics. The museum also highlights the town's past as a whaling port. A perfectly-preserved colonial town, full of 18th-century houses and souvenir shops, many owned by artists, Provincetown's narrow main street is also jammed with art galleries, craft shops and restaurants. Miles of beaches line the harbour and ocean shores. Off Race Point Road is a Visitor Centre where there is an observation platform, an auditorium programme and other exhibits.

Interesting places to see in the town are the Art Association and Museum of Art on Commercial Street which stages exhibitions in summer, and Seth Nickerson House, built in 1746, also on Commercial Street, which exemplifies Cape Cod architecture. The interior, constructed from shipwreck materials, includes a beehive-shaped oven in the fireplace.

Hotels

BEST WESTERN CHATEAU MOTOR INN: ¾ mile W on Bradford St W, tel 487 1286. 60 rooms. Expensive.

BRADFORD HOUSE & MOTEL; 41 Bradford St, tel 487 0173. 24 rooms. Moderate.

CORAL SANDS MOTEL: 3¼ miles SE on SR 6A, tel 487 1410. 33 rooms. Moderate.

HOLIDAY INN: 1½ miles SE on SR 6A, tel 487 1711. 139 rooms. Expensive.

Restaurants

BONNIE DOONE RESTAURANT: 35 Bradford St, tel 487 1185. A popular restaurant with an extensive menu. Moderate.

THE RED INN: 15 Commercial St, tel 487 0050. Overlooking ocean, excellent New England country cooking. Moderate–expensive.

Return on US 6 to Orleans. At the second interchange, take State Route 6A and drive along the bay shore for 32 miles to Sagamore. Join State Route 3 and drive for 15 miles to the third interchange. Turn right and drive one mile to State Route 3A for Plymouth.

Plymouth
A band of 102 weary English men, women and children chose to settle at Plymouth after a stormy 66-day ocean-crossing and a sojourn in Provincetown. Many died that first winter from pneumonia or starvation, but soon other settlers arrived from England to swell Plimoth Plantation.

Visit Plimoth Plantation on your way into the town. Established in 1627, the village is now a museum where costumed people enact life as it was in the Pilgrims' day.

The Pilgrim Village at Plimoth Plantation. Here events such as an English country wedding are staged in the style of the early settlers

At North Park the Plymouth Information Centre will shower you with details of 101 things to see in the town.

Plymouth Rock, on Water Street, now rests under a canopy of granite to protect it from souvenir hunters. Close by, moored at State Pier, is *Mayflower II*, a full-size replica of the original ship.

A short walk from here, to Carver Street, leads to the Plymouth National Wax Museum, which contains life-size tableaux of the Pilgrim Fathers and the first Thanksgiving.

From the wax museum, climb up to Coles Hill, the burial place of the Pilgrims who died during the first terrible winter. Massasoit, the friendly Indian chief who ratified the 1621 treaty with the Pilgrims, is commemorated by a statue here.

Stone steps beside the First Parish Church lead up to Burial Hill, which overlooks Town Square. It was the site of the old fort built in 1622 and the watchtower built in 1643. As well as a place of defence, the hill was used as a burial ground. The town established Brewster Gardens nearby, location of the Pilgrims' original gardens or 'meersteads'.

One of the oldest public museums in America, Pilgrim Hall, has an interesting collection of Pilgrim paintings and relics.

Hotels

COLD SPRING MOTEL: 188 Court St, tel 746 2222. 19 rooms. Inexpensive.

THE GOVERNOR CARVER MOTOR INN: 25 Summer St, tel 746 7100. 82 rooms. Moderate-expensive.

PILGRIM SANDS MOTEL: 3 miles S on SR 3A, tel 747 0900. 63 rooms. Moderate.

Proceed on State Route 3 for 5 miles north to the second interchange. Here turn right on State Route 3A and follow signs for Duxbury.

Duxbury
Alden House is located here – home of famous settlers John and Priscilla Alden. Built in 1653, there is a clamshell ceiling in one room, a borning room and gunstock beams.

At Powder Point, King Caesar House was built in 1808 to 1809 for Ezra Weston II, a 19th-century shipping magnate. A fine example of Federal architecture, two front parlours feature French wallpaper attributed to DuFour. A display of shipbuilding between 1800 to 1850 may be seen in a museum adjoining the house.

Rejoin State Route 3A and drive 4 miles north to Marshfield. Continue west on State Route 139 and rejoin State Route 3 after 3 miles. Drive for 15 miles, leaving at Interchange 27 for South Braintree. From South Braintree drive north on Washington Street to Braintree.

Braintree
Settled in 1634 and established in 1640. Braintree once included the towns of Quincy and Randolf. Robert Williams and Anne Hutchinson, exiled for their religious beliefs from Boston, found refuge here en route for Rhode Island.

General Thayer, the 'Father of the US Military Academy', was born here in 1785 in a house in Washington Street. The General Sylvanus Thayer Birthplace is now operated by the Braintree Historical Society as a house and barn museum, both of which include a Town Museum, a Military Museum and a Museum of Colonial Life.

Drive north on Independence Avenue for 2 miles to Quincy.

Quincy
During the late 18th century, this town, then part of Braintree, was home of the second US President, John Adams. His son, John Quincy Adams, also became President. The town, which separated from Braintree in 1792, is bursting with memorials to the esteemed Adams family.

Adams National Historic Site, 135 Adams Street, was the home of the family from 1788 to 1927. Original furnishings of four generations, including both Presidents, a 14,000-volume library and an 18th-century garden are on view.

The birthplaces of both presidents are on Franklin Street. John Adams was born in 1735 at number 133. The sixth President, John Quincy Adams, was born in 1767 at number 141, to where John and his wife Abigail had moved after the Revolution. Particularly interesting is the law office, in which was drafted the Constitution of Massachusetts, later used as a model for those of other states and for the US Constitution.

Built of Quincy granite in 1828, the Church of Presidents on Hancock Street has a crypt which contains the entombed remains of the two presidents and their wives.

Drive north on State Route 3A for 3 miles, then join State Route 3 at Interchange 20 and continue north for 5 miles to Boston.

Boston

Here, where the summers are warm but the winters bitterly cold, passions have always run high and hot.

In Boston, 350 years ago, early Puritan settlers, fired with religious zeal, strove to build a new life. Nearly 150 years later their descendants sparked off a rebellion and led the fight which freed America from British dominion. The Boston Tea Party, the Battle of Bunker Hill, Paul Revere's famous ride, episodes almost as familiar to British schoolchildren as to Americans – are all a part of the past in which Boston revels.

More recently Boston has been the scene of many of the milestones in the history of the city's most famous family, the Kennedys.

Yet Boston has another side – the broad avenues of the aggressive, modern city turn into the narrow, winding streets of the colonial town; the businessmen and industrialists responsible for Boston's growth mingle in the streets with 100,000 students from the city's several colleges and universities, some of them from Harvard, America's oldest and perhaps most famous university, which stands on Boston's doorstep – in Cambridge.

Links with Britain are strong, but stronger is the pride in its American history and its achievements, for Boston can boast of having given birth to a nation, the United States of America.

▲ *The 'Brig Beaver II' is a working replica of one of the ships attacked in the Boston Tea Party of 1773. A group of Bostonians thinly disguised as Mohawk braves boarded three ships in the harbour and threw their cargoes of tea overboard in protest against British taxes. Visitors who wish to re-enact this rebellion can do so with tea chests provided on board*

When in Boston, the British tourist is surrounded by reminders of home. This is a city which likes to show off its links with colonial England, and which recalls its part in the struggle for independence with pride.

The Massachusetts Bay area was first settled in 1630 by a British party led by the Puritan leader John Winthrop. They had followed in the footsteps of the Pilgrim Fathers, in search of religious freedom, but with certain advantages – there were more of them (nearly 1,000), and they were better equipped and financed – and therefore settled more quickly and developed faster. The settlements these early pioneers created were insular, religious, hard-working and self-governed. By their nature they attracted men of strong views, ambition and intellect. A tradition of intellectual fervour and political passion was established early in Massachusetts, and found its focus in the state capital, Boston, a city which has produced many of America's finest statesmen, philosophers and scientists.

Boston led the way towards independence. On 5 March 1770, an unruly crowd attacked British sentries. The troops, incensed by shouts of 'lobster back' and 'redcoat', fired on the mob, killing five. One of those who died was Crispus Attucks, a former slave who is believed to have been the first American to be killed by the British in the fight for independence. The incident, known as the Boston Massacre, is commemorated by a monument erected in 1888 by the Black community on the site on Congress Street where Attucks died.

Three years after the massacre, on a cold December night in 1773, 60 patriots, disguised as Indians,

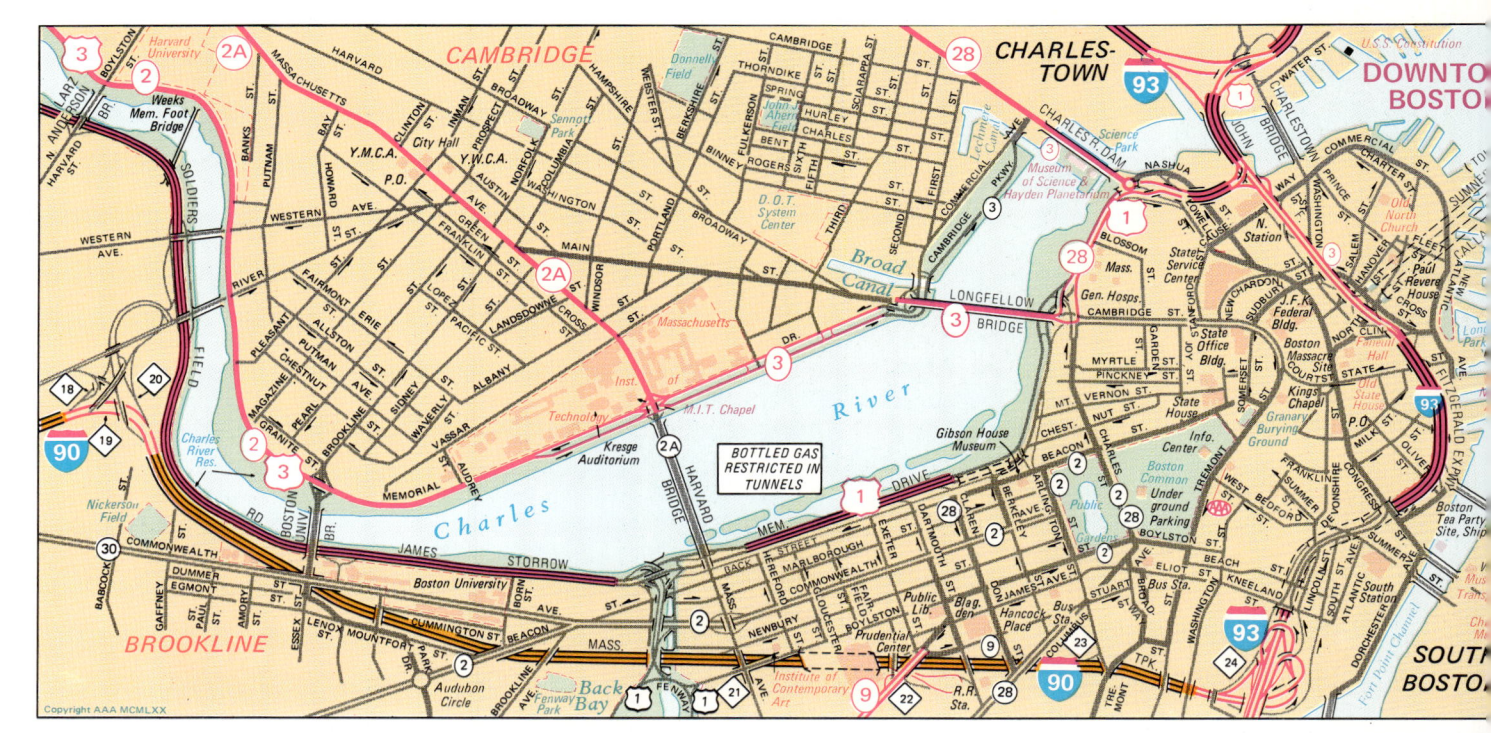

BOSTON

boarded three cargo ships at anchor in Boston Harbour, and threw the 342 chests of tea they were carrying overboard. This was a protest against taxes Britain wanted to impose on the colonists for tea and other goods, without allowing them the right to vote. The cry 'no taxation without representation' became a familiar one. Troops were sent to keep order, but this only angered the colonists more – the die was cast. Sixteen months after the Boston Tea Party, as it became known, the American War of Independence began, with Boston in the thick of it.

If you follow the one-and-a-half-mile Freedom Trail, marked by a red brick line set into the pavements, it will lead you to 16 of Boston's historic sites. You can begin at Boston Common, which served as a military parade and training ground during the War of Independence. In the middle, on Dorchester Hill, is the Soldiers Monument, erected to mark the spot where Washington drove the British out of Boston on 17 March 1776. Head north-east across the Common and you reach Beacon Hill, where the State House of 1795 stands, its dome covered with £100,000 worth of gold-leaf. The Trail continues, to take you past Brimstone Corner, where in Park Street Church gunpowder was made during the 1812 war with Britain, and where William Lloyd Garrison was the first to speak out against slavery in 1829. Next, the Granary Burying Ground is visited, where the bodies of the Boston Massacre victims lie alongside other luminaries of the Revolution, among them three signatories of the Declaration of Independence.

Among other sites visited by following the Freedom Trail are the 'oldest house in Boston', once owned by Paul Revere, and the house from which he set off on his fateful ride (see page 82), and Copp's Hill Cemetery, the vantage point on the south side of the Charles River from which the first bombardment was unleashed by the British on the Rebel position on Bunker Hill, the site of the first major encounter of the War of Independence. At Bunker Hill, in Charlestown, a monument marks the site. A spiral 294-step staircase leads to the top of the 221-foot-high obelisk.

In the docks at Charlestown Navy Shipyard lies 'Old Ironsides', a frigate which played a decisive part in the 1812–15 war with Britain. Christened the *USS Constitution* when she was launched in 1797, she earned her nickname because of the seasoned live oaks and red cedar timbers of which she was built, reputedly as strong as iron. This was the era before the techniques of iron-frame construction had been mastered, so her timbered skeleton was bolted together and lined with copper. The metal worker entrusted with the job was Paul Revere.

On another stretch of water, the Fort Point Chan-

BOSTON

tables under strings of fairy lights, Boston's fashionable young bring their friends to drink and dine. The three 500-foot-long buildings that make up the market are packed with reasonably-priced and exotic merchandise from all over the world.

At the other extreme, and yet only a stone's throw away, are the smooth, shining, giant 'glass-houses' of the modern commercial empires. They have grown up in recent years in what is generically called Government Center. The New City Hall dominates this area. Picked from 250 plans for its 'impressive, functional, economic and harmonious design', the building cost almost eight million pounds and has won several architectural awards. Nearby are the clean lines of the JFK Federal Building, named in memory of Boston's most illustrious 20th-century son, and a name as 'royal' in Boston's context as Windsor is in Britain's. As New England immigrants, the Kennedys came rather later on the scene than the forebears of Benjamin Franklin, John Hancock, Paul Revere and Josiah Quincy who formed the fabric of Boston's political past. Patrick Kennedy left Ireland in 1848 and set up as a cooper in Boston. Like other passionate political firebrands he inculcated into his family a social idealism that a century later was to give the dynasty an enduring place in history. His great grandson, John F Kennedy, was born on Beals Street in the Boston suburb of Brookline. The birthplace has been made a national historic site, and can be visited. The John Fitzgerald Kennedy Library and Museum, a 10-minute drive out of the city at Columbia Point, contains such personal items as the desk he used in the Oval Office of the White House, together with his famous rocking chair, and the tape recordings, books, films and documents he had around him. His political life, too, is traced in a half-hour film shown in a theatre at the museum.

Across the river at Cambridge stands the JFK School of Government. Built in the 1970s, it is one of the more recent additions to Harvard University's glittering array of disciplines. Though separate from the administrative area of Boston, Cambridge is linked to the city by more than three centuries of academic distinction derived from its illustrious university. Harvard itself was established because of a 30-year-old immigrant called John Harvard, who, when he died in 1637, left his 400 volume collection of books and £1,700 – half his estate – to a new college the colonists had founded a year earlier. The college was named after him in 1640. Until 1894, it was open only to male students, but in that year Radcliffe College was founded to educate America's brightest young women. The oldest university in the United States, Harvard can accommodate about 15,000 men and 1,100 women a year, and puts at their disposal 17 departments, the amenities of 9 faculties, 95 libraries, 7 botanical institutes, 2 astronomical stations and more than 50 laboratories of science, engineering and medicine. It also has 9 museums.

Another towering academic conglomerate in the Boston area is the Massachusetts Institute of Technology (MIT) which since 1916 has occupied a 125-acre campus along the northern bank of the Charles River. Like Harvard, it is richly endowed with intellectual and artistic riches, among them a concert hall, an art gallery and a nautical museum. With so many cultural resources on its doorstep, Boston enjoys a vigorous musical and theatrical tradition.

▲ *Harvard Yard, the original campus of America's oldest and most distinguished university. The statue of John Harvard was erected in the 19th century*

▶ *Quincy Market, one of Boston's oldest shopping areas, was built in the early 19th century by Major Josiah Quincy*

◀ *The 'new' State House, built in 1795, was one of the finest achievements of Charles Bulfinch, who designed many of Boston's historic buildings*

▼ *From this, Boston's oldest house, Paul Revere set off on his famous ride in 1775. The building, thought to date from 1676, was Revere's home for 30 years*

nel, a reconstruction of one of the Tea Party ships, the *Beaver*, allows an inspection on board of historic documents and a tea chest said to be one of those cast overboard in 1773.

But Boston, bounded on three sides by water – to the north by the bend of the Charles River, to the east by the Fort Point Channel, and to the west by the Back Bay Fens – is not just a history-student's happy hunting ground. It also has a brisk, topical, business-like air about it, reflected in its modern architecture and in the reincarnation of its older buildings.

Quincy Market, which for nearly 125 years was Boston's fruit market, has now been restored to its 19th-century glory. It is a modern shopping centre in the day, and a busy place at night. On pavement

BOSTON

Rivalling both the New York Metropolitan Museum of Art, and the Art Institute in Chicago, Boston's own Museum of Fine Arts in Huntington Avenue has acquired a tremendous range of exhibits of Asiatic, Classical, Egyptian, Near-Eastern, American and European decorative and 20th-century art and sculptures. The Symphony Hall, home of the world-famous Boston Symphony Orchestra, is one of more than 30 places providing a platform for musical and theatrical events.

There is plenty of sport and both outdoor and indoor recreation in Boston. Baseball at Fenway Park, American football and horse-racing in the suburbs, and basketball in Boston Garden draw the crowds regularly. And with many young people setting such a good example, Bostonians of all shapes and sizes are a familiar sight in running shorts, as they pound the pavements and the towpaths.

There is no shortage of good restaurants and hotels in Boston. Many eating places, some familiarly clad in the dark polished timber of English pubs, serve lobster as cheaply as the British sell fish and chips. Oysters are deliciously fresh, reasonably priced and widely available in snack portions of six or a dozen, and often sold in bars.

Among Boston's more than 50 downtown hotels, the Parker House claims to be the oldest continuously operated hotel in America. Since it opened in 1858, it has looked after many famous guests – among them Charles Dickens, who made it his home during a nine-months speaking tour of America in 1867, the famous British actress Sarah Bernhardt, and John Wilkes Booth who, eight days later went to Washington and assassinated Abraham Lincoln. In more recent years John F Kennedy and his brother Robert used the Parker House for their presidential campaign meetings.

Apart from the usual provision of modern shopping precincts and malls, Boston's older areas, and in particular the Back Bay District, have many interesting speciality shops. At the Prudential Center – a 31-acre complex of shops, restaurants, and covered walkways, dominated by the 52-storey Prudential Tower – many leading international names in shopping and merchandise are represented. While the 50th floor of the tower allows visitors a magnificent panoramic view of the city, a higher vantage point is available from the 740-foot John Hancock Observatory, where one can see not only all of Boston, but also the mountains of New Hampshire stretching into the distance.

▲ *Boston's Back Bay, beside the Charles River, as seen from the observatory of the John Hancock Tower. Lifts ascend the 60 floors in 30 seconds, and at the top telescopes enable visitors to view all the city's landmarks*

Boston Directory

Hotels and restaurants shown here are either recommended by the American Automobile Association (AAA) or are chosen because they are particularly appealing to tourists. As an approximate guide to cost, they have been rated as either expensive, moderate or inexpensive. Hotels all have private bathrooms and colour television.

HOTELS

BOSTON PARK PLAZA HOTEL: 64 Arlington St, tel 426 2000. 800 rooms. A well located hotel with bright rooms which have air conditioning and direct-dial phones. Health club, beauty salon, sauna. At selected times weekend bargains are available. Moderate.

THE COLONNADE: 120 Huntington Av, tel 261 2800. 300 rooms. Stylish contemporary hotel in the centre of town offering personalised service. Rooftop resort with putting green, pool, snack bar and occasional entertainment. Expensive.

COPLEY PLAZA: 138 St James Av, tel 267 5300. 450 rooms. One of America's finest hotels, run in the grand tradition. Elegant public rooms are decorated by mosaic floors, rich wood panelling and works of art. Guest rooms are gracious and plush. Outstanding dining and drinking facilities. Expensive.

57 PARK PLAZA HOTEL – HOWARD JOHNSON: 200 Stuart St, tel 482 1800. 350 rooms. One of Boston's newest downtown high-rise hotels near shopping district and theatres. Balcony to each of the well equipped rooms. Putting green, heated indoor pool, sauna. Moderate.

HAWTHORNE INN: 18 Washington Square West, tel 744 4080. 80 rooms. Hospitable service and old-world elegance in a completely modernised and redecorated inn. Inexpensive.

HOLIDAY INN: 5 Blossom St, tel 742 7630. 304 rooms. Close to Government Center and many tourist attractions. Lobster Trap restaurant on top floor, and coffee shop. Outdoor pool. Moderate.

HYATT REGENCY CAMBRIDGE: 575 Memorial Dr, tel 492 1234. 500 rooms. Boston showplace, terraced on the outside and with diamond-shaped glass lifts, fountains and balconies inside. Two restaurants and a revolving lounge on the glass-enclosed rooftop. 15 rooms for the handicapped and one for non-smokers. Bedroom furnishings include radio, television, in-house movie combination and air conditioning. Expensive.

LOGAN AIRPORT HILTON: Logan International Airport, East Boston, tel 569 9300. 559 rooms. Right at the airport, ten minutes by car to downtown Boston. The rooms are soundproofed and furnished in modern style, some with inner courtyard; swimming pool and lawn. Restaurant. Moderate.

LENOX HOTEL AND MOTOR INN: 710 Boylston St, tel 536 5300. 225 rooms. Incorporates Diamond Jim's Piano Bar, the Victorian Restaurant and Ye Olde London Pub, but this is a place for the family where children can stay free in their parents' room. Early American- and Oriental-style furnishings and homely touches such as digital alarm clock and coffee-maker in every room. Soft drinks and ice machines on alternate floors. Moderate.

SHERATON-BOSTON: Prudential Center, 39 Dalton St, tel 236 2000. 1,318 rooms. Spectacular views from this exciting, bustling skyscraper with five restaurants and lounges and covered passageway to shops and boutiques. Extra luxury in the top Sheraton Towers suites. Expensive.

BOSTON DIRECTORY

SUSSE CHALET MOTOR LODGE: 800 Morrissey Blvd, Dorchester, tel 287 9100. An economy-minded and family-oriented New England skiiing lodge. Convenient to Boston. Large, pleasant air-conditioned rooms are well furnished. Swimming pool in inner court and vending area with ice and snacks. The Swiss House Restaurant just across the car park offers varied meals and children's prices. Inexpensive.

RESTAURANTS

ANTHONY'S PIER 4: 140 Northern Av, tel 423 6363. Famous seafood restaurant at the end of a pier with splendid view of the harbour. Memorable meals served. Expensive.

BETTE'S ROLLS ROYCE: 1 Union St, tel 227 0675. The decor is 1890s-style in this enjoyable restaurant, with a good pianist adding to the fun atmosphere. Excellent seafood, chowder and onion soup. Moderate.

CAFE BUDAPEST: 90 Exeter St, tel 734 3388. Cuisine is Continental with strong Hungarian influence in this restaurant in the Copley Square Hotel. Excellent dishes, particularly the home-made soups and desserts. Expensive.

CHARLEY'S EATING AND DRINKING SALOON: 344 Newbury St, tel 266 3000. Authentic Victorian-style saloon cum restaurant with waiters appropriately dressed. Specialities are fish and beef, but excellent sandwiches are also served. Inexpensive.

THE CHART HOUSE: 60 Long Wharf, tel 227 1576. Nautical decor in a one-time (1760) tea store. Basically a steakhouse featuring top sirloin, prime ribs and marinated meats. Also fresh seafood and a portable chilled salad 'bar'. Moderate.

DU BARRY FRENCH RESTAURANT: 159 Newbury St, tel 262 2445. A little piece of France in Boston serving unpretentious French family fare, including frogs' legs, scallops and veal. Price includes soup or fruit juice and vegetables. Hors d'oeuvre and desserts are extra. Interesting wines. Moderate.

DURGIN-PARK: 340 N Market St, tel 227 2038. Everyone's favourite. A noisy, convivial restaurant serving hearty portions of good plain food such as Yankee pot roast, Boston baked beans and baked Indian pudding. Be prepared to queue – it's very popular. Inexpensive.

GOLDEN TEMPLE NATURAL FOODS: 95 Winthrop St, tel 354 0365. One of the few natural food restaurants in the city run by white-turbaned Sikhs. No additives, no sugar, no chemicals, but superb whole-wheat Syrian bread crammed with mushrooms, tomatoes, bean sprouts and hummus, topped with grilled cheese. Lots more delicious home-made fare. Inexpensive.

THE HERMITAGE: 955 Boylston St, tel 267 3652. A Russian restaurant in the Institute of Contemporary Art. Russian specialities such as caviar, borsch and chicken Kiev are included on a frequently changing menu. Moderate.

JIMMY'S HARBORSIDE RESTAURANT: 242 Northern Av, tel 423 1000. A long tradition of excellent seafood in this popular waterfront restaurant. Moderate.

THE MAGIC PAN: 47 Newbury St, tel 267 9315. Quincy Market, tel 523 6103. Dine outside in summer at these pleasant restaurants where the pancake is king. Complete crêpe and salad lunches available, with crêpes St Jacques a favourite dinner dish. Soups and desserts also good. Inexpensive.

MEDIEVAL MANOR: tel 262 5144. 'Jest a Minute' at a three-hourly Knightly Banquet which parodies the Middle Ages. Eat and drink American style and enjoy the fun. Moderate.

NO NAME: 15½ Fish Pier, tel 338 7539. Possibly the best, if not the most glamorous, seafood restaurant in Boston 'where the fish jump from the ocean into the frying pan'. Unlicensed, so take your own wine and avoid peak mealtimes to miss queues. Inexpensive.

RITZ-CARLTON: 15 Arlington St, tel 536 5700. Famed for its superb continental cuisine, this internationally acclaimed restaurant-within-a-hotel offers a splendid choice of gourmet dishes served in glamorous surroundings. Expensive.

TOP OF THE HUB: 800 Boylston St, Prudential Center, tel 536 1775. Where you can eat 52 floors up and get the best view of Boston. Steaks and local seafood are specialities. Entertainment. Moderate.

VOYAGEURS: 45½ Mt Auburn St, Cambridge, tel 354 1718. Creative and sometimes unusual menus and a comprehensive wine list are features of this striking restaurant, where you can eat to harp or harpsichord music. Resembling a museum, it is decorated with bronze ornaments and jade Buddhas. The roof garden has a fountain, goldfish and gardenias. Open only for dinner. Expensive.

YE OLDE OYSTER HOUSE: 41 Union St, tel 227 2750. Louis Philippe lived here in exile before becoming King of France. It is now Boston's oldest (150yr) restaurant. Seafood, wine by the carafe and a children's menu.

TRANSPORT

AIRPORT: Logan International, East Boston: The airport is linked to the city by two, one-way toll tunnels which run under the Inner Harbor, and is served by most of the major airlines. There is an inexpensive limousine 'shuttle' between the airport and the larger hotels. Alternatively, by using a Share-A-Cab system to outlying suburbs, the normal fare can be halved.

BUSES AND SUBWAYS: The Massachusetts Bay Transportation Authority (MBTA) runs both the buses and the subway (underground) systems. A circle containing the letter T indicates subway stations, where there are displays of direction and location maps. Bus and subway fares are cheap, but on buses only the correct fare will be accepted. For information tel 722 3200.

CAR HIRE: Weaving through Boston's narrow, crowded, one-way streets is something of a problem, but for out-of-town trips it is possible to hire a car from major rental agencies; these are: Avis, 60 Park Sq, tel 267 8500; Dollar, 230 Porter St, tel 569 5300; Hertz, Motor Mart Garage, Park Sq, tel 482 9100, and National, Logan International Airport, tel 567 3261. Check in Yellow Pages for a complete list of companies.

TAXIS: There are a lot of taxis about, either cruising or waiting at stands, and they are relatively inexpensive. The major companies are Checker, tel 536 7000, Independent Taxi Operators' Association, tel 426 8700, and Town Taxi, tel 536 5000.

TRAINS: Boston is served by two stations: Trains to and from the south and west use South Station on Atlantic Av at the corner of Summer St. North Station, 120 Causeway St, near Charles River, is the terminus for local northern trains.

TOURING INFORMATION

AAA: Offices of the Massachusetts Division of the AAA are at 141 Tremont St, Boston, tel 482 8031. There are other branches at Chestnut Hill, tel 738 6900 and Fairhaven, tel 997 7811. All are open Monday to Friday during normal office hours.

SIGHTSEEING: Gray Line (tel 426 8800) is one of the many bus companies which run sightseeing tours around Boston and its surroundings. A complete list of operators can be found in the Yellow Pages of the telephone directory. There are walking tours organized from Boston Common Information Center, tel 482 2864. They offer walks of several areas at a small cost, which varies according to the length of the tour.

Several cruise lines sail from Boston's downtown wharves for daily sightseeing and fishing trips in the harbour. There are also cruises along the Charles River and to Provincetown and Gloucester. Companies include A C Cruise Line, 28 Northern Av, tel 426 8419 and Great Congress Street and Atlantic Steamship Co, 300 Congress Street, tel 426 6633.

'Made to measure' walking tours are arranged by Boston by Foot, 77 N Washington St, tel 367 2345. These highlight the history and architecture of the City.

VISITOR INFORMATION: Throughout the year the information centre on the Tremont St side of Boston Common provides street maps, brochures and information concerning current events. In addition, an official guide magazine to Boston, *Panorama*, is published twice weekly and is usually available at stations, hotels and the airport.

PLACES TO SEE

BUNKER HILL MONUMENT: Monument Sq, Charlestown. Centre of the Battle of Bunker Hill on 17 June 1775 which resulted in a defeat for the American Colonists. However, the British were driven out of Charlestown in 1776 – hence the Monument. It is a 221-foot-high granite obelisk and visitors can climb 294 steps to the top – there is no lift.

BUNKER HILL PAVILION: 55 Constitution Rd, Charlestown, tel 241 7575. Contains a specially built theatre with 14 screens, seven sound channels and 22 life-size costumed figures which vividly recreate, through sights, sounds and special effects, the Battle of Bunker Hill – America's first full-scale battle.

CUSTOMS HOUSE TOWER: State and India Sts. Take a lift to the observation platform 500 feet up for a fascinating view of Boston.

FANEUIL HALL: Faneuil Hall Square, at Merchants Row. Merchant Peter Faneuil gave the building to the city in 1742 as a market and meeting hall. It became known as the Cradle of Liberty because of the numerous protest meetings held there before the Revolution. It contains a library, museum and paintings of famous battles.

GRANARY BURYING GROUND: Tremont and Bromfield Sts. Some illustrious Americans are buried here, including Paul Revere, Benjamin Franklin's parents, the victims of the Boston Massacre (six colonists shot by British troops in 1770) and the wife of Isaac Goose – the Mother Goose of nursery-rhyme fame.

BOSTON DIRECTORY

JOHN HANCOCK OBSERVATORY: Copley Square, St James Av and Trinity Pl, tel 247 1976. New England's tallest (740ft) building from which you can see right across Boston as far as the mountains of New Hampshire. Also exciting multi-media exhibits.

LEAD SOLDIER SHOP: 728 St Louis, tel 524 0548. Toy soldiers everywhere and there are full-scale models of soldiers dressed in complete military uniforms. Specially appealing to youngsters.

LOUISBURG SQUARE: Beacon Hill. An English courtyard atmosphere to this lovely old square with railed private garden, which was, and is, the centre of wealthy 'old' Boston.

NEW ENGLAND AQUARIUM: Central Wharf, tel 742 8830. Famous for its educational displays of 2,000 species of aquatic life, including sharks, sea lions, turtles and dolphins in natural surroundings. Daily displays in a floating amphitheatre.

OLD NORTH CHURCH: 193 Salem St. Built in 1723, this is the oldest church in Boston. In April 1775 lanterns were hung in the steeple as signals to the patriots that the British were on their way to Lexington and Concord. One lantern was lit if the Redcoats approached by land, two if by sea.

PAUL REVERE HOUSE: 19–21 North Sq. Built about 1677, this is the oldest home in Boston and was occupied by silversmith Paul Revere from 1770 to 1800. He left here for the Boston Tea Party in 1773 and for his historic ride to Lexington in April 1775 to warn his fellow colonists of the approach of the British.

THE PRUDENTIAL CENTER: Between Huntington Av and Boylston St. A massive architectural complex, featuring a shopping arcade full of interesting boutiques, book shops, men's and women's shops; also restaurants, squares and gardens surrounding the 52-storey Prudential Tower. Superb views from the 50th-storey Skywalk.

STATE HOUSE: Beacon and Park Sts. The shining gilded dome (the copper for which was bought from Paul Revere) of this 1795 house marks the government seat of the Commonwealth of Massachusetts today. The archive museum in the basement displays many fascinating old documents, Indian treaties, historical records and relics.

MUSEUMS

THE BOSTON TEA PARTY SHIP AND MUSEUM: Congress St Bridge on Fort Point Channel, tel 338 1773. The notorious Tea Party dramatically recreated in audio-visual form and through the period museums. There is also a full-size working replica of one of the Tea Party ships.

CHILDREN'S MUSEUM: Museum Wharf, 300 Congress St, tel 426 8855. Great fun for everyone here, where there are 'touch-and-feel' participative exhibits: work on a production line, explore a city street through a manhole, try on grandparents' clothes, explore the Giant's Desktop, and a lot more. Reduced rates for children and senior citizens.

GIBSON HOUSE MUSEUM: 137 Beacon St. An old Boston brownstone house furnished in Victorian style. It is full of 19th-century curios, including one of America's oldest telephones and a petrified-tree hat-rack.

ISABELLA STEWART GARDNER MUSEUM: 280 The Fenway, tel 734 1359. Like a Venetian palazzo with a breathtaking courtyard of fresh flowers, this one-time home of a wealthy Bostonian is now a gallery for many works of art, including paintings by Matisse, Titian and Whistler. Stained glass windows, tapestries and exquisite antique furniture are also on display. Concerts are held here in summer.

MUSEUM OF SCIENCE: Science Park, tel 723 2500. A lively 'look-and-touch' science centre for all ages. Exhibits range from the human body to the stars, from live animals to a model of Tyrannosaurus Rex – and a lot more besides. The Hayden Planetarium next door offers special programmes of astronomy.

MUSEUM OF TRANSPORTATION: Museum Wharf, 300 Congress St. Trace the history and development of transport systems in Boston from 1630 to the present. An amazing collection of exhibits from roller skates to aeroplanes. Fun, too, at the activity centre.

MUSEUM OF FINE ARTS: 465 Huntington Av, tel 267 9300. One of the world's finest collections of paintings and sculpture from nearly every age and culture. There is also a satellite branch at Faneuil Hall, South Market Building.

MAPPARIUM: Massachusetts Av and Clearway St, tel 262 2300. Walk in and find yourself in a huge room the exact shape of the globe, around which you then travel. Stained glass colours and distinct acoustics make it a fascinating tour which points out where the International Dateline falls, which are the deep-water parts of the ocean, and so on.

USS CONSTITUTION MUSEUM: Charlestown Navy Yard, tel 426 1812. 'Old Ironsides' was one of America's great fighting ships. It is a 44-gun frigate which was launched in 1797 and has been restored and is on view to the public. Art and preservation galleries bring to life her building and life aboard in the 1800s.

'WHERE'S BOSTON?': 60 State St, tel 661 2425. A 200-seat theatre in which over 3,000 slides and quadrophonic sound paint a historical and contemporary multi-image portrait of Boston and its people. Shows are daily, on the hour.

PARKS AND GARDENS

ARNOLD ARBORETUM: Arbor Way, tel 524 1717. This is perhaps Boston's most beautiful park – it's certainly one of its oldest. Wander through some of the 265 acres which contain over 6,000 varieties of ornamental trees, shrubs and vines. It is especially beautiful in spring when the air is heavy with fragrance. Specially famous for its varieties of lilac.

BOSTON COMMON: Noted for its trees, this historic site is a pleasant place for cool shade on sunny days. A recently planted oak tree, called the Liberty Tree, is at the corner of Boylston and Tremont Streets – a one time rallying place for Revolutionary patriots. It is a replacement for the tree cue down by the British in 1775. The park is the oldest in the United States.

PUBLIC GARDEN: Adjacent to Boston Common, this is a superbly pretty flower garden, especially in spring when tulips and pansies are blooming. An ideal place to relax, rest or watch the world go by. Alternatively, ride round the pond in a swan boat with the children.

SPORT

BOSTON TENNIS CLUB: 653 Summer Street, tel 269 4300. Offers eight tennis courts, nine racquet ball courts, plus steamheat and a whirlpool. Instruction is available.

FENWAY PARK: tel 267 8661. This is the venue for baseball matches and the home team are the Boston Red Sox.

BOSTON GARDEN: is the place to see the Boston Celtics (basketball) and the Boston Bruins (hockey). American football can be seen at SCHAEFFER STADIUM in Foxboro.

SUFFOLK DOWNS RACETRACK: US Route 1, tel 567 3900. Thoroughbred horse racing daily (January to July and September to December) except Tuesday; harness racing from April to October.

There are several public tennis courts and golf courses which are run by the Metropolitan District Commission, tel 727 5250.

THE PERFORMING ARTS

THEATRE: Experimental theatre is sometimes featured at The American Repertory Company Theatre, Loeb Drama Center, 64 Brattle St, tel 547 8300; The Charles Playhouse, 74 Warrenton St, tel 426 6912 and the Boston Repertory Theater, 1 Boylston Place, tel 423 6580. Before and after Broadway productions are staged at the Colonial Theater, 100 Boylston St, tel 426 9366; Schubert Theater, 265 Tremont St, tel 426 4525 and Wilbur Theater, 252 Tremont St, tel 423 4008. Universities and colleges in the area often put on very good productions, usually in the winter season. These include chapel organ music, choral and band concerts. For opera lovers there is the first-rate Opera Company of Boston, whose offices are at 539 Washington St, tel 426 5300. Tickets, sometimes at discount prices, for performances and all kinds of attractions, can be bought at Bostix, the ticket booth at Faneuil Hall, tel 723 5181. Recorded information tells of the day's offerings.

MUSIC: The Boston Symphony Orchestra at Symphony Hall, corner of Huntington and Massachusetts Avs, tel 266 1492 is one of the world's biggest names in symphony orchestras. The BSO winter season runs from September to April and though most tickets are taken by subscription, the house is not always sold out. Alternatively, you can attend an open rehearsal on Wednesday evenings. The Boston Pops Orchestra is also at Symphony Hall in early May for a nine-week season of popular to light classical music. Drink punch and light beverages as well as listening to the music, surrounded by garden-green decor. Later in the summer the Pops musicians go to the Hatch Shell of the Charles River Esplanade where delightful concerts are held under the stars. Free classic concerts are given frequently at the New England Conservatory of Music, 290 Huntington Av, tel 262 1120; the Berklee College of Music, 1140 Boylston St, tel 266 1400; and also at the Handel and Haydn Society, which is America's oldest performing arts organisation, now in its 171st season. *Panorama*, a bi-weekly publication, lists events.

CLIMATE

Boston's spring and autumn are cool – rather like those in Britain – while summer is hot and sticky. In winter, however, it is a lot colder than in most parts of Britain. Snow can be expected and can stay for long periods.